Collective Dynamics and Territories

Territorial Entrepreneurship and Innovation Set
coordinated by
Didier Chabaud, Florent Pratlong and Carlos Moreno

Volume 3

Collective Dynamics and Territories

9 Issues for Competitive, Innovative and Sustainable Territories

Edited by

Anne Albert-Cromarias
Thérèse Albertini
Patrice Terramorsi

ISTE

WILEY

First published 2024 in Great Britain and the United States by ISTE Ltd and John Wiley & Sons, Inc.

ISTE Ltd
27-37 St George's Road
London SW19 4EU
UK

www.iste.co.uk

John Wiley & Sons, Inc.
111 River Street
Hoboken, NJ 07030
USA

www.wiley.com

Library of Congress Control Number: 2024932053

British Library Cataloguing-in-Publication Data
A CIP record for this book is available from the British Library
ISBN 978-1-78630-930-3

Contents

Introduction

Managing Territorial Dynamics: Why? How?

I.1. People and territories: an unquantifiable harmony

From time immemorial, people and territories have maintained a relationship that combines measure and excess. It is in this dialectical relationship that the living theater of human societies is formed, with its share of hubris, conflict and predation.

Originally nomads, seeking the resources necessary for their subsistence in ever-changing environments, humankind gradually became sedentary. This occupation of progressively domesticated spaces went hand in hand with the development of agriculture and animal husbandry, as well as the beginning of modern social organization (Cauvin 1977). This period also corresponds, according to a number of researchers (Ruddiman 2003), to the beginning of the Anthropocene era (Crutzen and Stoermer 2000), characterized by the fact that "Human activities have become so pervasive and profound that they rival the great forces of Nature and are pushing the Earth into planetary *terra incognita*" (authors' translation, Steffen et al. 2007)[1]. Indeed, over time, the burden of human activities on the planet has led to profound disruptions that are now affecting both physical (e.g. global warming, extreme weather events) and ecological (e.g. reduced biodiversity) balances (Crutzen 2006).

Introduction written by Thérèse ALBERTINI, Anne ALBERT-CROMARIAS and Patrice TERRAMORSI.

1 Cited by Federau (2017).

In this movement linking people and territories, the industrial revolutions represent a significant break. The technical, scientific and social developments of the 18th and 19th centuries opened up new horizons, while at the same time increased humans' insatiable appetite. The territory, dominated as it has perhaps never been, is now the site of ever larger and more efficient factories (see, for example, Ford's giant factories on the Red River site in Michigan, built between 1917 and 1928)[2], and also of the unbridled exploitation of the natural resources necessary for modern society, be they coal, copper or oil.

Globalization marks another turning point. The scope of human activity then changes scale, bringing with it an unprecedented increase in the production of wealth, and also in the impact of human activities on the planet. The grounding of the *Ever Given*, a container ship that blocked the Suez Canal for several days in March 2021[3], and the shortage of medical devices and basic pharmaceutical substances in many countries as a result of the Covid-19 pandemic show better than any words how often profit optimization is the only variable of choice, and how illusory this *limitless* world can be. Consumed by the economic and financial activities, the "world territory" needs to be populated.

In this context, from ecological transition to innovation, competitiveness, employment, training, solidarity and the creation of the Commons, the territorial dimension is now everywhere. It expresses the urgent need for humankind to rediscover its bearings, so that it can take measure of its actions and face up to the unprecedented challenges it faces.

I.2. Management Sciences and further better relations between people and territories

Isolated responses are not enough to tackle the consequences of the Anthropocene. Only a global mobilization that cuts across societies and questions the relationship between humankind and the Earth is likely to enable us to develop responses that are both acceptable and relevant. In order to achieve this, all scientific disciplines, from education to engineering, to geography and biology, need to be mobilized.

2 See, for example: https://www.thehenryford.org/visit/ford-rouge-factory-tour/history-and-timeline/fords-rouge/.

3 See, for example: https://www.lemonde.fr/afrique/article/2021/03/26/canal-de-suez-bloque-ce-que-l-on-sait-de-l-echouage-du-cargo-ever-given_6074575_3212.html.

How do the Management Sciences fit into this? How can they, often accused of being an extension of ultra-liberal thinking, shed light on the paths to harmonious development of human activities within territories? Before outlining these answers, which will be further developed in this book, we need to look back at the very concept of territory and its gradual appropriation by the Management Sciences.

Initially considered to be negligible, the territory, conceived solely as a geographical space, was gradually integrated by standard economic theory as a variable enabling companies to benefit from comparative advantages. The aim is to optimize the location of activity in order to "locate where it will be most profitable" (Porter 1990). Despite Marshall's pioneering work in 1890 on the location of industry and the effects of industrial concentration, it was not until the 1970s that the territory became the focus of renewed interest.

With the oil shocks putting a stop to the growth of *Les Trente Glorieuses*[4], and thus to the development of ever larger and more international companies, the virtues of "small is beautiful" were (re)discovered (Piore and Sabel 1984). Beyond location, it became clear that the competitiveness of organizations could be based on their ability to forge links between themselves and within a given territory. The work carried out by researchers on the industrial districts of the "Third Italy", under the impetus of Arnaldo Bagnasco and his "disciples", sought to explain the success of clusters of small, often family-run, companies. The concept of the Marshallian industrial atmosphere was revived. They emphasized that cooperation and noneconomic ties in the local community (Becattini 1991) were fostered by the cultural, social and political homogeneity observable in these districts (Garofoli 1992).

Subsequently, the work of the "French proximity school[5]" demonstrated the relevance of addressing the question of relationships between organizations in a given territory. Indeed, while the territory can facilitate or hinder the coordination of actors (Zimmermann 2008), other factors come into play in this complex interaction: socio-economic proximity (Bouba-Olga and Grossetti 2008), organized proximity (Rallet and Torre 2004), institutional proximity (Kirat and Lung 1995), cognitive proximity (Boschma 2005) and political proximity (Talbot 2010). This is followed by the search for the ideal

4 *Les Trente Glorieuses* was a 30-year period of economic growth in France between 1945 and 1975, following the end of World War II.

5 L'école française de la proximité.

territorial structure (technopoles, competitiveness clusters and other local production systems) to optimally coordinate the various agents according to preestablished objectives. However, in the face of prescriptive approaches, accused of being disconnected from the reality of the actors, a so-called "problem-solving" logic has emerged (Landel and Pecqueur 2016). From then on, it was no longer a question of applying a standard response to a given territory, but of accompanying stakeholders in the development of collective territorial dynamics, from the analysis of the situation to the definition of the problem, via the generation of ideas, their selection, implementation and evaluation. From this perspective, Management Science, as a set of disciplines dedicated to "analyzing and designing the steering mechanisms of organized action" (authors' translation, David 2000), seems to be the most appropriate field of study. Bringing together 22 researchers in strategic management, human resources management and marketing, this book offers a synthetic, systemic and operational vision for better understanding, and acting upon, collective territorial dynamics. For each of the nine territorial challenges identified, theoretical and conceptual benchmarks, as well as analysis and action tools, derived from problems encountered in different territories, are presented in Table I.1.

	Territorial challenges
Chapter 1	Setting Up in a Rural Environment: A Sustainable Strategic Management Approach
Chapter 2	Organizing a Network of Actors to Preserve and/or Enhance the Common Resource
Chapter 3	Building Collective Environmental Action Within Territories
Chapter 4	Innovating and Regenerating Territories Through the Development of Ecosystems
Chapter 5	Reconciling Individual and Collective Territorial Dynamics
Chapter 6	Supporting Social Innovation Within Territories
Chapter 7	Tackling Medical Deserts in Rural Territories
Chapter 8	Identifying and Valorizing Human Resources Within Territories
Chapter 9	Attracting and Retaining Talents in Organizations and Territories

Table I.1. *Nine territorial challenges*

I.2.1. *Challenge 1: setting up in a rural environment: a sustainable strategic management approach*

The first challenge is to read the territory, in the rural sense of the term, as a strategic asset for a company. Alexandre Asselineau's starting point is the observation that setting up in rural territories is an option that is all too often neglected, even though it can be a strategic choice with high economic, social and environmental value. Setting up in a rural environment can align resources, culture and local actors around a coherent vision, reducing production costs, enhancing differentiation and attracting talent. Through the example of the *Institut de Tramayes*, located near Cluny, the author demonstrates that it is possible to revive a territory's dynamism, even when it does not appear to have major assets and resources, by enabling the company setting up there to draw upon the territory's resources to generate a highly coherent and adapted value proposition.

I.2.2. *Challenge 2: organizing a network of actors to preserve and/or enhance the common resource*

The second challenge, taken up by Christophe Assens and François Coléno, is that of developing (or sustaining) a competitive advantage linked to the territory, combining the economic imperative of greater competitiveness with respect for the common good that is the territory. Two examples from the agri-food sector, corn production in Alsace and potatoes from Noirmoutier, illustrate the need for a network strategy that reconciles the individual interests of each partner within the cooperative with the collective interests of the territory. Two conditions are essential: first, cultural proximity and identity, which creates a climate of trust sufficient to facilitate collaboration despite rivalries; and second, industrial collaboration, which brings together the different actors within a genuine network strategy for the territory.

I.2.3. *Challenge 3: building collective environmental action within territories*

The third territorial challenge, addressed by Solange Hernandez and Camille Fiore, is linked to environmental issues, and more specifically to the problem of air pollution, responsible for several thousand deaths every year in France. In this public health context, territorial organizations can, through collaborative management, act to improve air quality by drawing on two types of strategic management: *collaborative strategic management and the "On-The-Way Strategy"*. A multiple case study was carried out on three territories (Greater Paris, Grenoble-Alpes-Métropole and the Eurometropole of Strasbourg), showing that, when faced with a complex problem such as improving air quality, the implementation of collaborative strategic management and *"On-The-Way Strategy"* by the territory's stakeholders is not easy.

I.2.4. *Challenge 4: innovating and regenerating territories through the development of ecosystems*

The fourth challenge deals with collective and open innovation within a given territory, where proximity facilitates exchanges between actors. Innovating within an ecosystem with partners enables us to offer greater value than would have been created individually by each member of the ecosystem. In fact, the complementarities that develop between ecosystem members are just as many opportunities for business development. Thomas Loilier, Magali Malherbe and Guillaume Detchenique offer a fresh perspective on ecosystems, discussing the role played by the territory in the dynamics of an ecosystem, which in turn can contribute to its development or regeneration. Using two examples – the Norman cider ecosystem and the NFC technology ecosystem, also in Normandy – they demonstrate, through the notion of proximity, the mechanisms that enable a territory to unblock or renew an ecosystem: development of shared projects, sharing of values and representations by actors in the territory concerned, writing or rewriting a common history, without minimizing the risk of "territorial myopia".

I.2.5. *Challenge 5: reconciling individual and collective territorial dynamics*

The fifth challenge facing territories is how to reconcile individual and collective entrepreneurial outlook logics. Colette Fourcade, Christophe Leyronas and Stéphanie Loup propose an analysis that combines these two dimensions. For these authors, territorial development is definitely linked to available resources, and also to the ability of actors to perceive, integrate and exploit them. In order to achieve this, the individual and collective levels must maintain a fruitful relationship. This observation has led to the proposal of a diagnostic grid, cross-referencing, on the one hand, the perception associated with the value of a resource and, on the other hand, the level of convergence or divergence of this appreciation. For each of the four positions identified by the authors, perspectives for action are outlined, based on an analysis of the Pézenas commune, internationally renowned for its crafts.

I.2.6. *Challenge 6: supporting social innovation within territories*

The sixth challenge, addressed by Yamina Vierge and Nathalie Raulet-Croset, has a more direct societal dimension. The authors show how, thanks to a dedicated process, it is possible to coordinate the plurality of actors involved in the creation and appropriation of social innovations within territories. In this chapter, the reader will find both theoretical reference points for understanding the process of institutionalizing social innovation, notably through the concept of the middleground, and a concrete illustration based on an analysis of the various support mechanisms set up by the Occitanie Region and the City of Toulouse. We will then identify the factors that have fostered the dynamic development of social innovation initiatives in this territory.

I.2.7. *Challenge 7: tackling medical deserts in rural territories*

The seventh challenge is that of tackling territorial inequalities regarding access to healthcare, and the health, social and economic consequences that accompany them. Questioning this major issue, Corinne Rochette first shows that, when faced with the complexity of the problem posed by medical deserts, instrumental logic alone will not suffice. She argues that, if we are to find a solution, we need to move away from a highly centralized mode of operation to a collaborative model that is more in tune with territorial singularities. She bases her argument on a study of two schemes designed to provide a collective response to the problems of access to healthcare and medical deserts within a given territory: *CPTS (Communautés Professionnelles Territoriales de Santé)* "territorial professional health communities", and *CLS (Contrat Local de Santé)* "local health contracts". The author emphasizes that the cognitive, social, institutional and organizational proximities that accompany these mechanisms contribute to the durability and relevance of these collective responses.

I.2.8. *Challenge 8: identifying and valorizing human resources within territories*

The eighth challenge, addressed by Ingrid Mazzilli, Isabelle Bories-Azeau and Truong Giang Pham, is that of identifying and making the most of the competencies present in local territories/areas. The authors emphasize that, beyond isolated initiatives, we need to initiate collaboration between territorial authorities, socio-economic actors and local residents. The authors first present a summary of research carried out in the field of Territorial Human Resources Management (T-HRM), and then, based on this work, they propose a framework for studying T-HRM projects. The dimensions thus identified (territorial context; purpose of the project and of the methodology adopted; collective and partnership properties) make it possible to adapt the institutional work essential to the project's success. This proposed analysis is then applied to two cases from research-actions carried out in north-western and southern France.

I.2.9. *Challenge 9: attracting and retaining talents in organizations and territories*

Ève Saint-Germes and Christophe Alaux tackle the final challenge in this book. This concerns the attraction and retainment of talent. Beyond focusing solely on job vacancies, some territories/regions are moving towards promoting a quality of life that combines professional opportunities and well-being. This perspective has led to the development of tools such as the *QVT (Qualité de Vie Territoriale*[2]*)* "quality of territorial life", which combines quality of life at work and quality of life in a given territory. Its assessment is based on multiple indicators (human development, socio-economic conditions, quality of life, etc.), and its mobilization can encourage new marketing approaches based on *MET (Marques Employeurs Territoriales)* "territorial employer brands". Based on the case study of Attitude Manche, the authors show that the attention paid to territorial quality of life enables the development of a double-entry approach that simultaneously questions the organizational and territorial levels.

I.3. References

Becattini, G. (1991). Italian industrial districts: Problems and perspectives. *International Studies of Management & Organization*, 21(1), 83–90.

Boschma, R. (2005). Proximity and innovation: A critical assessment. *Regional Studies*, 39(1), 61–74.

Bouba-Olga, O. and Grossetti, M. (2008). Socio-économie de proximité. *Revue d'économie régionale et urbaine*, 3, 311–328.

Cauvin, J. (1977). Les fouilles de Mureybet (1971–1974) et leur signification pour les origines de la sédentarisation au Proche-Orient. *Annual of the American Schools of Oriental Research*, 44, 19–48.

Crutzen, P.J. (2006). The "Anthropocene". In *Earth System Science in the Anthropocene*, Ehlers, E. and Krafft, T. (eds). Springer, Berlin/Heidelberg.

Crutzen, P.J. and Stoermer, E.F. (2000). The Anthropocene. *Global Change Newsletter*, 41, 17–18.

David, A. (2000). Logique, épistémologie et méthodologie en sciences de gestion : trois hypothèses revisitées. In *Les Nouvelles Fondations des sciences de gestion : éléments d'épistémologie de la recherche en management*, David, A., Hatchuel, A., Laufer, R. (eds). Vuibert, Paris.

Di Méo, G. (1998). De l'espace aux territoires : élément pour une archéologie des concepts fondamentaux de la géographie. *L'information géographique*, 62(3), 99–110.

Federau, A. (2017). Genèse et géologie de l'Anthropocène. In *Pour une philosophie de l'anthropocène*, Federau, A. (ed.). Presses Universitaires de France, Paris.

Garofoli, G. (1992). New firm formation and local development: The Italian experience. *Entrepreneurship & Regional Development*, 4(2) 101–126.

Gilly, J.-P. and Torre, A. (2000). *Dynamique de proximité*. L'Harmattan, Paris.

Kirat, T. and Lung, Y. (1995). Innovations et proximités : le territoire, lieu de déploiement des processus d'apprentissage. In *Coordination économique et apprentissage des firmes*, Lazaric, N. and Monnier, J.-M. (eds). Économica, Paris.

Lamara, H. (2009). Les deux piliers de la construction territoriale : coordination des acteurs et ressources territoriales. *Développement durable et territoires* [Online]. Available at: https://journals.openedition.org/developpementdurable/8208 [Accessed 15 March 2015].

Landel, P.A. and Pecqueur, B. (2016). Le développement territorial : une voie innovante pour les collectivités locales. In *Développement durable des territoires*, Carrières, J.P., Hamdouch, A., Iatu, C. (eds). Économica, Paris.

Mcluhan, M. and Fiore, Q. (1967). *The Medium is the Massage: An Inventory of Effects*. Bantam Books, New York.

Piore, M.J. and Sabel, C.F. (1984). *The Second Industrial Divide: Possibilities for Prosperity*. Basic Books, New York.

Porter, M.E. (1990). The competitive advantage of nations. *Harvard Business Review*, March–April, 73–93.

Rallet, A. and Torre, A. (2004). Proximité et localisation. *Économie rurale*, 280, 25–41.

Ruddiman, R.F. (2003). The anthropogenic greenhouse era began thousands of years ago. *Climatic Change*, 61(3), 261–293.

Steffen, W., Crutzen, P.J., McNeill, J.R. (2007). The Anthropocene: Are humans now overwhelming the great forces of nature? *AMBIO. A Journal of the Human Environment*, 36(8), 614–621.

Talbot, D. (2010). La dimension politique dans l'approche de la proximité. *Géographie, économie, société*, 12(2), 125–144.

Torre, A. (2010). Jalons pour une analyse dynamique des proximités. *Revue d'économie régionale & urbaine*, 3, 409–437.

Zimmermann, J.B. (2008). Le territoire dans l'analyse économique. Proximité géographique et proximité organise. *Revue française de gestion*, 84(4), 105–118.

1

Setting Up in a Rural Environment: A Sustainable Strategic Management Approach

1.1. Introduction

This contribution is taken partly from work carried out over the last 10 years in collaboration with Anne Albert-Cromarias (co-author of the present book); and, more broadly, from a reflection on the essential role that we believe the strategic management of organizations and territories should play, as a teaching and research discipline, and as a practice, in the current and future mutations of our societies (see Asselineau 2021; Albert-Cromarias et al. 2022).

On the one hand, there are important issues to be addressed in terms of territorial dynamics and planning. In France, public policies over the last few decades have confirmed the trend towards the creation of imposing metropolises that attract activity, employment and inhabitants. However, while they enjoy a marked economic dynamism, many of these large cities have probably reached their critical size, and now accumulate numerous disadvantages in environmental terms (air and water pollution, insalubrity, congested transport) and social terms (housing costs, distance between work and home, insecurity, quality of life). All of this is happening at a time when large swathes of the territory feel abandoned, suffering from a lack of economic prospects, and paying dearly for the phenomena of deindustrialization, demographic devitalization, and the impoverishment of

---

Chapter written by Alexandre ASSELINEAU.

public services (education, health, transport, places to live). Is this model of territory development viable and sustainable? If not, how can the process be curbed or reversed?

On the other hand, public and private sector organizations are faced with a number of important issues: economic, strategic, social and environmental, without necessarily having the tools or methodologies to formulate appropriate responses. Faced with hyper-competition and globalization, how can we formulate value propositions that are both differentiating and economically efficient, while taking full account of social and environmental imperatives: paradoxical injunctions?

While we do not claim to have the answers to these questions, we wish to investigate the hypothesis that setting up in rural areas, an option that is all too often neglected, is, under certain conditions, a strategic choice for high economic, social and environmental performance; not least because it can reconcile the constraints and challenges associated with these three inescapable dimensions. Better still, this strategic choice offers the opportunity to align them around a vision that is coherent with local resources, culture and actors, thereby reducing production costs, increasing differentiation and attracting talent.

Nevertheless, there are numerous obstacles and difficulties that cannot be underestimated. In particular, much remains to be done in order to define the conceptual and methodological framework, both rigorous and available to actors in the field, for a "responsible" strategic management approach that would contribute to reconciling the economic, social and environmental dimensions, on the one hand, and companies and territories, on the other hand. It seems to us that, far from being opposed to each other, these dimensions simply need to be combined.

Experiments carried out in rural areas attest to the fact that it is possible to revive the dynamism of a territory, even when it does not seem to have major assets and resources, by enabling the company setting up there to draw upon the territory's resources to generate a highly coherent and adapted value proposition. By way of illustration, we are studying the case of a project to create a training institute in Tramayes, in the Cluny region (71). Based on a strategic vision and economic viability objectives that are clearly defined by the project's initiators, which are strongly consistent with those of the host territory, it relies on local actors (public and private) and strong ecological and social values to offer unique training programs.

1.2. High stakes for territories… and companies

1.2.1. *"Metropolization" and "clusterization"*

"Metropolization" or "metropolarization" (Godet et al. 2018)? By "metropolarization", the authors refer to the "ideological vision according to which metropolises are automatically destined to attract the bulk of activities" (author's translation, *ibid.*, p. 4); they thus highlight the potential role of public policies in the spatial planning choices of recent decades, which would have contributed, at the very least, to reinforcing the weight of metropolises in a country such as France.

This is an undeniable fact, and not a new one. Whether it is a question of public choices or the direct or indirect consequences of unbridled globalization, the weight of the French economy, as in most developed countries, is focused on its cities (metropolises), which account for a large share of wealth production and job creation (Altaber and Le Hir 2017), and concentrate assets in terms of dynamism and attractiveness.

The rationale is based on a premise that can be summed up as follows: economic development in the 21st century is based on European and global competition between large groups of "world cities", which must reach a critical size sufficient to radiate and fuel a dynamic that is beneficial to themselves and their peripheries. The State-Metropolis Pact, signed on July 6, 2017 following the 2015 NOTRe law, is notably based on this approach.

This perspective, which led to the creation of ambitious cities of competitive size, is in line with the cluster concept proposed by Michael Porter in the early 1980s (Porter 1990). The central concept of clusters and their close derivatives (Italian industrial districts, French competitiveness clusters) is based on the relevance of grouping organizations with common business logics in close geographical proximity, thereby generating attractive clusters with a strong international reputation. Porter often cites the examples of the Milan shoe industry and Silicon Valley technology start-ups. Local partnerships foster innovation, thanks to collaboration and cross-fertilization of skills, mutual recognition mechanisms to encourage investment, and the existence of key skills, such as universities and research centers, specialized banks, etc. (Asselineau and Cromarias 2011); an "industrial atmosphere" (Marshall 1906 [1890]), specific to a given territory, is generated, as well as a form of international division of trades and skills.

Fundamentally, these approaches are based on two standard principles of strategic thinking. On the one hand, the theoretical recognition that "big is beautiful", including those regarding territorial matters (Camagni and Capello 2020): economic dynamics derive a great deal from the ability of territories and the companies located in them to activate the coherence of the ecosystem they constitute. On the other hand, "national prosperity is created, not inherited. It depends on the capacity of its industry to innovate and grow" (author's translation, Porter 1990, p. 73); "economic space is a relational space capable of innovation" (Camagni and Capello 2020, p. 595), translated by the term "innovative environment". In other words, actors have the capacity to generate a territorial dynamic, an observation that refutes the idea of an unsurpassable "territorial determinism"; this opens the way to the definition of territorial strategies to support their development.

While this logic of "metropolarization" may seem appealing in terms of the economic development of the country and the towns concerned, it does seem questionable, particularly when environmental and social issues are taken into account.

First of all, "metropolarization" seems questionable. As Godet et al. (2018) point out, there are many examples of entrepreneurial successes that are regularly based on endogenous innovation, and not on a principle of dissemination by a metropolitan center. In France, for example, Michelin, Limagrain, Legrand, Fleury-Michon, Saint James, Mauviel and many others have developed without any link to a major economic center. This led these authors to suggest drawing inspiration from the best local innovation practices, without imposing a single model.

Second, "metropolarization" has serious limitations. It is fair to say that many metropolises have now exceeded their equilibrium point. They accumulate disadvantages detrimental to the quality of life of their inhabitants, and interfere with the objectives of building a more socially and environmentally responsible society: air and noise pollution, congested transport, stress, increased transport times and distances to be traveled daily, difficulties in access to housing, cost of living, insecurity, even insalubrity, etc. The Covid-19 crisis may have accentuated these observations, but the trend is more profound: in France, as in other countries, the ratio between arrivals and departures in these metropolises has reversed, and to cite only the most emblematic case, inhabitants are leaving Paris for so-called "human-sized" cities, an indication therefore that the capital would no longer be so.

Another striking fact is that these large, congested metropolises are surrounded by vast areas devoid of economic and social life. With the decline of traditional agriculture in recent decades, whole swathes of the territory feel abandoned and neglected, suffering from a seemingly inexorable demographic decline and a lack of essential public services – education, social services, healthcare (see Chapter 7), means of transport (creating dependence on the private car), places to live and socialize, etc.

These different dimensions need to be examined. However, in the final analysis, is this panorama of territorial dynamics the result of a will on the part of public authorities, of collective choices supported and assumed by society as a whole? Also, is it the inevitable fruit of a fatality that some attribute to globalization or the excesses of disconnected financial capitalism?

In order to help answer these questions, our research is based on a hypothesis, the starting point for all strategic reasoning: there is no such thing as territorial determinism. If there is a collective will, local actors can contribute to the positive transformation of their environment, attracting companies, funding and skills. However, there are strong conditions: this depends on the ability to rethink established ideas and behaviors, first and foremost on the collaborative links between companies and territories, and between public and private actors.

1.2.2. *Territory: a simple variable adjustment?*

Any approach aimed at better understanding territorial dynamics, in order to contribute to supporting them, presupposes an adapted conception of territory. This is a well-known and complex problem, and is related to the role attributed in economic theory to both territories and companies (Loup and Leyronas 2021). In the standard neoclassical economic view, the company is an entity driven solely by the pursuit of profit, and need not concern itself with social or societal considerations (Friedman 1970). Schematically, under such a framework, the territory is seen simply as a location endowed with production factors, a receptacle for activities. In management, the work of Michael Porter has brought territorial issues into sharper focus; however, thinking about location remains anchored in questions pertaining to competitiveness/competition between companies. Territory appears to be an adjustment variable for rational strategic choices, from which it is largely absent (Asselineau and Cromarias 2011); all the more so, as industrial competition is based on production cost differentials. However, are companies' location choices really always the result of a rational economic calculation? While the logic of clusters, as set out by Porter, rests on an analysis based on criteria that are potentially convincing from the point of view of objective rationality, other considerations that preside over location decisions are more akin to subjective criteria or dimensions that relate to the psychology of actors.

This is true, for example, of the mimetic behavior of decision-makers in a given industry, who form a unanimous conviction (founded or unfounded) about the factors they believe will lead to success or failure in their business (Di Maggio and Powell 1983; Baretto and Baden-Fuller 2006). Similarly, decisions based on accounting and financial approaches are likely to overlook the essential weight of extra-accounting dimensions, which may conceal important sources of hidden performance.

These elements leave room for doubt: are "world cities" and territories "devoid" of economic development an inevitability of our modern societies? Could not other, perhaps better balanced, approaches and models reveal their relevance, at least in some cases? If so, what theoretical concepts and tools can we, as researchers, practitioners and local actors, draw upon?

One starting point is to revisit the assumptions that guide relations between companies and territories:

> Territory is not just a meaningless geographical location, but takes the form of an asset that corporate strategy aims to specify, in order to reinforce the founding strategic dimension of cooperation (author's translation, Fourcade 2008, p. 13).

This is a fully integrated actor in the entrepreneurial project (Pecqueur and Zimmermann 2004), and not just a simple provider of natural or human resources.

1.3. What is the strategic relevance of setting up in a rural environment?

1.3.1. *Responsible strategic management and differentiation*

In other words, we need to include the territory, in all its different meanings and components, as a full and integral part of strategic thinking. Also, we need to consider that the company is much more than a knot of contracts designed to meet the sole objective of profit: it is necessary to integrate into modeling the affective, emotional and relational dimensions, which every practitioner knows is an integral part of decision-making processes within organizations.

These dimensions open up a wider, more vertiginous field of possibilities in economic, social and environmental terms. All the more so, as the principle of maximizing corporate profit is hardly a tenable position (Chanteau et al. 2017, p. 11), and "contemporary societies expect, more than ever, a significant contribution from companies to the collective interest and strong social and environmental engage, far from the excesses of faceless, stateless financial capitalism" (author's translation, Asselineau 2021).

While these observations seem to be relatively widely shared today, the challenge of implementation and concrete action remains.

Our reflection falls within the field of strategic management. This discipline, whose aim is to propose a global coherence between strategic intention and operational implementation, offers a suitable framework for responding to the challenges posed by the links between companies and territories, as confirmed by Régent et al. 2021:

> Strategic management literature provides a solid theoretical basis for examining territory and studying territorial projects in order to understand how they can help differentiate a territory and make it more attractive and competitive (author's translation, Régent et al. 2021, p. 23).

More specifically, we propose the concept of "responsible" strategic management, which advocates the full integration of corporate social responsibility (CSR) schemes, defined as "the voluntary integration by companies of social and environmental concerns into their business activities and their relations with stakeholders" (European Commission 2001), at the heart of strategic thinking (Asselineau 2021).

Responsible strategic management postulates that the company cannot prosper at the expense of the community. On the contrary, it is intended to offer a model that generates a peaceful and coherent complementarity between economic, social and environmental considerations, based on proposals for "shared value creation" (Porter and Kramer 2011) or "socially responsible capitalism" (Savall et al. 2021).

Research studies show that there is a positive correlation between a company's competitiveness and the implementation of coherent CSR approaches. At the very least, CSR seems to offer observable direct and indirect positive benefits (Asselineau and Cromarias 2011; Chanteau et al. 2017), and many companies are adopting a "mission company" status or obtaining B Corp certifications (Asselineau 2021).

Issues of territorial dynamics are thus bound to fit naturally and harmoniously into these approaches to responsible strategic management. In our view, territories offer a particularly suitable crucible for companies committed to CSR, wishing to differentiate themselves intelligently, and to give meaning and coherence to their development projects, outside the logics of critical mass and metropolarization.

At this stage, however, the methodologies and tools available are a stumbling block for researchers wishing to better understand these approaches, for actors in charge of territorial development and for companies seeking economic, social and environmental performance.

1.3.2. *The territory: the backbone of the strategic project*

We believe that this approach is socially useful, both for companies seeking to improve their economic and social performance, and for public sector actors concerned with issues of general interest, territorial attractiveness, and social and environmental best practice. We therefore agree with Chabaud and Maurand-Valet:

> The study of the relationship between territory and Management Science has become an important theme in Management Science [...]. The stakes are essential in this period of

> globalization, because the territory – this social construct – is a vector of job creation and increasingly appears as the place of proximity (or mediation) that allows us to grasp the relationship of the organization (company, association, etc.) to the country (author's translation, Chabaud and Maurand-Valet 2016, p. 6).

However, the matter is complex: the use of the notion of territory is accompanied by a conceptual vagueness, not least because the analysis of links between organizations and territory implies a meso-level of reflection that is inherently more complex than the study of inter-individual/organizational relations. Zardet and Noguera thus emphasize the absence of hierarchical links between the actors involved, who are numerous, of varied status and are legally independent: "In this respect, the territory can be likened to a network, in the sense that the network qualifies the nature of inter-organizational relations that are cooperative and non-hierarchical" (author's translation, Zardet and Noguera 2013, p. 8). It is within this framework that these actors envisage developing multiple cooperations and creating synergies (Zardet and Noguera 2013, p. 8).

A central question regards the territorial anchoring of the corporate project, defined as a "process and result of interactions between a company and its territory, based on the will to collectively create specific and localized common resources, enabling a long period of sedentarity for a company" (author's translation, Loup and Leyronas 2021, p. 54). There are "interactions" because the territory is not an external element of the project: the influence is mutually reciprocal, and therefore complex, between individuals and organizations (Chabaud and Maurand-Valet 2016).

How does the territory, in its various components, fit into the company's strategy? Also, how can the company's project make a lasting contribution to a sustainable territorial dynamic? Answering these questions requires collective action and the active participation of all project stakeholders, and must involve identifying and taking into account all their respective interests, which may diverge (Régent et al. 2021, p. 23) or generate inconsistencies. This implies a real sense of purpose, mobilization and cohesion on the part of the people involved, in the light of a clearly defined strategy in everyone's interest.

Once these observations have been made, what tools and methodologies can be mobilized to help the actors concerned? Undoubtedly, much remains to be done, as research into the strategic management of territories is still in its infancy. However, a number of points of support have already been identified for fully reintegrating the territory into strategic thinking. At the conceptual level, the use of stakeholder theory, inspired by Freeman (1984), and the resource or capability approach seem to offer a fruitful framework. Loup and Leyronas (2021), for example, mobilize the latter to propose an interpretive grid for a dynamic understanding of territorial anchoring. However, these authors admit that the concrete success mechanisms of a project associating companies and territories remain to be fully identified or modeled.

The next step is identifying a number of good practices that lead to the success of experiments carried out. Among these, several factors are highlighted in the literature and confirmed by our own research. For example, the dynamics of a territory seem to be based on the coherent articulation of ecosystem elements by local governance: alignment of actors, projects, resources and skills. It is worth stressing the importance of high-quality collaboration between the actors involved, whether public or private, which is sometimes difficult to achieve.

In concrete terms, cooperation can take a material form, such as the provision of premises, equipment or land. However, it can also take an intangible form, often overlooked as less easily quantifiable, but with potentially high added value: bringing actors together in local networks, access to elements of local culture, inter-organizational skills exchange systems, proactive support for cooperation, structuring actors around the territory's reputation, etc.

1.4. A textbook case study: the *Institut de Tramayes*

1.4.1. *The project*

The *Institut de Tramayes*[1] is a higher education establishment based in the town of Tramayes (Saône-et-Loire, population 1,056), already recognized for its remarkable commitment to the environment (the first town with over 1,000 inhabitants to use 100% renewable energy). The project is led by five entrepreneurs close to the *Arcenciel France* association[2]. It was presented with the *Fabrique des Territoires* award and recognized by the

1. See: www.institutdetramayes.fr.

2. See: www.euromed-france.org/arcenciel-France.

French Ministry of Territorial Cohesion for its innovative role as a driving force within the territory. "To think, to work, to undertake, in the service of rurality and the world" (author's translation): the "vision" conveyed by these entrepreneurs sums up the nature of the project, combining learning, rurality and economic, social and environmental sustainability.

The project's origins can be traced back to a number of factors: the changing aspirations of young people, who, in their search for meaningful careers, are increasingly turning to manual trades; the advantages of these trades for the attractiveness of rural territories, which represent a desirable alternative for tackling the problems posed by global metropolization; and the benefits of working together with territorial actors (municipalities, craftsmen, farmers, entrepreneurs, local councilors, etc.) as part of a social economy approach. In concrete terms, the project involves the creation of a post-baccalaureate school that offers a three-year curriculum unique in France, enabling students to obtain a double diploma and combine theoretical knowledge (economics, philosophy, sociology, history, law, English, etc.), management methodologies (finance, marketing, project management) and a manual trade (construction, catering, agriculture), notably through partnerships with specialized organizations (apprentice training centers, family and rural homes). Throughout the course, students are encouraged to carry out applied projects in the real world that meet the needs identified by territorial actors and communities, in a spirit of active learning and co-creation of knowledge. The Institute aims to have a medium-term enrolment of around 100 students, sufficient to ensure the viability of its business model: although tuition fees are required (calibrated according to students' social situations), additional funding is made accessible through a sponsorship program and policy of responding to calls for "third-party training" projects. The guiding principle is that "money should never be an obstacle to enrolment: we will find a solution", explains Valentin Bertron, who is project leader and head of the pedagogical department. For future graduates, the potential outlets are varied: crafts and manual trades, social entrepreneurship in rural areas, project management in associations and social enterprises, and territorial government.

At this stage, the Institute is still in the seed phase. The five entrepreneurs are responsible for the Institute's governance. They have divided up the operational roles (teaching models and lecturers, engineering, administrative and financial management, links with the commune, local actors and partners, commercial aspects, communication, student recruitment), and recruited two employees to manage partnerships and communication.

1.4.2. *Discussion: what is at stake?*

For a researcher, being able to approach a case study from the outset of a project is an opportunity: through longitudinal monitoring, it enables the dynamics of the project to be understood, and avoids the pitfall of reinterpretation after the event.

In this case, the project's entrepreneurial and societal aims are inspiring. Can higher education be provided anywhere other than in major cities, at a time when large cooperative groups are being set up to achieve critical mass and enter the global competition in education? Can a significantly differentiated proposal that is likely to attract students to rural areas, in occupations that may be meaningful, but remain unattractive (construction, catering, etc.) be developed? Can we reconcile an economically viable entrepreneurial project with a strong social and environmental dimension?

There is no doubt that the project cannot be transposed. However, at a time when traditional economic models are struggling to be restructured to tackle the challenges of the 21st century, in-depth analysis of innovative experiments is an ideal way to formulate new, relevant approaches.

In addition to a particularly welcoming natural environment, visitors to Tramayes are immediately struck by the apparent dynamism of the area, with its many local shops. The data collected on Tramayes, and direct observation and discussions with locals, all point to the existence of an "atmosphere" geared towards sustainable development, driven by the determination of the town council and local actors over several decades, even though the territory is isolated (Mâcon, the nearest town is 30 minutes away by car; the tourist site of Cluny is 20 minutes away).

While other communes were reluctant to welcome a student population, preferring to focus on tourism, for example, Tramayes immediately took interest and became involved in the Institute's project, making the former elementary school and adjoining premises available, and organizing meetings with local residents. The municipality was quick to realize that the arrival of students would disrupt habits and generate new needs (consumption, housing, travel, living spaces, etc.), and immediately embraced the project. However, not everything is set in stone: while the project has a clear vision and the support of local development and municipal authorities, the problems common to many rural communities are also present: transport, funding, health services, public services, housing, etc. The project must be seen in the context of the local economy.

The coherence of the project with the host territory, the active participation of local actors and cooperation mechanisms, the support of the town council and collective creativity, allow for innovative, relevant and coherent solutions to emerge: "There are a lot of shutters closed in Tramayes, and we hope to help reopen them through this project. The boarding school is relevant and creates a link with the territory," explains Valentin Bertron (author's translation). Transformed barns and accommodation are available. The town council is going to make them available for a program of renovation into passive housing, social housing and intergenerational shared accommodation (with the *Villages Solidaires* association) to enable elderly people to remain at home, thanks to the presence of students, thereby creating a virtuous dynamic.

Analysis of this ambitious entrepreneurial project confirms the messages conveyed by the concepts of "responsible" strategic management, applied to the territory, as defined above. Foremost among these is the rejection of a deterministic approach to rural territories: generating a sustainable, responsible territorial dynamic seems possible. However, this requires a number of restrictive conditions. Firstly, there needs to be a real intention to transform the area, based on a proactive approach and the active collaboration of the public and private actors concerned to find and implement solutions. There is no room for infighting. The expression of a vision shared by stakeholders at the territory level – in this case, the community – enables us to focus on projects that are consistent with the territory's history, geography, sociology, culture and resources. It does not hesitate to open up to a variety of partnerships, providing access to skills and resources that are lacking: at all levels, a logic of openness, collaboration and networking is essential.

1.5. Conclusion

The *Institut de Tramayes* is a fascinating case study for researchers and practitioners working on issues of territorial dynamics, the social economy, and sustainable development. Developing a higher education structure in a rural environment, with the emphasis on manual trades, is a prefiguration – still in its exploratory stages – of models that could possibly be successful in the territory. Even if a particular case is not necessarily intended to be generalized, it nonetheless represents a laboratory of potentially inspiring ideas. The awards and recognitions already obtained by the Institute show the interest of public actors and local authorities concerned by the issues of rurality and sustainable development. However, if the project is clearly relevant and coherent "on paper", it is the actual implementation that will be the judge of the structure's viability.

The project has a clear vision, a philosophy rooted in the social and solidarity economy, and values coherent with the territory in which it is set up (particularly its ecological and social dimensions), all of which the strategic management literature identifies as key factors in a project's success. This is necessary, but not sufficient. For implementation, this involves resolving questions, both large and small, which are part of the day-to-day work: does the proposed model provide an answer to students in search of meaning and alternative training offers? Will they accept the specificities of student life in a rural environment? Will they find solutions to the challenges they face? "Where there is a will, there is a way," said the English poet William Hazlitt in 1822, summing up the spirit of strategic management long before its advent.

1.6. References

Albert-Cromarias, A., Asselineau, A., Blanchard, G. (2022). Value creation, appropriation, and destruction in coopetitive relationships among micro-firms. *Industrial Marketing Management*, 104, 366–375.

Altaber, C. and Le Hir, B. (2017). Dynamique de l'emploi dans les métropoles et les territoires environnants. *France Stratégie, Note d'analyse*, 64, 1–12.

Asselineau, A. (2021). Rigueur et pertinence du management stratégique "responsable" : apports de la théorie socio-économique. In *Traité du management socio-économique. Théorie et pratiques*, Savall, H. and Zardet, V. (eds). EMS Editions, Caen, 727–735.

Asselineau, A. and Cromarias, A. (2011). La RSE, un catalyseur d'innovations au service de la "vision" stratégique. *Revue Sciences de Gestion*, 84, 29–48.

Barretto, I. and Baden-Fuller, C. (2006). To conform or to perform? Mimetic behaviour, legitimacy-based groups and performance consequences. *Journal of Management Studies*, 43(7), 1559–1581.

Camagni, R. and Capello, R. (2020). Towards a new interpretation of regional evolution: Convergence between quantitative and qualitative approaches. *Revue d'Économie Régionale et Urbaine*, 4, 591–616.

Chabaud, D. and Maurand-Valet, A. (2016). Territoire, gouvernance et acteurs : 10 ans après les pôles de compétitivité. *Gestion 2000*, 2(33), 5–14.

Chanteau, J.P., Martin-Chenut, K., Capron, M. (2017). *Entreprise et responsabilité sociale en questions*. Classiques Garnier, Paris.

Di Maggio, P. and Powell, W. (1983). The iron cage revisited: Institutional isomorphism and collective rationality in organizational fields. *American Sociological Review*, 48(2), 147–160.

European Commission (2001). Promoting an European framework for corporate responsibility. Green Paper.

Fourcade, C. (2008). Stratégies de coopération de proximité : des modes d'innovation organisationnelle en PME. *Actes du 9e colloque CIFEPME*, Louvain-la-Neuve.

Freeman, E. (1984). *Strategic Management: A Stakeholder Approach*. Pitman, London, and Harper & Row, New York.

Friedman, M. (1970). The social responsibility of business is to increase its profits. *New York Times Magazine*, September 13.

Godet, M., Jarry, B., Chabaud, D. (2018). Innovation et territoires : les limites de la "métropolisation" en France. *Population & Avenir*, 3, 4–7.

Loup, S. and Leyronas, C. (2021). L'ancrage territorial : proposition d'une grille d'analyse. Une application aux artisans d'art de Pézenas. *Question(s) de Management*, 33, 53–64.

Marshall, A. (1906). *Principes d'économie politique* (translated by Sauvaire-Jourdan, F). Giard et Brière, Saint-Amand [Original published 1890].

Pecqueur, B. and Zimmermann, J.-B. (2004). Les fondements d'une économie de proximité. In *Économie de proximités*, Pecqueur, B. and Zimmermann, J.-B. (eds.). Hermes Lavoisier, Paris, 13–41.

Porter, M. (1990). The competitive advantage of nations. *Harvard Business Review*, 68(2), 73–93.

Porter, M. and Kramer, M. (2011). Creating shared value. How to reinvent capitalism – and unleash a wave of innovation and growth. *Harvard Business Review*, January-February, 62–77.

Régent, B., Favre-Bonté, V., Da Fonseca, M. (2021). Le management stratégique comme clé de lecture du développement des projets de territoire. *Gestion et Management Public*, 9(2), 9–30.

Savall, H., Péron, M., Zardet, V., Bonnet, M. (2021). Le capitalisme socialement responsable, environnement pertinent du management socio-économique. In *Traité du management socio-économique. Théories et pratiques*, Savall, H. and Zardet, V. (eds). EMS Éditions, Caen, 1206–1215.

Zardet, V. and Noguera, F. (2013). Quelle contribution du management au développement de la dynamique territoriale ? Expérimentation d'outils de contractualisation sur trois territoires. *Gestion et Management Public*, 2(2), 5–31.

2

Organizing a Network of Actors to Preserve and/or Enhance the Common Resource

2.1. Introduction

In the context of economic globalization, each territory is faced with the challenge of "glocalization", a term coined by Fourcade and Torres (2003), that is, the ability to develop distinctive skills on a local scale while ensuring a global reach. This challenge raises a number of strategic questions:

– How can we develop a competitive advantage in a given territory that cannot be transferred or relocated to other territories?

– What are a territory's distinctive skills?

– How can we manage the resources on which a territory's local dynamics and global reach depend on?

The competitive advantages of territories are based on the ability of local companies to develop a territorial brand image, a strong reputation and industrial efficiency, gaining recognition in the market economy through the applied combination of these expertises.

In order to sustain these competitive advantages, the problem for companies is not to lose sight of the notion of the common resource. Under the pretext of striving for greater competitiveness, they must not neglect the

---

Chapter written by Christophe ASSENS and François COLÉNO.

territory's sociological, environmental and identity-related specificities or else they may risk destroying the *common resource*. In the agri-food sector, this issue is central to the strategies pursued by French agricultural cooperatives.

In fact, the status of these companies is defined by rural law. This applies in particular to the geographical areas in which they operate. From this point of view, the agricultural cooperative is faced with a double constraint: on the one hand, the reality of the territory, which pushes the cooperative to settle close to its member farmers; and on the other hand, the constraint of agri-food markets and agro-industrial intermediaries, which impose on the cooperative a capacity for global development beyond the limits of the territory, to improve the economic well-being provided to farmers.

To reconcile these two issues – *terroir* and market – cooperatives often adopt network strategies to manage agri-food chains, while respecting the common resource of the territory. How is it possible to initiate a network strategy with cooperatives whose activities are complementary and often rivalrous? Who embodies the network? To what extent does the network strategy preserve the common resource and make a lasting contribution to territorial dynamics? In order to answer these questions, we will begin with a theoretical presentation of the concepts of common resource and territorial network strategy. We will then present two case studies on network strategies: the concerted management of genetically modified organisms (GMOs) of the corn sector in Alsace, and the implementation of a registered designation of origin for the potato sector in Noirmoutier. In conclusion, we draw lessons from the network strategies observed.

2.2. Territory and the common resource

By definition, the territory has the characteristics of a common resource, that is, a resource with cultural specificities in terms of reputation and brand image, economic properties in terms of resources and skills, and geographic aspects that collectively benefit all the actors established in the territory, without belonging to any one of them in particular. More precisely, based on the work of Baumol and Bowen (1966) and Samuelson's definition (1954), we can define territory as a common resource according to two criteria:

– Rivalry between actors on the territory: consumption of the territory's resources by one actor may prevent consumption by others, due to the physical limits of the territory, and the limited capacity for renewal of the territory's resources and properties. At a certain stage, the consumption of a common resource by one citizen prevents its consumption by others as capacity saturation approaches. For example, on a beach in summer, the capacity to accommodate holidaymakers may become saturated during peak times.

– The "non-exclusion" of actors from locating in the territory: in principle, it is not possible to exclude certain citizens from consuming the common resource in the territory, insofar as access to the territory is free and not subject to protectionist restrictions or quotas. If the free movement of goods and people is established, it is not possible to exclude from consumption, for technical and cost reasons, citizens located within the boundary of the territory or jurisdiction to which the good refers. For example, on the coast, access to a public beach is not restricted.

"Common resources" are therefore those whose use no one can exclude, but for which there is rivalry in their use. These resources are mainly natural resources, which are eroded by excessive consumption. On this subject, Hardin (1968) evokes the tragedy of the commons, which leads to their disappearance in the event of overuse. This theory is illustrated by a livestock farming village, where everyone can graze their animals in a meadow belonging to no one in particular. Since use of the meadow is free and unrestricted, and the herder earns their income from their livestock, it is in every herder's interest to take their animals to the meadow as often as possible, as soon as possible and for as long as possible. Inevitably, the meadow turns into a field of mud, making it unusable for all the farmers. Hardin (1968) proposes two alternatives to avoid this disappearance of the commons:

– The first is a "dirigiste" or authoritarian approach. The meadow remains the common property of the village, but an authority, with the power to penalize, is charged with administering the resource (the meadow) and distributing its use among each herder. The common resource is transformed into a public good of general interest, non-divisible, by being administered by a public power such as the state or a deconcentrated authority.

– The second is a "capitalist" approach. Each and every farmer benefits from a right of ownership over a parcel of meadowland and is therefore responsible for managing the resource. The common resource is distorted. It is fragmented into a multitude of private assets placed under the aegis of market forces of supply and demand, with the risk of losing the overall cohesion of the territory.

This theory shows that managing the commons requires collective action, perpetually re-evaluated by the state to compensate for market failures. For a long time, this theory was seen as proof of the need for public intervention in the administration of the commons, following the example of the work of Tinbergen (1956) and Musgrave (1959), part of the public economics school.

Since then, other research studies have contradicted this postulate. Williamson's Theorem (1983), for example, introduced the notion of transaction costs, and showed that no law could conclude that public intervention was superior to the market and vice versa, and that good management of the common resource was rather the fruit of a pragmatic, case-by-case study, comparing the respective costs and benefits (both in terms of economic efficiency and general interest) of each management mode. Clearly, collective action can be substantiated without state intervention (Arrow 1970). The management of common resources requires us to examine the emergence of collective mechanisms on a territorial scale, outside of public power and the strict rules of market negotiation. We therefore need to examine the conditions for the existence of such mechanisms.

The work of Ostrom (1990) completes our thinking, by imagining autonomous regulation of the commons by the resource users themselves. This evokes an image of a condominium, where everyone has the right to vote in order to make collective decisions on common parts. Beyond the logic of state intervention and market regulation, Ostrom (1990) envisages mechanisms of self-regulation of the commons by consumers of the resource.

According to Assens (2021), these self-regulatory mechanisms correspond to collective strategies carried out in a collaborative framework within a network that federates territory stakeholders.

2.3. The common resources and the network

The socio-economic benefits derived from belonging to a territory – agglomeration economies in Marshall's (1920) sense – are non-divisible, in that no single member of the territory can appropriate them alone. They benefit everyone, and no one in particular. They cease to exist for the company that decides to leave the territory. These advantages are specific, as they cannot be transferred or copied outside the territory concerned. In these conditions, managing the common resource of a territory requires a collective strategy within a network, which has a local dimension and an indivisible character.

The concept of a network is a very old one. Its origin comes from the Latin *retiolus*, diminutive of *retis* meaning *net*, whose semantic extension led to *reticulum*, meaning *small net*, which gave rise to the noun *reticule*, and the adjectives *reticulated* and *reticular*. The notion of network thus refers to objects with the appearance of a net with mesh-like properties, that is, an assembly strong enough to support the weight of a load by distributing it between the links, and flexible enough to adapt to the shape of the load due to the vacant space at the intersection of the links. The analogy of the net is taken up by Musso (1997) in his description of the network, where he explains that the fishing net holds back and at the same time lets the water flow. The nature of a network results from this ambivalence, which is specific to the net: being able to trap objects and let flows circulate at the same time. Transposed to the management of common resources, the network is seen as a net of lasting alliances between independent partners, which requires the removal of disloyal market intermediaries or bureaucratic state intermediaries and their replacement by trusted intermediaries chosen for their bond to the territory and for their shared objective of managing the common resource.

In this conceptual framework, there are three network configurations (Assens and Courie 2014):

– the piloted network, with a central pilot whose performance depends on the pilot's legitimacy to coordinate and regulate the network;

– the managed network, whose performance is linked to the co-voting arrangements between elected and nonelected members, with a concern for equity in the sharing of relational rents;

– the distributed network, which eliminates all forms of power with the absence of a pilot or governance charter, and whose performance is linked to self-management mechanisms to avoid the dissolution of the network or the need for authority.

In a star-shaped piloted network, the pilot centralizes information and resource interfaces. They represent the network, and as such must maintain overall cohesion with peripheral partners, ensuring compliance with specifications on information systems, quality, logistics and the sharing of gains from collaboration.

In a daisy-chain network, the management of collaborative interfaces is based on a charter of rights and duties, drawn up by representatives chosen or elected from among the members. In this context, care must be taken to ensure that the political dimension of elected representatives does not take precedence over issues of solidarity between all members: elected and nonelected.

Finally, in a distributed network in the form of a point cloud, interfaces are usually of a social or technical nature, based on tacit conventions of exchange and sharing. In this type of network, collaboration enables innovation and unmanned economies of scale to be achieved, provided a balance is maintained between a degree of mesh closure embodied in the "between-us" principle and a degree of mesh openness to extend relational possibilities.

According to this thinking, a territory's strength and attractiveness lies in the ability of local actors to organize themselves into networks, in order to preserve or develop the common resource, whose universal character is asserted within identitarian, political, social, economic and geographical boundaries. We will illustrate this point with two case studies.

2.4. Two case studies on territories managing a networked common resource

2.4.1. *A distributed network: the case of corn production in Alsace*

Alsace is a major producer of corn for human consumption. The warm summer climate of the Alsatian plain is particularly favorable to corn production, and the region's proximity to the Rhine River is also conducive. The river is the preferred transport route for supplying processing plants in northern Europe. Furthermore, the Alsace corn industry has developed specific know-how in terms of production, storage and primary processing, enabling it to meet the exacting demands of the food industry. As a result, the Alsatian corn industry enjoys a reputation for superior quality, which justifies higher production costs than in other regions.

The Alsatian industry is structured around four Collection and Storage Enterprises (CSEs), two of which are cooperatives (*CAC* and *Comptoir Agricole*) and the other two are private companies (*Ambruster Frères* and *Gustave Muller SAS*). They play a structuring role in the industry, as they are both the farmers' main suppliers and their main customers. They benefit from government approval, which is essential if they are to allot the produce of different farmers (i.e. combine the produce of several farmers into a single batch). These companies hold around 95% of the corn market in Alsace and compete fiercely for new farmers.

Competition is based on the quantities to be delivered to manufacturers. These are principally dependent on the quantities delivered by farmers. Each operator is therefore seeking to expand its collection area. This competition takes place not only between private operators, but also between cooperatives, which do not hesitate to acquire stakes in private operators in order to collect in each other's collection zones. *Gustave Muller SAS*, for example, is owned by *Comptoir Agricole.*

Conversely, the reputation for quality of the Alsace corn industry is a collective asset that each operator is keen to protect. The GMO crisis of the late 2000s showed that this reputation could be subject to a tragedy of the commons (Hardin 1968).

When GMOs were first introduced in France in 1998, CSE Alsace offered its farmer customers *Mon 810* corn seed, resistant to the European corn borer. However, these companies were soon alerted by starch and semolina manufacturers, CSEs main downstream customers, as to European consumers' aversion to GMO food products. These manufacturers therefore offer specific contracts to guarantee the absence of GMOs in the corn delivered to them. This situation led the various CSEs in Alsace to adopt a common position. Therefore, the directors of the three main companies decided to coordinate their efforts to develop a common position on GMOs, and to convince the other stakeholders (competitors, farmers and their representatives, and seed companies) to adhere to this position.

For the managers of the three main CSEs, the only way to preserve outlets for human food is to exclude all GMO production in Alsace, to guard against the risk of cross-pollination between GMO and conventional plots (Le Bail et al. 2010). Indeed, given the configuration of the Alsace plain and the high proportion of corn grown there, it could take just a few GMO plots for the GMO content of all crops to be higher than that expected by downstream food manufacturers. To prevent this undesirable spread of GMOs in Alsace, the leading CSEs have convinced their smaller competitors to join them in their vision of a GMO-free Alsace, and to participate in the implementation of production management methods that include other actors. This led to the implementation of specific policies for farmers and seed companies, as well as a collective and informal system for managing the risk of "contamination".

The success of this collective strategy depended first and foremost on the support of farmers. To this end, meetings were quickly organized with corn growers, attended by the heads of the major CSE companies, representatives of farmers' unions and chambers of agriculture, as well as downstream industry representatives. The aim of these meetings was to convince farmers of the danger that the use of GMO varieties represented for the entire Alsatian corn industry. Alongside this information, the companies set up a social pressure mechanism to limit the use of GMO seeds by farmers. To this end, they carry out a daily test by taking a sample from each delivery. In the event of GMO detection, CSE sends a letter to all farmers concerned, including the test result and the list of farmers who have delivered that day.

To ensure that Alsatian farmers have access to GMO-free seed batches, all CSEs have collectively set up procedures for controlling seed batches entering Alsace, so as to exclude any batches containing traces of GMOs.

Finally, all CSEs have set up an "informal risk management system". They rely on their network of technical sales representatives to identify seeds purchased in Alsace, and to prevent the risk of batches of varieties not marketed in Alsace entering the human food collection.

All of these actions have helped to strengthen the reputation for quality of Alsatian corn, not only in the eyes of the actors involved, but also internally for all of those involved in the production process. As a result of this collective strategy implemented by all CSE actors, this reputation has become a specific collective asset. Failure to respect it could lead to the loss of this asset through the delivery of GMO-contaminated batches to the semolina or starch industry. This strategic asset is therefore subject to a tragedy of the commons. The management strategy implemented by the CSE network is a form of commons management (Ostrom 1990) of this asset (see Table 2.1).

Management principles	Their application in Alsace
Clearly defined boundaries	Only Alsatian farmers and their CSE can capitalize on the reputation of the Alsace corn industry.
Matching appropriation rules to local conditions	The rules for managing and preserving these assets are specific to Alsace.
Collective decision mechanisms	The entire strategy was put in place informally by CSE managers.
Monitoring	There are many different monitoring systems for different actors (seed companies, farmers, etc.).
Gradual penalties	Penalties are linked to social pressure.
Conflict resolution mechanisms	The informal network enables conflicts to be quickly identified and resolved.
Minimal recognition of organizational rights	The collective mechanism is recognized by customers and suppliers outside Alsace.
Interlocking organizations	There are systems adapted to each level of the industry.

Table 2.1. *Managing the reputation of Alsatian corn as a common resource*

This informal way of operating, which characterizes the Alsatian industry, is based on relationships of trust and a very specific culture in which consultation is an almost systematic practice. The original way in which the Alsatian system operates is partly due to the socio-cultural characteristics of the territory in which it is located. It is a territory with a strong identity and its own dialect.

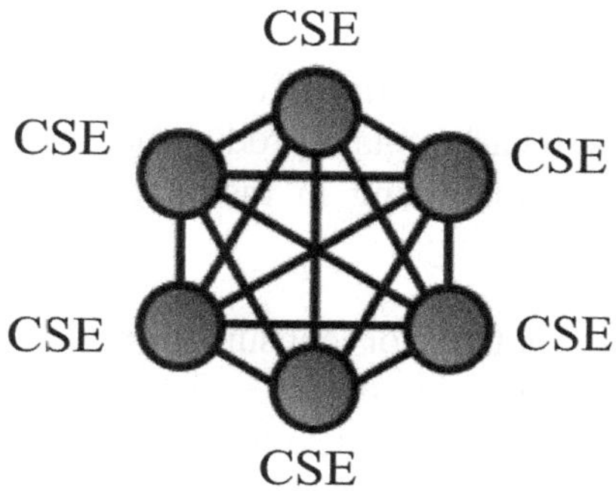

Figure 2.1. *Point cloud network*

This mode of organization corresponds to a point-cloud network configuration (see Figure 2.1). Interactions between CSE managers are regular and informal. They mainly concern technical issues relating to the GMO-free management system: how to set up monitoring mechanisms or how to share information between CSEs on GMO management.

Apart from these specific issues, the competitive relationship between network members is maintained, and building alliances with other actors is entirely possible. Nevertheless, when it comes to issues that could harm maize production in Alsace or the reputation of the Alsace maize industry, actors turn to the network. For example, when a corn pest appeared (corn rootworm larvae), all network members coordinated to adopt a collective treatment response (Hannachi 2011).

2.4.2. *A daisy chain network: a case study on the Noirmoutier cooperative*

Situated on the French coast, the island of Noirmoutier is a small territory with a surface area of 49 km^2 (site of the *communauté de communes*[1]) consisting of four communes. The island's climate is oceanic. The northern part of the island has sandy soils that are particularly well-suited to potato cultivation. Potatoes have been grown on the island since the early 20th century. It was, however, a food crop, as the island was more oriented towards cereal production, as evidenced by the presence of 32 mills at the time. Early potato production began to develop in the 1920s with the development of the *Barfleur* variety. This agricultural activity was mainly carried out by women, while men were more involved in fishing and salt-making. The creation of the Noirmoutier agricultural cooperative in 1945 accelerated the development of early potato production, which was far more profitable than other activities. Today, the Noirmoutier agricultural cooperative specializes in early potato production, that is, potatoes harvested before full maturity and remaining in the ground for less than 100 days between planting and harvesting.

In comparison to a potato for consumption, the early potato has an excellent taste, a higher vitamin content and a lower starch content. As the potato skin does not have time to thicken, early potatoes cannot be kept out

1 A *communauté de communes* is a federation of municipalities in France. It forms a framework within which local tasks are carried out together. It is the least-integrated form of intercommunality.

of the ground for more than a few days if their organoleptic qualities are to be preserved. For these reasons, potatoes are exported the same day or the day after harvesting, after washing and packaging at the cooperative.

Since the 1960s, the island's farmers have practiced potato monoculture. The cooperative's efforts have led to the development of the "Noirmoutier potato" brand, whose early and artisanal character (the potatoes are planted and harvested by hand) gives it significant added value. This authenticity is reinforced by a quality label (*label rouge*) obtained in 2019. In order to develop the early potato market, farmers have set up, via their cooperative, a major industrial facility for washing and bagging potatoes. The cooperative is also responsible for marketing and communicating about the early potato, and defines the marketing strategy for the "Noirmoutier potato" brand. Farmers grow several varieties adapted to each market. To guarantee equal access to the most profitable markets, each farmer receives the same percentage of each variety.

In the interests of fairness, farmers have drawn up "regulations governing the organization and discipline of the production and marketing of early potatoes and other products" (authors' translation). These regulations are reviewed each year at the cooperative's general meeting. It defines the percentage of the variety each member will receive, the planting and harvest delivery periods to the cooperative (so that each member can benefit from access to the most profitable markets).

There are several ways in which farmers can monitor the use of resources and compliance with jointly developed specifications. The first, of course, is proximity between farmers. The island of Noirmoutier is small, and each farmer's plot is close enough to the other to know if their neighbor is not respecting the rules. In addition to this close proximity, inspections of the plots carried out with the cooperative's technical advisor enable the latter to ensure that the rules are being respected. Last but not least, the cooperative recently set up an island-wide information system recording the practices carried out on each plot. This information system is inputted by the farmers themselves.

This collective management system is recognized outside the island. Noirmoutier has been granted a derogation by the French Ministry of Agriculture to continue producing potatoes despite the presence of nematodes. The granting of this derogation is linked to recognition of the original system put in place by Noirmoutier farmers.

As we can see, the farmers of Noirmoutier have succeeded in implementing collective management of potato production and their brand as a common resource. Nevertheless, this collective management encompasses other components. For farmers, collective management has become a habit, a recurring way of dealing with the problems at hand. In this way, collective management concerns not only the direct production and marketing of potatoes, but also the management of varietal resistance, land and water.

Within this joint management of their brand, the cooperative plays a central role. It not only manages the marketing of potatoes, but also provides technical support to farmers and distributes varieties. The cooperative is run both by a director, who is an employee of the cooperative, and by an elected president. The president is supported by a board of directors made up of around 10 farmers. The board of directors is renewed every year. This enables each farmer to play an active role in the management of the cooperative, and prevents any one group from controlling it. In addition to managing their brand and production as a common asset, the 23 Noirmoutier Island farmers have built a daisy-like network (see Figure 2.2) that ensures the brand's development while leaving room for individual maneuvering.

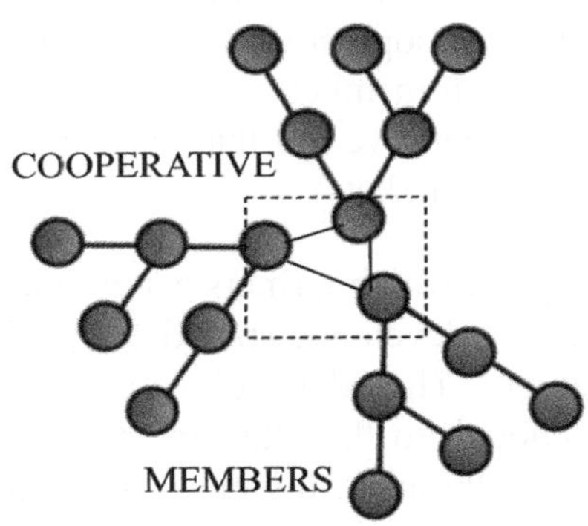

Figure 2.2. *Daisy chain network*

Concurrently, at the initiative of one of its members, the cooperative is exploring new markets (Noirmoutier onion) to develop new sources of revenue, while meeting an agronomic constraint of crop rotation.

2.5. Conclusion

What can we learn from this reflection? There are a number of similarities between our two case studies. First of all, we can measure the inefficiency of the state or the market in defending the common resource on a territorial scale. Let us return to the case of the corn industry in Alsace. State legislation is too prescriptive to take account of the specific features of each territory, which can be detrimental, for example, to the reputation of the corn industry in Alsace when it comes to the introduction of GMOs. Relying on the market to regulate the actions of Alsace's agricultural cooperatives is not a solution, at the risk of reinforcing a form of intensive agriculture with the widespread use of GMOs and the gradual loss of biodiversity and the Alsatian quality label. In order to strike a balance between the economic stakes of the market and the sustainable preservation of natural resources in an agri-food industry, cooperative networking provides solutions, reconciling the individual interests of each partner with the collective interests of the territory.

The success of a network strategy on a territorial scale is always based on two essential conditions: cultural proximity and a sense of identity between the actors based on the territory, which creates a climate of trust sufficient to facilitate collaboration despite rivalries; the presence on the territory of all links in a value chain, as in Alsace, or of all elements of an ecosystem, as in Noirmoutier, legitimizing industrial collaboration based on a climate of trust. When the two conditions of cultural and industrial proximity are reunited, a network strategy emerges. It is not necessarily planned, and unfolds in the form of a point cloud with the mutual adjustment of partners, as in Alsace, or in the form of a daisy chain with offshoots coordinated by a cooperative acting as a trusted third party for members and their stakeholders.

In each case, these network strategies illustrate the principle of agglomerative economics as defined by Marshall (1920), insofar as the location and concentration of farmers in the same territory enables each of them to benefit from economies of scale, productivity gains and development capacity, without increasing the size of their farms. This agglomeration principle reinforces the territory's influence and attractiveness in certain sectors, such as corn in Alsace and potatoes in Noirmoutier, areas of regional specialization that are considered common assets. In this context, to preserve and enhance agricultural regionalism, a network strategy appears more effective than regulation by the state or the market.

2.6. References

Arrow, K. (1970). *Social Choice and Individual Values*, 2nd edition. Yale University Press, New Haven.

Assens, C. (2021). *Réseaux : les nouvelles règles du jeu.* VA Éditions, Versailles.

Assens, C. and Courie, A. (2014). Du réseau à la fédération de réseaux : l'évolution des mécanismes de gouvernance. *Question(s) de management*, 8, 27–36.

Baumol, W.J. and Bowen, W.G. (1966). *Performing Arts. The Economic Dilemma.* Cambridge University Press, Cambridge.

Fourcade, C. and Torres, O. (eds) (2003). Les PME entre région et mondialisation : processus de "glocalisation" et dynamiques de proximité. *Cahier de l'ERFI*, 10(4), 136.

Hannachi, M. (2011). La coopétition au service du bien commun. Les stratégies des entreprises de collecte et de stockage face aux OGM. PhD Thesis, Université Versailles Saint-Quentin-en-Yvelines, Paris.

Hardin, G. (1968). The tragedy of the commons. *Science*, 162(3859), 1243–1248.

Le Bail, M., Lecroart, B., Gauffreteau, A., Angevin, F., Messéan, A. (2010). Effect of the structural variables of landscapes on the risks of spatial dissemination between GM and non-GM maize. *European Journal of Agronomy*, 33(1), 12–23.

Marshall, A. (1920). *Principles of Economics*. Macmillan, London.

Musgrave, R.A. (1959). *The Theory of Public Finance*. McGraw Hill, New York.

Musso, P. (1997). *Télécommunication et philosophie des réseaux, la postérité paradoxale de Saint-Simon*. Presses Universitaires de France, Paris.

Ostrom, E. (1990). *Governing the Commons. The Evolution of Institutions for Collective Action*. Cambridge University Press, Cambridge.

Samuelson, P.A. (1954). The pure theory of public expenditure. *The Review of Economics and Statistics*, 36(4), 387–389.

Tinbergen, J. (1956). *Economic Policy: Principles and Design*. North Holland Publishing Company, Amsterdam.

Williamson, O.E. (1983). *Markets and Hierarchies*. The Free Press, New York.

3

Building Collective Environmental Action Within Territories

3.1. Introduction

In France, air pollution is responsible for between 48,000 and 67,000 premature deaths every year (Lelieveld et al. 2019). The consequences of pollutant emissions are also environmental (depletion of pollinator species, ecosystem imbalance) and financial (total cost of outdoor air pollution estimated at €68 billion)[1]. The main sources of pollutant emissions (PM10 particles, NOx, etc.) are linked to road transport, residential sector (wood heating, burning of green waste, etc.), agricultural activities (tractors, spreading, livestock rearing, etc.) and industrial activities (building materials, chemical processes, etc.)[2].

While air pollution has been considered a public health issue since 1987 by the World Health Organization (WHO), France recognized the right "for everyone to breathe air that is not harmful to their health"[3] in 1996. Today,

---

Chapter written by Camille FIORE and Solange HERNANDEZ.

1 Examples: medical expenses, hospitalization, work stoppages, reduced life expectancy, etc. See: Sénat (2015). Commission d'enquête sur le coût économique et financier de la pollution de l'air, 18 [Online]. Available at: http://www.senat.fr/commission/enquete/cout_economique_et_financier_de_la_pollution_de_lair.html.

2 ADEME (2019). La pollution de l'air en 10 questions, 6–7 [Online]. Available at: https://librairie.ademe.fr/cadic/592/guide-pratique-pollution-air-en-10-questions.pdf?modal=false.

3 Article 1 of the French law on air and the rational use of energy, known as the LAURE law.

air quality is considered the third most important environmental concern for the French[4].

Faced with these challenges, public policies have evolved to be more effective. Therefore, since 2014, with the implementation of the *MAPTAM* "Law of Modernization of the Territorial Public Action and Affirmation of the Metropolises", the State has granted cities abilities aimed at developing policies that permit the improvement of air quality in a harmonized way over an enlarged geographical perimeter. In concrete terms, territorial organizations are expected to draw up new strategic documents, such as *PCAET* and *PCAE* "Territorial/Metropolitan Climate–Air–Energy Plans", in addition to *PPA* "Atmosphere Protection Plan" and *SRCAE* "Regional Climate–Air–Energy Plans".

Furthermore, in view of the various European legal disputes, air quality roadmaps have been commissioned for the 12 French zones concerned, in order to demonstrate to the European Court of Justice the efforts being undertaken. The French government therefore strongly encourages territorial authorities to take collective action to combat air pollution. However, after being repeatedly called to order, the French government was doubly condemned[5] by the courts for repeatedly exceeding its limits on nitrogen dioxide and PM10 particle emissions. It faces a fine of €100 million.

While the State's willingness to act – or have someone act – on a territorial scale is quite clear, there is considerable uncertainty about *how*. According to the French National Assembly[6] (2016, p. 250), air quality governance "remains to be built". The complexity of the situation is heightened by the consequences of the *territorial big bang* (Carmouze et al. 2019), because when it comes to air quality, the abilities assigned to the territorial authorities sometimes overlap. This is the case for cities, which are responsible for drawing up policies for their territory, and for regions, known as "leaders"[7], for ensuring the coherence of climate–air–energy policies.

4 ADEME (2020). Les représentations sociales du changement climatique, 8 [Online]. Available at: https://librairie.ademe.fr/changement-climatique-et-energie/4057-representations-sociales-du-changement-climatique-21-eme-vague.html.

5 A first condemnation from the Court of Justice of the European Union came in October 2019, and a second, from the *Conseil d'État* in August 2021.

6 National Assembly (2016). Rapport d'information sur l'évaluation des politiques publiques de lutte contre la pollution de l'air, no. 3772.

7 Proposed translation for: *chefs de file*.

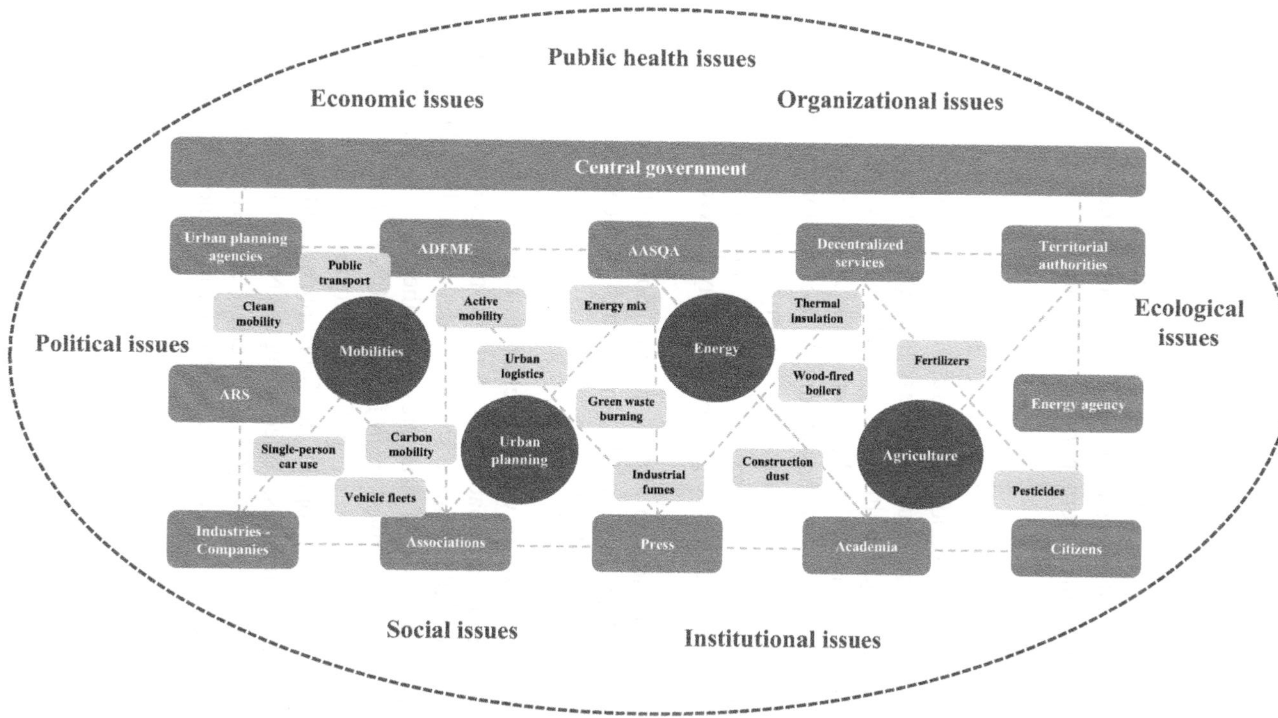

Figure 3.1. *A research object with transversal and interdependent elements (source: Fiore (2022, p. 123)). For a color version of this figure, see www.iste.co.uk/albertcromarias/collective.zip*

Territorial authorities are faced with a government injunction to work collectively and coherently across a vast area. However, there is no practical indication of this in the regulations. What is more, air pollution is a cross-cutting issue, involving both the public sphere – at the state and territorial level – and the private market and non-market spheres. The multiplicity of stakeholders, existing political tensions, the fragmentation of competencies, the technical nature of the subject and citizens' modes of action are all interrelated elements; this interdependence is a marker of complexity (Morin 1995, pp. 110–111).

Finally, in a complex context, two types of strategic management seem appropriate. On the one hand, collaborative strategic management, defined as "the organized and structured process through which public and private inter-organizational and multi-actor collectives develop, implement and evaluate collective strategies"[8] (Favoreu et al. 2016, p. 470); on the other hand, strategic management based on "a conception of the processes involved in formulating/implementing an organization's strategy, giving priority to adapting the strategy as it is put into action, so as to take advantage of situations that emerge along the way"[9] (Avenier 1999, p. 5).

With this in mind, to what extent does collaborative strategic management facilitate the establishment and implementation of public policies to improve air quality?

To answer this question, we first return to the concept of collaboration, then detail the various approaches to strategic management (Favoreu et al. 2016), the model of collaborative strategies developed by Clarke and Fuller (2010) and the dimensions of strategies along the way (Avenier 1999). Next, we present the results, derived from Fiore's (2022) thesis work, based on a multiple case study of three metropolitan territories (Grand Paris, Grenoble-Alpes-Métropole, Eurométropole de Strasbourg) and 49 semi-structured interviews and 228 documents, coded using the NVivo 12 software as part of a thematic content analysis (Gavard-Perret and Helme-Guizon 2018). Finally, we offer advice and recommendations for public managers.

8 Authors' translation.
9 Authors' translation.

3.2. Inter-organizational relations and air quality policies: an appraisal of collaborative strategic management

Since this chapter examines the concept of collaborative strategic management, we need to begin by understanding what collaboration is. Like cooperation and coordination, collaboration belongs to the concept of inter-organizational relations (IORs), which are conceptualized as a continuum that highlights the order of magnitude and intensity of these different types of interaction, as shown in Figure 3.2.

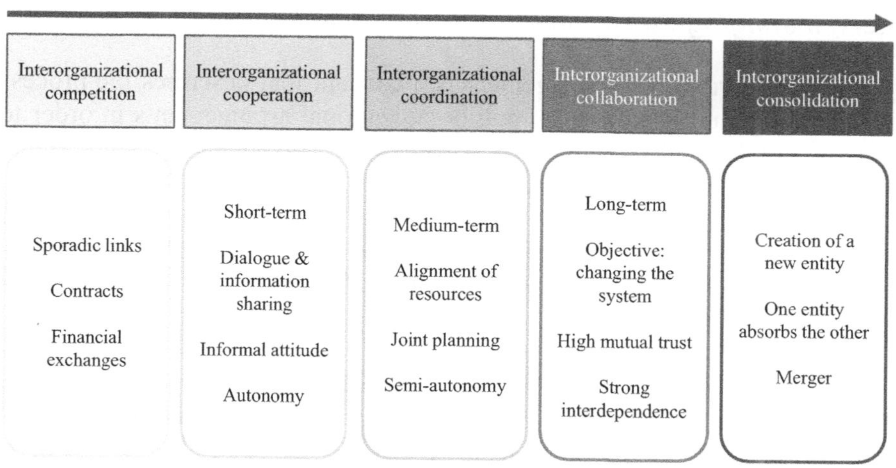

Figure 3.2. *The IOR continuum (source: Fiore (2022, p. 83), after Keast (2016))*

In the public sphere, collaborations in the form of IORs appear in the literature as the most appropriate apparatus to develop, since it aims to respond to complex problems and a changing environment (McGuire 2006; Thomson and Perry 2006; Clarke and Fuller 2010; Clarke 2011). As we indicated in the introduction to this chapter, the air issue and the way it is dealt with in the context of public action are characteristic of complexity.

For McNamara (2016), collaboration can take two forms: mandated or voluntary. In *mandated collaboration*, organizations are brought together under a higher authority to address a complex problem. This organization is thus placed "in a position of authority over other partnering organizations" (McNamara 2016, p. 72). A *voluntary collaboration*, on the other hand, is set up with a view to significant long-term change. Indeed, it "required much closer relationships, connections, and resources and even a blurring of the boundaries between agencies" (Keast et al. 2007, p. 19). In other words, "participants relinquish some autonomy to the collective arrangement" (McNamara 2016, p. 74). This is not straightforward, and Vangen (2017) points out that achieving collaboration does not necessarily signify project success.

Therefore, let us see how public organizations can collectively develop a strategy and implement it through collaborative strategic management.

3.2.1. *Managing stakeholders through a collaborative approach*

Collaborative public management is a concept that describes the process of facilitating and operating in multiorganizational arrangements in order to remedy problems that cannot be solved – or solved easily – by single organizations (McGuire 2006, p. 33).

For Favoreu et al. (2016), the formation of strategies in a public environment can be analyzed through three approaches: rational, political and collaborative.

In short, the *rational approach* sees strategy as the result of a cognitive process, enabling objective decision-making. The *political approach*, on the other hand, is based on the principle of bounded rationality. Here, strategy is the result of "a multiplicity of local rationalities, each with its own objectives and interests"[10] (Favoreu et al. 2016, p. 468), and therefore involves conflict logics and the formation of coalitions. Negotiation between actors therefore plays an important role, since the strategic formation process in this case is based on a "quest for social legitimacy and phenomena of mimetic or coercive isomorphism"[11] (Favoreu et al. 2016, p. 469). Finally, as part of the *collaborative approach*:

> Strategy formation [...] is seen as a complex phenomenon, made up of interactions and exchanges being established between groups or networks of interdependent actors, which leads to the co-production of collective solutions and strategies[12] (Favoreu et al. 2016, p. 469).

10 Authors' translation.

11 Authors' translation.

12 Authors' translation.

	Rational planning	Political approach	Collaborative strategic management
Role of strategy	– Ensuring fit between and organization and its environment	– Ritual and symbolism – Function of legitimization and mimeticism	– Strategy as a practice of learning, innovation, and knowledge sharing
Strategy organization	– Steering development by defining objectives and action plans	– Strategy as discourse	– Developing interactions and exchanges between stakeholders
Strategy as a learning process	– Deductive and rational – Formalized and sequential – Optimization	– Disorganized – Inductive and bottom-up – Highly dynamic and unpredictable – Logic of conflict management and political pressures	– Vertical and horizontal – Deductive and inductive – Top-down and bottom-up – Selected solutions enable key players to be mobilized and resources realized for collective strategies
Nature of tools and concepts used	– Diagnostic, evaluation and decision-making tools	– Not available	– Mechanisms for establishing relationships and managing interactions – Stakeholder mapping – Strategic intent and vision
Strategy content and degree of formalization	– High degree of formalization – Definition and hierarchization of objectives, action plans	– Low degree of formalization: multiple, ambigious objectives with little involvement – Discontinuity of strategies	– Mixed – Existence of stable global orientations (vision, missions) but co-constructed solutions and actions plans
Role of a public manager	– Technical and methodological management	– Management of conflicts, dissensions and coalitions of support	– Relational governance – Management of interorganizational interactions and arrangements
Designing organizations	– Mechanical, hierarchical and neutral structures	– Political arenas and networks	– Complex and diverse open systems

Designing change	– Intentional and organized changed – Radical or progressive change – Programmatic approach	– Reactive and discontinuous change – Managing conflicting interests	– Mixed conception: change framed in its broad outlines but emergent in its realization

Table 3.1. *The three approaches to strategy formation in public settings (source: Fiore (2022*[13]*, p. 117), after Favoreu et al. (2016, p. 482))*

This approach is naturally accompanied by "collaborative costs" (Favoreu et al. 2016, p. 479), such as financial or time resources, but ultimately this leads to collaborative benefits, such as the decompartmentalization of actors.

Favoreu et al. (2016) indicated that the latter approach was currently the most common, not least because of the complexity of the issues inherent in the public sector. Table 3.1 shows the differences between these three approaches.

3.2.2. *Strategic collaborative management: which method?*

Clarke and Fuller define collaborative strategy as:

> … the joint determination of the vision and long-term collaborative goals for addressing a given social problem, along with the adoption of both organizational and collective courses of action and the allocation of resources to carry out these courses of action (Clarke and Fuller 2010, p. 86).

We understand that this includes the work done by each organization, as well as the inter-organizational work aimed at achieving the objectives shared by all partners. Collaborative strategy focuses on the collaborative formulation of the strategic plan and its implementation at organizational and inter-organizational levels, in five stages (see Figure 3.3).

13 Authors' translation.

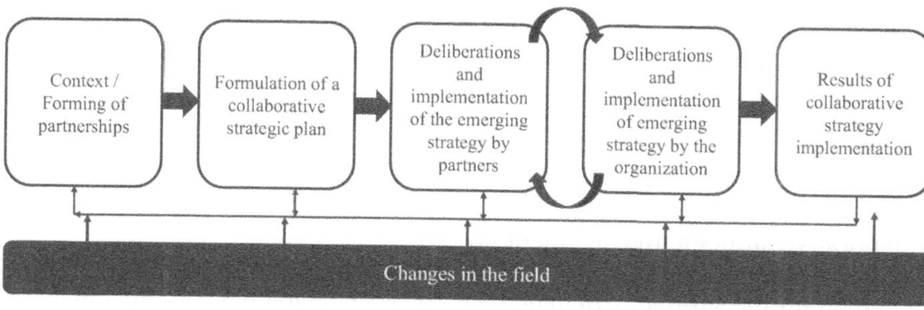

Figure 3.3. *The collaborative strategic management process (source: Clarke and Fuller (2010, p. 90))*

The first step in the process is to *assess the context*, that is, "different situational considerations related to the social problem(s) being considered" (Clarke and Fuller 2010, p. 88), and to *form the partnership(s)*. The aim is to map out potential stakeholders and the necessary resources. Based on this, an organization would bring all the partners together and put them in contact with each other.

The second stage, known as "*collaborative strategic plan formulation*" (Clarke and Fuller 2010, p. 90), should lead the various partners to develop a shared vision and ultimately define a collaborative strategic plan, notably through negotiations. While the objectives must naturally relate to the actions to be carried out, they can also be understood through statements of vision or values. In terms of timing, this stage takes place quickly, or on the contrary, can take years. It all depends on the nature and scope of the issues under consideration.

The third and fourth stages take place simultaneously. The *implementation of the collaborative strategic plan* is divided between aspects handled collectively, and those carried out by a single organization. Moreover, this implementation is the result of both deliberate and emergent approaches, allowing for adaptation to contextual hazards and changes. This can be seen in what the authors call "feedback loops" (Clarke and Fuller 2010, p. 97), which are illustrated by arrows in Figure 3.3.

The final stage is the *realization of results*, following the implementation of various actions.

Also, to reflect the complexity inherent in inter-organizational collaboration, Clarke and Fuller (2010, p. 90) add a "*changes in the domain*" box to their model, as external factors can influence the process at any moment, with the result that the formulation of the strategic plan can be reversed. These various elements highlight the potential for corrective action, overlapping activities, and cyclical decision-making inherent to the collaborative strategic management process.

Collaborative strategic management is both a deliberate and emergent strategy. This raises questions about the advantages and disadvantages of this back-and-forth process, as well as how it should be managed. To this end, let us take a look at "Strategizing On-the-Way" (Avenier 1999).

3.2.3. *Strategizing on-the-way management*

A mix of deliberate and emergent strategy, *Strategizing On-the-Way* is "a conception of the processes involved in formulating/implementing an organization's strategy, emphasizing adaptation of the strategy as it is put into action, so as to take advantage of situations that emerge along the way"[14] (Avenier 1999, p. 5). This is based on "a principle of intentional intervention that is constantly reconsidered in the light of phenomena that arise in the course of action"[15] (Avenier 1999). The main idea behind "strategizing on-the-way by doing" is to overcome the debate between pre-established or deliberate strategy, on the one hand, and unintentional or emergent strategy, on the other hand. This is a matter of implementing step-by-step actions that represent both an initial strategic intention and an adaptation to contextual emergences. It is this dialogical approach that responds to the complexity experienced by organizations.

In terms of process, the starting point is strategic intent. This "implies a strategic vision, defined over the long term, and embodying what the organization aspires to become. This intention represents a dream, a desired future rather than an extrapolation of the present"[16] (Hernandez 2017). The adaptation of strategy then passes through two distinct moments. First, there are moments when initially planned strategic actions are ready to be implemented. Before taking this next step, it is essential for organizations to take the time to look back and consider the changes that have taken place in

14 Authors' translation.
15 Authors' translation.
16 Authors' translation.

the context, as well as the feedback from previous stages. Second moments occur when certain contextual evolutions render the current strategy obsolete. They concern both phenomena “monitored” by the organizations and emerging phenomena that had not been envisaged.

Finally, the back-and-forth takes place between vision and action.

Added to this is the distinction to be made between different levels of actors. Avenier (1999, p. 2) talks of global, peripheral and local levels. In the case of air quality improvement policies, we can divide the actors, for example, into state and territorial levels. On the one hand, the state sets out its vision – to improve air quality – and asks territorial authorities to work collectively to achieve greater coherence. On the other hand, territorial organizations adapt this global vision to the specific characteristics of their territory, depending, for example, on whether it is urban or rural. In metropolitan areas, for example, action on mobility (local) translates into a desire to reduce air pollution (global), notably through the introduction of a restricted traffic zone.

3.3. Air quality improvement policies: development, implementation and limits

In France, the fight against atmospheric pollution is organized around two missions: firstly, the measurement and monitoring of pollution levels; secondly, the implementation of public policies. It is the latter that is of interest here.

Within this framework, the central government sets strategic national guidelines, notably through the *PRÉPA*, the “National Plan to Reduce Emissions of Atmospheric Pollutants”[17], which was established in 2016.

At the local level, two types of projects can be undertaken to improve air quality. On the one hand, local actors are obliged to produce regulatory documents, such as *PPA* “Atmosphere Protection Plan”[18] or Air Quality

17 Proposed translation: *Plan national de réduction des émissions de polluants atmosphériques*.

18 The *PPA* is the regulatory document that defines the strategy for improving air quality in a given territory. It includes the information needed to draw up an inventory and assessment of air quality in the territory concerned, as well as preventive and corrective measures, whether permanent or temporary, for all pollutant-emitting sectors, with the aim of reducing atmospheric pollutants in the area.

Roadmaps[19]. Also, territorial authorities can choose to implement certain actions to combat the pollutant emissions most prevalent on their territory.

For example, the Greater Paris region and the Strasbourg Eurométropole have placed greater emphasis on the issue of mobility, with the introduction of a low-emission zone (LEZ)[20]. In the Grenoble metropolitan area, local actors attempted to solve the problem of emissions linked to wood heating by setting up a *Fonds-air-bois* ("Wood-Air Fund")[21]. Both initiatives were supported by the central government, which launched calls for projects to help territorial authorities finance them.

As we will see, the projects carried out, whether regulatory or voluntary, are built within a framework of collaborative strategic management. However, there are a number of obstacles at various levels.

3.3.1. *Building and implementing a territorial air quality policy through hybrid management*

Our findings on strategic management (Fiore 2022, pp. 284–293) are in line with those of Favoreu et al. (2016), since it is 1) the collaborative approach that appears to have the highest adoption among local actors. However, the 2) rational and 3) political approaches are also prominent in project development. As such, we are tasked with finding a hybrid strategic management approach.

1) All projects are based on meetings between stakeholders, so that they can collectively move forward in their thinking and decision-making. For example, in the context of the *PPA* "Atmosphere Protection Plan" for the Grenoble metropolitan area, one respondent explained:

"We've had a *PPA* since 2006, quite a long time. And at the invitation of the Prefect, so the State services, a certain number of actors have been around the same table since about that time"[22].

19 Fourteen zones in France have been obliged to produce one. It is a tool designed to coordinate players in a given territory, and to reinforce actions to combat air pollution.

20 LEZs (Low-Emission Zones) are traffic zones reserved for cleaner transport.

21 The Fonds air-bois or Prime air-bois, launched in 2016, offered financial assistance for individuals wishing to change their old wood-burning appliance or open fireplace for a "Flamme verte" ("Green Flame") – labeled wood heater.

22 Authors' translation.

On the Strasbourg Eurométropole territory, several projects were carried out in "local air committees". This format enables local actors to work on air quality actions *across the board*, while *mobilizing ever more stakeholders*. One respondent stated that:

> Local air committees are forums for debate at local level within the framework of *PPA* "Atmosphere Protection Plan", involving the State, State operators, ADEME, etc. […]. […] In these forums, we say here are the actions that have been decided upon, those that are underway, and those that could be taken. Therefore, there's a debate and we can say to an association or a company present, here's what we can do. So spread the word in your networks, get your projects off the ground. We can help you. Then we'll put the project together with the actors involved[23].

These meetings are also an opportunity for stakeholders to offer *feedback* on actions taken, as explained by a respondent from the Greater Paris region in the context of the *PPA* "Atmosphere Protection Plan" review:

> Since 2017, an annual review meeting has been organized by the State services and the Region. Everyone gives feedback on the actions implemented, especially innovative ones. We share, we all work in the same direction to improve air quality. It is an interesting novelty[24].

Strategy therefore becomes a means of learning and generating new knowledge, which is one of the hallmarks of *collaborative management*.

2) Rational planning, on the other hand, can be seen in the various tools used by stakeholders to build a territory's strategy, from an informed initial assessment to the *setting of precise objectives*. These include territorial diagnostics, preliminary studies and monitoring indicators. For example, several preliminary studies (impacts on air quality and public health, economic consequences) enabled the actors in the Greater Paris region to make decisions about the future low-emission zone (LEZ). A respondent from Strasbourg also indicated how studies can be used:

23 Authors' translation.

24 Authors' translation.

> We have quantified actions based on pollutant emissions, industrial emissions, car fleet emissions [...]. We also evaluate actions qualitatively, for the behavioral aspect: do people discipline themselves, do they burn green waste less? [...] And every ten years, there are mobility surveys to see what changes have taken place in behavior and choices. Are we cycling more often? Or are we still using the car?

3) Finally, the *political approach* can be viewed from two angles. It can be used to encourage actors to make a greater commitment to air quality, as part of the pursuit for legitimacy. It can also be used to demonstrate that organizations are already investing in air issues. For example, certain actions are presented as powerful levers for improving air quality, when in fact it is difficult to predict their real impact. In this context, the strategy becomes a symbol, or even a discourse. This last element is present in the revision of the *PPA* "Atmosphere Protection Plan", judged by some as lacking ambition:

The *PPA* is not ambitious enough: even in the self-assessment, we did not meet European regulations in 2020; whereas, normally a *PPA* is designed to do just that.

Let us turn our focus now towards the project implementation phase.

3.3.2. *The strategic process: a mix of the collaborative approach and "strategizing on-the-way"*

With regards to the process of defining and implementing collaborative strategies, our results (Fiore 2022, pp. 294–304) did not entirely correspond to the model proposed by Clarke and Fuller (2010) (see Figure 3.3).

Initially, projects to improve air quality were launched either in response to an injunction from a higher authority, as with the case of the *PPA*, or as a result of a desire on the part of local actors, particularly elected representatives who wished to make a commitment to the health of citizens in their territory. In such cases, experimentation takes place at the local level. In this context, *partnerships are formed.*

The formulation of a *collaborative strategic plan* involves moments of negotiation, based on an informal search for meaning. Stakeholders debate which actions to implement, how, and by what means. Negotiation also concerns the operationalization of actions (financing, communication).

The *implementation of the strategic plan* can be seen in its organizational dimension. For example, in the case of the low-emission zone (LEZ) project, each organization acts alone, as each mayor signs a traffic decree for their city. Collective implementation does not appear to be taking place.

However, *Feedback loops* appear in the course of projects. Punctuated by meetings, they provide an opportunity for local and national actors to go back and forth. They enable iterative reflection on the strategic vision of the actions to be implemented, as well as on feedback. Projects are thus built *on-the-way* (Avenier 1999), in the image of the collaborative strategic management process defined by Clarke and Fuller (2010) (see Figure 3.4).

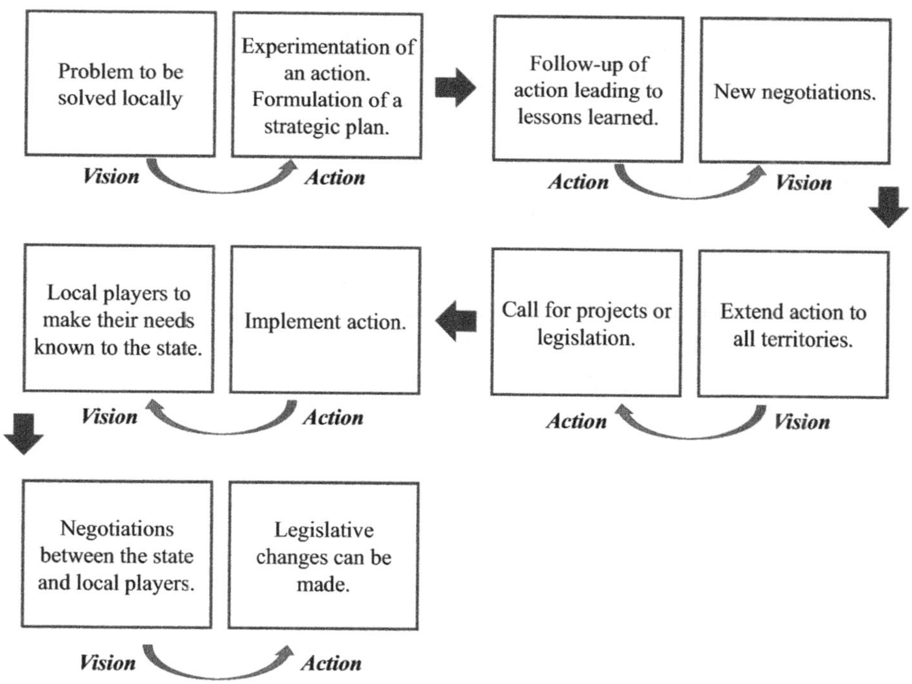

Figure 3.4. *The step-by-step aspect of actions to improve air quality (source: Fiore and Hernandez, based on Fiore (2022, p. 373))*

Based on these results, let us examine the effectiveness of this hybrid strategic management and project implementation process. Is the collaboration of actors effective when they are managed in this way? Is the work “on-the-way” approach always appropriate to the project being implemented? Also, what problems are local actors likely to encounter?

3.3.3. *Difficulties encountered by stakeholders*

Various factors slow down or prevent public action to improve air quality, as Table 3.2 shows.

Taking action to improve air quality is not easy, and requires a certain courage in the face of political, institutional and societal difficulties.

Although public managers are setting up collaborative approaches to bring the whole territory to progress in terms of knowledge about air and to act for the health of citizens, many elements demonstrate the dysfunction of air governance.

Finally, there are three main obstacles to project effectiveness. First, the existence of an institutional brake, that is, due to a lack of human, financial or legal resources, and the distribution of powers and competencies, directly linked to decisions taken by the central government. Second, a lack of knowledge hinders the ability of stakeholders to reach agreement. Lastly, as improving air quality requires action that is binding for its citizenry, political actors may be reluctant to commit themselves to such a course of action.

Therefore, the main problem is to get all actors, at both national and local levels, to understand the need to improve air quality and to value this approach.

In section 3.4, we highlight some observed practices that could help overcome these obstacles.

Heterogeneity of knowledge makes it difficult to make a diagnosis, and slows down decision-making	*"The level of knowledge of the players around the table is extremely variable. Some are passionate […] Others know next to nothing, or only preconceived ideas. Sharing a diagnosis is not easy. And building a common goal is even harder if you don't agree from the start…". "It's a nightmare […] You really have to fight against misconceptions at every meeting […] So it's very complicated, and you really have to educate people at every stage, at every meeting, and remind them of the figures."*
The difficulty of arbitrating between issues such as air pollution and global warming, which sometimes collide	*"The difficulty for a local authority is: on the one hand, there's the Air-bois bonus, which helps replace old wood-burning appliances with new ones, and on the other, the bonus for replacing gas boilers with wood boilers. Of course, the particle levels are much higher afterwards. So, we have a scheme that reduces CO_2 emissions but not particulate matter."*
A lack of political support due to the unpopularity of the measures to be taken, which are often liberticidal	*"If there isn't the political will at the outset, I don't see how it can work. Today, the State is not the driving force! […] When it comes to experimenting with automated control, the State hasn't given us the tools to implement it, nor the financial resources. Sometimes you get the impression that it's actually optional to improve air quality […] "Local authorities may wonder whether it's worth putting this issue on the table. It's not very positive for territorial marketing. It's not what brings people in (laughs)."*
Political conflicts between different organizations	*"As long as there's political opposition between a regional executive and more local governance, it's going to be complicated. Especially when you have strong personalities like Anne Hidalgo and Valerie Pécresse at the head of these executives."*
A division of powers and competencies that holds back local players	*"Competence isn't very clear: the regions are in charge of air quality, but that doesn't mean much. They don't really have any operational powers. They do have funding powers, so they can help local authorities to set things up, but they can't impose anything on local authorities."*

A contradiction between the scale of power and the scale of action	*"We created the 'metropolitan echelon' because we wanted coherent action. But for the LEZ, the 79 mayors are still in charge."*
Cumbersome consultations and a slow bureaucratic system	*"It's a big job for the technical staff to run all these validation bodies in addition to the deliberations [...] At the same time, we have to keep the elected representatives and directors who take part in these meetings informed on an individual basis. All this with a fairly long hierarchical line. So there are a lot of intermediary stages: prepare the documents two weeks in advance, before the meeting, so that each level of hierarchy can have its say [...]."*
Difficulty in evaluating actions both ex-ante and ex-post	*"If you want this system to work, you have to put in place controls, and the French governent is not putting any resources into it. In the absence of adequate monitoring resources, bad habits return. Yes, it scared people at first, and some are changing their behavior a little. But without the means to control and evaluate...."*

Table 3.2. *The main obstacles to public actions seeking to improve air quality (source: Fiore (2022, pp. 315–338))*

3.4. Recommendations for managers

We present here a number of approaches that can help overcome, to a certain extent, the difficulties associated with stakeholder learning. Indeed, setting up moments of prospective reflection that bring together numerous stakeholders is a means of inter-organizational learning, as well as of defusing conflicts. We then explain how the creation of new inter-territorial organizations fosters dialogue with the national stratum, initiating collaborative management on the global scale of air governance.

3.4.1. *Fostering inter-organizational learning through forward-looking, cross-functional thinking*

Despite numerous training courses and the support of experts, the level of knowledge among stakeholders does not seem to be sufficient. How can this be explained? Fiore's research (2022, p. 397) indicates, for example, that perceptions of mobility are associated with beliefs that are part of the collective imagination, and constitute obstacles to learning. In fact, public action depends on general awareness and reflexive work on our lifestyles and the adaptations they require. Without a paradigm shift, this objective seems difficult to achieve. A double-loop learning approach (Argyris and Schön 1995) is recommended, inviting us to question the values and paradigms that underpin the way organizations function, rather than simply seeking to adapt to changes in the environment.

To put it another way, improving air quality requires organizations to take risks, since they have to experiment with actions that require citizens to change their behavior. These policies are therefore the bearers of a new vision of society, and require everyone to make an effort and deconstruct the way we act.

To this end, the organization of cross-functional, forward-looking reflection sessions is an interesting option. This approach proved extremely positive in the Greater Paris and Strasbourg Eurométropole areas. For the former, the construction of a White Paper on Mobility, published in March 2018, helped to overcome political conflicts and other disagreements. One respondent explained:

> When we started this work, we never thought we'd come out with a book saying we had to optimize freeways, meet air quality challenges, promote cycling and new innovative and technological forms of mobility. […] However, as this forum was a rather vague structure in the political arena, with no decision-making power, strangely enough, we made a lot of progress! Maybe because it's so vague, all the elected representatives come and talk […]. It's interesting in terms of management, because it's a powerful tool. When you can't make decisions, when it's not politically mature or too complicated, you have to disseminate knowledge, share information, debate solutions… And it works![25]

In Strasbourg's case, the *Grenelle des mobilités* was held between 2017 and 2020, to collectively determine the future of mobility in the area. One of the participants explained the benefits:

> In the *Grenelle des mobilités*, we asked all the regions, Alsaciens and Germans, within a 100 km radius, "What do we

25 Authors' translation.

> expect from mobility in the future?" As the mission was entrusted to the urban planning agency, the actors were on neutral ground [laughs]. So, they were able to talk to each other. That was a breakthrough. When you get out of an institutional, political and formal framework, it helps[26].

To set up this informal framework, a specific organization was put in place, as the same respondent explained to us:

> From the outset, we clearly involved an extremely broad panel of local users and actors [...]. Finally, in this non-formal setting, everyone can take part in the debate, the small member of the association with the president of a community of communes in person. It's not institutionalized like a big public meeting. The point was to work around small tables, where everyone is treated as an equal. And in terms of form alone, the workshops ensured that no one felt constrained by an elected official monopolizing the floor, for example[27].

Dialogue between numerous stakeholders, supported by experts in a non-decision-making consultative framework, therefore seems to be an effective way of overcoming, at least for a time, the divergences between organizations with objectives that are both convergent (to bring about changes in mobility, to meet air quality challenges) and divergent, and which are therefore unable to find a common solution. Although these approaches do not lead to concrete action, they are the result of collective reflection and learning, which would leave their mark and enable progress to be made towards improving air quality.

3.4.2. *Joining forces to encourage greater government involvement in air quality issues*

As seen, local public managers are held up, or even blocked, by decisions taken by the state, or because the latter fails to modify the regulatory framework when necessary. In an attempt to overcome this serious difficulty, some elected representatives have decided to join forces and create an association, the *Alliance des collectivités françaises pour la qualité*

---

26 Authors' translation.
27 Authors' translation.

de l'air[28], one of whose aims is to establish, or re-establish, a dialogue with the state.

This inter-territorial collaborative body was set up in Strasbourg following a series of conferences on air quality organized by the Eurométropole. The association's president, who was the city's air quality delegate at the time, recounted:

> We held a conference in 2016, on practices, initiatives that territorial authorities could take in terms of air quality. We invited our Swiss and German neighbors, cities like London and Milan, cities that had done some interesting things, the winners of the "*Villes respirables en 5 ans*"[29] call for projects. At the end, the elected representatives present came up to me to say: it's very interesting to find out what's being done elsewhere, to discuss it amongst ourselves, to see if it's effective, if it's acceptable, etc. And thus, the idea of a network was born; this idea of an informal network between us came from there. The first meeting was in 2017. After a year, there were around forty communities in this informal network. [...] We organized theme days: low-emission zones, urban planning and air, climate and air, micro-sensors and citizen mobilization, and so on. Then we started to be invited to symposiums and national events. We then decided to create a legal entity, an association.

The association became a key player in the fight against atmospheric pollution, particularly due to its role as a bridge-builder between local and national authorities:

> This alliance of territorial authorities for air quality emerged in the wake of the "*Villes respirables en 5 ans*" call for projects, when territorial authorities said to each other: "We need to share our difficulties, our needs and to equip ourselves to make our needs known at the national level. So, we share our findings and see how we can make adjustments at national level. It's quite new but very interesting, it's a form of lobbying at the national level."

28 Proposed translation: Alliance of French Local Authorities for Air Quality.

29 Proposed translation: Breathable Cities in 5 Years.

This lobbying role was also played by the *Groupement des Autorités Responsables du Transport (GART)*[30] in connection with the drafting of the 2019 *Loi d'Orientation des Mobilités (LOM)*[31], which was of interest to local actors in terms of traffic control in the LEZs. A respondent from the Grenoble territory explained the role played by one of their territory's elected representatives, in the context of their duties regarding GART:

> *GART* is a strong lobbying body for the Ministry on mobility issues. So [the elected representative in question] is very involved in this area. He was listened to, particularly during the preparatory work for the *LOM*, which has served us well for the territory[32].

The mission carried out by these two associations is a form of institutional work, that is, "the purposive action of individuals and organizations aimed at creating, maintaining and disrupting institutions" (Lawrence and Suddaby 2006, p. 215). By bringing local actors together, these organizations have the power to establish a form of inter-territorial collaborative management, a real avenue for increasing the weight of the local voice, influencing at the national level, with the objective of upsetting current norms and bringing about regulatory change.

3.5. Conclusion

The aim of this chapter was to understand whether collaborative, strategic management facilitates the establishment and implementation of public policies conducive to improving air quality. The results presented indicate that this type of management, while encouraging dialogue, meetings and ongoing strategic adaptation, does not overcome all the difficulties faced by local public actors. The adage "alone we go faster, together we go further" is not as easy to achieve as it might seem.

The experience of the managers we interviewed shows that, in order to move forward collectively to tackle a complex problem, it is necessary to organize moments of forward thinking that do not call for decision-making. Although at first glance this may seem counter-intuitive, this exercise helps to break down barriers between stakeholders that previously seemed

30 Proposed translation: Group of Authorities Responsible for Transport (also GART).

31 Approximate translation: "French Mobility Orientation Law."

32 Authors' translation.

insurmountable. Similarly, the results of our study clearly indicate that managing the local territory is not enough, since the central state remains the master of the game. It therefore seems necessary to set up bottom-up inter-territorial management approaches to get all national and local public actors to move forward together within a framework of collective intelligence.

3.6. References

Argyris, C. and Schön, D.A. (1995). *Organizational Learning II: Theory, Method, and Practice*. Addison-Wesley, Boston.

Avenier, M.-J. (1999). La complexité appelle une stratégie chemin faisant. *Gestion 2000*, 5(99), 13–44.

Carmouze, L., Hernandez, S., Serval, S. (2019). Through the looking glass: What does strategic planning reveal in French local governments? [Online]. Available at: https://hal-amu.archives-ouvertes.fr/hal-02277944 [Accessed 27 May 2022].

Clarke, A. (2011). Key structural features for collaborative strategy implementation: A study of sustainable development/local agenda 21 collaborations. *Management & Avenir*, 50(10), 153–171.

Clarke, A. and Fuller, M. (2010). Collaborative strategic management: Strategy formulation and implementation by multi-organizational cross-sector social partnerships. *Journal of Business Ethics*, 94(S1), 85–101.

Favoreu, C., Carassus, D., Maurel, C. (2016). Le management stratégique en milieu public : approche rationnelle, politique ou collaborative ? *Revue Internationale des Sciences Administratives*, 82(3), 465.

Fiore, C. (2022). Le management des relations interorganisationnelles : le cas des politiques publiques d'amélioration de la qualité de l'air. PhD Thesis, Aix-Marseille Université [Online]. Available at: https://hal.archives-ouvertes.fr/tel-03671252 [Accessed 27 May 2022].

Gavard-Perret, M.-L. and Helme-Guizon, A. (2018). Choisir parmi les techniques spécifiques d'analyse qualitative. In *Méthodologie de la recherche en sciences de gestion : réussir son mémoire ou sa thèse*, Gavard-Perret, M.-L., Gotteland, D., Haon, C. and Jolibert, A. et al. (eds). Pearson Education, London, 241–274 [Online]. Available at: https://halshs.archives-ouvertes.fr/halshs-00325144 [Accessed 26 October 2021].

Hernandez, S. (2017). *À la recherche du management territorial : construire les territoires entre idéologie, paradoxe et management*. Presses Universitaires de Provence, Marseille.

Keast, R. (2016). Shining a light on the black box of collaboration: Mapping the prerequisites for cross-sector working. In *The Three Sector Solution*, Butcher, J. and Gilchrist, D. (eds). ANU Press, Canberra [Online]. Available at: http://press-files.anu.edu.au/downloads/press/n1949/pdf/ch08.pdf [Accessed 29 January 2020].

Keast, R., Brown, K., Mandell, M. (2007). Getting the right mix: Unpacking integration meanings and strategies. *International Public Management Journal*, 10(1), 9–33.

Lawrence, T.B. and Suddaby, R. (2006). Institutions and institutional work. In *The SAGE Handbook of Organization Studies*, Clegg, S.R., Hardy, C., Nord, W.R., Lawrence, T.B. (eds). SAGE Publications, New York, 215–254 [Online]. Available at: http://sk.sagepub.com/reference/hdbk_orgstudies2ed/n7.xml [Accessed 31 January 2017].

Lelieveld, J., Klingmüller, K., Pozzer, A., Pöschl, U., Fnais, M., Daiber, A., Münzel, T. (2019). Cardiovascular disease burden from ambient air pollution in Europe reassessed using novel hazard ratio functions. *European Heart Journal*, 40(20), 1590–1596.

McCann, J.E. (1983). Design guidelines for social problem-solving interventions. *Journal of Applied Behavioral Science*, 2(19), 177–189.

McGuire, M. (2006). Collaborative public management: Assessing what we know and how we know it. *Public Administration Review*, 66(s1), 33–43.

McNamara, M. (2016). Unraveling the characteristics of mandated collaboration. In *Advancing Collaboration Theory: Models, Typologies, and Evidence*, Morris, J.C. and Miller-Stevens, K. (eds). Routledge, New York, 65–86.

Morin, E. (1995). La stratégie de reliance pour l'intelligence de la complexité. *Revue Internationale de Systémique*, 9(2), 105–112.

Poister, T.H., Pitts, D.W., Hamilton Edwards, L. (2010). Strategic management research in the public sector: A review, synthesis, and future directions. *The American Review of Public Administration*, 40(5), 522–545.

Thomson, A.M. and Perry, J.L. (2006). Collaboration processes: Inside the black box. *Public Administration Review*, 66(s1), 20–32.

Vangen, S. (2017). Developing practice-oriented theory on collaboration: A paradox lens. *Public Administration Review*, 77(2), 263–272.

4

Innovating and Regenerating Territories Through the Development of Ecosystems

4.1. Introduction

Innovation does not take place in weightlessness, but in one or more geographical locations where project leaders and their allies work: Silicon Valley, the Paris region, the Toulouse (for aeronautics) or Grasse (for perfumes). Since, in order to innovate, these actors regularly need to see each other and exchange ideas, it is not surprising that these exchanges are facilitated if they live next to one other (even if, in our digital world, conversing at a distance is greatly simplified by WhatsApp, FaceTime, Skype, etc.). Territories are also places where it could be useful to develop a country's capacity for innovation and renewal. A whole branch of economics, often referred to as "regional", has long been interested in the development of a country's territories and their relationship with innovation.

When innovation is collective and open, the ecosystem concept takes on its full meaning, when analyzing these innovative creative phenomena. Since Moore's seminal work (1996), this concept has been the subject of growing interest in academic circles. Defined as a "structure through which partners interact to deliver a value proposition to the end customer" (Adner 2021, p. 12), ecosystems constitute a space where heterogeneous actors become interdependent and align their contributions to propose a main offer absorbed from several complementary offers (Cusumano et al. 2019; Autio and Thomas 2020). They therefore propose a new approach to collective value creation – and the relational dynamics that support it – that fits in with

Chapter written by Guillaume DETCHENIQUE, Magali MALHERBE and Thomas LOILIER.

current preoccupations of open innovation and the breaking down of industrial boundaries (Adner 2021).

Having studied the relationship between ecosystems and innovation, and also innovation and territory, it is tempting to think of ecosystems and territory in the same breath. Literature on ecosystems has long ignored the question of territory, even though the biological notion of ecosystem is itself inseparable from a predefined geographical area. Today, changes in our lifestyles, driven by the challenges of sustainability and ubiquity, give rise to ecosystems rooted in a given territory, such as smart cities and initiatives supporting the circular economy. Similarly, the cultural and institutional specificities of the territory explain the incapacity of certain ecosystems to establish themselves in a given territory (e.g. eBay's defeat in its conquest of the Chinese market[1]) or, on the contrary, the success of ecosystems facilitated by the support of public authorities (e.g. the incentive policy of the US government behind the adoption of the shared medical record[2]).

This chapter is part of this renewed perspective on ecosystems, discussing the role that the territory plays in the dynamics of an ecosystem, which, in turn, contributes to its development or regeneration. It is based on the study of two contrasting cases – the dynamics of the cider ecosystem and those of the NFC technology ecosystem – both of which are inseparable from the Normandy territory. In particular, it shows the specific situations and mechanisms (based on the notion of proximity) that enable a territory to unblock or renew an ecosystem.

4.2. Collective innovation in a territory

4.2.1. *The ecosystem for innovation in a territory*

The concept of the ecosystem can be used to account for these phenomena of collective innovation. The underlying logic is quite simple: collectively, ecosystem members are stronger. Innovating within an ecosystem with partners enables us to offer greater value than would have been created individually by each member of the ecosystem. This phenomenon is linked to the fact that the complementarities that develop

1 For more on this subject, see Cusumano et al. (2019).

2 For more on this subject, see Adner (2021).

between ecosystem members have as many opportunities to develop their activities (Jacobides et al. 2018; Cusumano et al. 2019; Adner 2021).

Seizing these opportunities is not a matter of course, since it can only be the product of the will of all the actors in the ecosystem. Being a collective of actors only multiplies the capacities of each one on two conditions. First, these same actors must be complementary; and second, they must share the same desire to embark on the same development path. In other words, a company's success is at least partly determined by that of its partners in the ecosystem.

The challenges faced by ecosystem members are therefore considerable, and should not be underestimated. They are all the greater during the nascent phase of an ecosystem, when the contours of the value proposition remain unclear, offering individual opportunities to actors whose interests overlap and conflict as they strive to seize the same opportunities (Malherbe and Tellier 2022). The links between actors are therefore not stabilized, but take shape step by step, reflecting awareness of their belonging to the ecosystem and acceptance of the role entrusted to them.

The convergence of ecosystem members towards a common goal is a key factor in its development and sustainability. This naturally raises the question of member coordination and leadership. The literature has seen the emergence of different conceptions on this subject[3]. Early works defined the ecosystem as a community of actors, orchestrated by a pivotal organization and bound by the same strategic destiny (Moore 1996). A second trend sees ecosystems in terms of a platform whose access is governed by a leading firm, and on which a set of organizations will graft themselves to offer complementarities that, in turn, increase the platform's value (Cusumano et al. 2019). This trend developed around now emblematic examples, such as Android, iOS, Uber and Airbnb. Finally, a third approach focuses analysis on the value proposition and underlying value creation mechanisms (Adner 2021). According to this approach, there is no such thing as a self-proclaimed leader. This role is built up according to the choices made by the actors and the resulting alignment, just as it can be challenged by the seizure of new opportunities. For example, Apple is not the leader of a single ecosystem, but participates in several ecosystems

3 For a detailed presentation on these different approaches, readers can consult the work of Adner (2017) and Jacobides et al. (2018).

(healthcare, education, home automation, mobility, etc.) structured by different actor alignments, and in which it plays different roles.

Whether we consider the ecosystem from the angle of a leading firm that pre-exists the collective, or from the angle of a value proposition whose alignment structure determines the roles of the participants, the management of innovations that complement the main offer is a fundamental challenge for ecosystems. The existence of an ecosystem depends on the participation of a heterogeneous group of actors, known as "followers", "niche actors" or "complementors". By enriching the value proposition, these actors increase the value created by the ecosystem and boost its attractiveness, not only for the end-user, but also from the point of view of the niche actors who are encouraged to join the ecosystem. The key to success therefore lies in creating a virtuous circle fed by network externalities (Cusumano et al. 2019).

However, such a dynamic is not self-evident, and actors need to consider the existence of bottlenecks. As the ecosystem's offering is made up of all the contributions of its members, any failure on the part of one of them will create a break in the chain of activities and jeopardize the whole. It is therefore necessary for certain members, often leaders, to provide their support to ensure that these activities come to life.

Two main strategies need to be assessed. On the one hand, actors can subsidize these activities through financial incentives or, more generally, the provision of resources to help members develop their activity (Cusumano et al. 2019; Adner 2021). On the other hand, actors may decide to carry out the bottleneck activity themselves, in order to drive the value proposition to market. This second strategy is not insignificant, and can have the opposite effect to that intended, by discouraging potential members from investing in the ecosystem. Indeed, expanding into several activities, even on a temporary basis, risks being interpreted as an ambition to conquer and dominate, and thus send out a negative signal.

Surprisingly, the concept of ecosystem has tended to develop without mobilizing the concept of territory, even though both are intimately linked to innovation. However, several remarkable cases, such as the industrial districts of the "Third Italy" or Silicon Valley, demonstrated the advantages of physical agglomeration for collective innovation. Territory offers advantages when it comes to innovation.

4.2.2. *Innovation mechanisms for a territory: proximity*

When it comes to collective innovation, the emergence of new ideas through the confrontation of points of view and the disclosure of strategic information can only be achieved through frequent interaction, with face-to-face relations enabling fluid, truly interactive discussions. Geographical proximity is therefore seen as a means of facilitating (in number and quality) relations between network members, particularly in the early stages of a project. Furthermore, this physical proximity is generally seen as a means of disseminating non-codifiable knowledge and limiting information costs.

Defined as the physical distance between actors, geographical proximity is partly subjective, since it also depends on the availability of transport and communication infrastructures that actors are able to use. It can also be permanent or temporary (Torre 2008), as ecosystem members do not necessarily need to be close at all times. For example, the need for face-to-face exchanges may be high during the birth of the ecosystem, until the value proposition has been stabilized.

Geographical proximity acts as a genuine "confidence-builder". For Saxenian (1996), friendly, even quasi-familial relations between engineers do more for technology transfer and innovation than any formal means of communication. The creation of an ecosystem can therefore take time, and it does no good trying to speed it up. The key is to take part in seminars, technical conferences, associations and other clubs, to demonstrate your skills and your ability to provide as much information as you receive. Formal and informal relationships, both commercial and non-commercial, and habits of working together, generate a work ethic and principles of solidarity and mutual aid that are essential in building territorial networks. As the skills, information or goods exchanged remain uncertain, network actors must "socialize" their exchanges; this means inscribing them in a social group with its own rules of operation, customs, rituals, etc.

While it is well understood that proximity facilitates innovation, there is no mistaking it. The notion of proximity can be dissociated from space. Two actors may consider themselves close because they share different things: values, rules of coordination, knowledge or language. This notion is not geographical, but relational. A distinction is made, for example, between institutional, cognitive and social proximity (Boschma 2005). Institutional proximity covers the laws, regulations, language and habits shared by different organizations, while cognitive proximity characterizes their common knowledge. Finally, social proximity defines the level of trust between organizations.

We use the approach of Rallet and Torre (2004), which distinguishes between geographical proximity and organized proximity. The latter can be based on two different logics: the logic of belonging and that of similarity. In the first case, ecosystem members are said to be close because they interact, their interactions being facilitated by the rules or behavioral routines they follow. This logic becomes stronger if the ecosystem has been able to develop and rely on such rules and routines. Following the logic of similarity, the actors of the ecosystem are supposed to share the same system of representations, beliefs or knowledge. Two organizations in an ecosystem are close because they share the same system of representations.

The territory offers high development potential for these two types of proximity, which are also effective innovation mechanisms for an ecosystem. The following two cases, both inseparable from the Normandy region, shed light on the dynamics at work.

4.3. Regenerating an ecosystem through territory: four lessons from the cider ecosystem in Normandy

Along with Brittany, Normandy is one of the two regions with the largest cider production in France. In the early 2000s, the Normandy ecosystem mainly consisted of competing industrial (notably Pernod-Ricard, then market leader) and artisanal processors, who produced and distributed beverages made from cider apples harvested and supplied by local growers, who cultivated and maintained high- and low-stem orchards. Alongside these actors, a number of private and public organizations supported the cider market through technical, promotional and representative operations. These included the CRAN[4], IFPC[5] and UNICID[6]. However, an announcement from the leader upset the ecosystem.

---

4 CRAN: *Chambre d'agriculture de Normandie*, the French Chambers of Agriculture of Normandy.

5 IFPC: *Institut Français des Productions Cidricoles*, the French Institute for Cider Production.

6 UNICID: *Union Nationale Interprofessionelle Cidricole*, the French "National Inter-professional Cidricole Union".

In December 2000, Pernod-Ricard announced that it was refocusing on spirits and wines, which meant its future withdrawal from the cider market. After several years of domination, which began in the 1970s, and of reorganization and concentration in the cider sector through the purchase of various companies (such as Loïc Raison in 1983), the French group finally sold its cider business to CCLF in 2002. Although the multinational is internationally recognized for its know-how, resources and expertise in beverage manufacturing and marketing, it has never managed to boost cider sales, apart from its only notable success: the creation of *Champomy*, a sparkling, alcohol-free drink made from cider apples. At the time of Pernod-Ricard's departure, annual per capita consumption of cider in the UK was 8 liters (rising to 12 liters in Ireland), while French consumers drank just 2 liters[7] (compared with 38 liters of beer and 58 liters of wine)[8], with consumption peaking in January and February and sales concentrated mainly in cider-producing regions.

While the leader's departure, coupled with sales difficulties, could have slowed the evolution of the cider ecosystem, its members instead saw it as a salutary and necessary opportunity for a collective rebound, not least to preserve jobs and growers' dependent on the particular raw material of the cider apple. A study of their collective reaction, based on 30 semi-directive interviews with cider executives, managers and experts, and a literature review (Detchenique 2012), revealed four lessons about ecosystems.

4.3.1. *Lesson no. 1: taking advantage of the ecosystem leader's departure*

The departure of the leader of an ecosystem forces the remaining actors to react; particularly, when the activity concerned is a strong symbol of a region, such as cider in Normandy. Therefore, the announcement of Pernod-Ricard's departure prompted a collective awareness and reaction from several actors concerned about the future of the ecosystem. Above all, the future disengagement of the leader has prompted these actors to really question the difficulties of the traditional business and the conditions for its sustainability without the support of a global company. In fact, the

7 See XERFI 2009.

8 CESER Normandie: *Conseil économique et social régional de Basse-Normandie* (2002), the cider industry in Lower Normandy.

difficulties encountered were not new, and had already begun in 1972 with the end of the outlets provided by State-owned spirits[9].

An audit, carried out between November 2001 and March 2002 by CESER[10] of Lower Normandy, led to the identification of a successor to Pernod-Ricard, which was an organization familiar with the agricultural world. Indeed, the cider ecosystem had long been marked by a lack of organized proximity and, more particularly, a lack of understanding and confidence in Pernod-Ricard. For example, the leader's relations with cider apple growers, described as exclusively commercial (in exchange, however, for advantageous supply contracts), and the French group's demands for regularity and frequency of apple production, demonstrated, according to several actors in the ecosystem, a lack of knowledge and sensitivity to the specificities of the agricultural world. In addition, a point of no return was reached when Pernod-Ricard refused to renew several of the contracts and stopped participating in the financing of the generic communication on cider elaborated by UNICID.

In 2004, the torch was finally taken up by Agrial, a Normandy-based cooperative specializing in agricultural and agri-food production, through its acquisition of CCLF. Several of its members urged an expansion in investment in cider, which had previously been limited to apple collection and storage, or juice production. Agrial quickly demonstrated its willingness to move away from the practices of the former leader, and to forge closer links with (and between) the actors in the ecosystem. To regenerate the cider business, the cooperative launched a new orchard development plan, in agreement with growers and in exchange for a renegotiation of their apple supply contracts.

This major episode for the cider ecosystem shows how the departure of a leader can become an opportunity to recreate proximity, according to the logic of similarity. In other words, it is a question of erasing the negative

9 State-owned spirits were initiated in preparation for World War I and to meet the alcohol needs of the armaments industry. In particular, a major expansion of orchards enabled the manufacture of explosives.

10 CESR: *Conseil économique social régional* (known today by the acronym CESER) for *Conseil économique social et environnemental régional*, the Economic, Social and Environmental Council (ESEC) is a constitutional consultative assembly represents key economic, social and environmental fields, promoting cooperation between different socio-professional interest groups and ensuring they are part of the process of shaping and reviewing public policy.

effects resulting from the perceived incompatibility between different systems of representation by identifying a new leader whose status and mode of operation will be considered legitimate and consistent with the general interest of the ecosystem.

4.3.2. *Lesson no. 2: building a common history and shared interpretation*

The arrival of Agrial as leader improved the organized proximity within the ecosystem. However, this settlement was also facilitated by the systematic comparison and reprimand of the practices of the former leader, who was then held solely responsible for the ills of the cider business. By way of illustration, when actors refer to Pernod-Ricard's company takeovers, these operations are systematically likened to a logic of domination desired by the French group, as expressed by one of the directors of Celliers Associés, a cider cooperative:

> The problem with Pernod-Ricard was that they did not really want to increase the size of the pie so that everyone could have a piece. They wanted to buy up as many companies as possible so they could have the whole pie.

When, in 2009, Agrial bought out its main competitor (Val-de-Vire), the actors involved had different opinions about an operation that was essential for the future of the ecosystem, and, in particular, to preserve the jobs of several producers and employees. As one Agrial member put it:

> There was a logic in trying to find an industrial and commercial solution for this company, because behind it there are cider producers too. And then there are employees, there is a tool, there is a past.

Ultimately, it is not so much the actual designs of Pernod-Ricard and Agrial that interest us here, but the way in which the shared interpretation of the "Pernod-Ricard years" fostered the coming together of the actors in the ecosystem. In other words, the facts are less important than the collective rejection of the former leader, which, in addition to his departure (more precisely, the announcement of his departure), facilitated this rapprochement.

In this way, the construction of a shared history, blaming Pernod-Ricard for the results of the cider business as a whole, helped to unite the actors. The case of cider thus highlights a second lesson: how the renewal of an ecosystem can be achieved not only through a common vision, but also through the construction and sharing of a common history (in other words, a proximity based on similarity) that serves as a mechanism to bring actors together; and, as we will see in section 4.3.3, as a referent for the new actions implemented.

4.3.3. *Lesson no. 3: changing industry rules for innovation*

Since Pernod-Ricard's departure, several companies have come up with new products to complement cider sales and to try to attract new consumers. For example, Val-de-Vire, Agrial's main challenger until its takeover (see section 4.3.2), created new drinks based on flavored beers[11]. Agrial also sought to move away from the traditional drink, marketing a rosé cider among other products.

However, the cider ecosystem has long been marked by a strategic homogeneity symbolized by the implementation of a pricing strategy (in Porter's sense) by several companies. This common competitive positioning, while failing to attract new consumers, led to a reduction in margins and capacity for innovation. Above all, this strong proximity based on belonging (in other words, sharing and following common competitive rules) had a negative impact on the overall perceived quality of cider beverages. The departure of the former leader was seen as an opportunity to challenge the rules of the competitive game.

The cider case study illustrates how, within an ecosystem, actors can justify and encourage the questioning of sector-specific rules. The departure of the leader ultimately led to a reconciliation of the ecosystem actors around a representation of a desired competitive environment more conducive to innovation, and in opposition to a competitive environment rejected because, in their view, this emanated from an actor outside the ecosystem. This rapprochement was made possible by strengthening proximity based on similarity (a shared belief system about the former leader) and evolving proximity based on belonging. It is no longer a question of strictly following

11 For more on this subject, see Detchenique and Joffre (2012).

the same competitive rules, but of accepting that the future of the ecosystem depends on heterogeneous strategic choices.

4.3.4. *Lesson no. 4: focusing on new collective projects*

The previous sections have shown the value of a shared understanding of the ecosystem's history and the need to perceive a competitive environment conducive to innovation. However, the new collective rationale is also illustrated by the launch of several projects to revitalize the ecosystem on a commercial level and to acquire new knowledge. For example, under the umbrella of the National Inter-professional Cidricole Union, a number of actors have backed the "*cidre d'automne*" ("Autumn Cider") collective brand, designed to create a new consumption moment. In another way, new organizations with different resources and skills were also mobilized. A collective project, for example, involved INRA[12] Dijon, and ESA[13] Angers, among others, to develop knowledge about cider non-consumers, and to gain a fresh perspective on cider-making issues.

The evolution of proximity based on similarity and belonging makes it possible to facilitate collective projects between geographically close actors, as well as to be free, if necessary, from this geographical proximity. In particular, this makes it possible to call on and mobilize resources and skills that are different from those already present in the ecosystem.

4.4. Unlocking an ecosystem through territory: four lessons from the NFC ecosystem in Normandy

The 2000s marked the entry of our economies into a digital era. The cellphone became a growth driver for many manufacturers, who imagined transforming this tool – with its hitherto limited functionalities – into a must-have gadget for our daily lives. A decade later, these ideas are gradually becoming part of our daily lives, with the advent of smartphones marking a

12 INRA: *Institut National de la Recherche Agronomique* was a French public research institute dedicated to agricultural science. It was founded in 1946 and is a Public Scientific and Technical Research Establishment under the joint authority of the Ministries of Research and Agriculture.

13 ESA: *École supérieure des agricultures* was a French engineering College created in 1898. The school trains engineers in agronomy and agriculture. Located in Angers, the ESA Angers is a private higher education institution of general interest recognized by the state.

turning point in the history of mobile telephony. Most of us now believe that Internet giants such as Apple, Google and Windows have revolutionized our lives by building global innovation ecosystems.

However, appearances are deceptive. Private and public sector organizations also worked together to develop local ecosystems on a territorial scale. This was notably the case in Normandy, which became the cradle for the development of an innovative range of "contactless" mobile services. These services facilitate and enrich our everyday activities, such as making a purchase from a retailer, taking public transport, enjoying community facilities (swimming pool, library, theater, etc.) or, more simply, obtaining a wide range of information accessible from an interactive terminal (loyalty offers, tourist sites, traffic conditions, booking services, etc.).

Historically, the Normandy region has been home to organizations operating in various industries (semiconductors, telecommunications) with strong expertise in "secure electronic transactions". The development of near-field communication (NFC) technology by semiconductor manufacturer Philips (which a few years later became NXP) brought these organizations together around a common goal, driving the convergence of different industries within a single ecosystem. Much more than a local phenomenon, the standardization of NFC technology paved the way for the emergence of a global ecosystem that brought together organizations that were dominant in their respective markets. Semiconductor, SIM card and cellphone manufacturers, cellphone operators, financial institutions and transport authorities all aimed to build an ecosystem whose technical foundations would be shared throughout the world. However, this ambitious goal ran up against two main difficulties.

Firstly, the different actors coveted the same share of the value created by the ecosystem, which did not favor the alignment of their individual interests and gave rise to several conflicts. Secondly, the ecosystem had to rely on service providers who operated in local markets, such as access to communal infrastructures, and whose concerns were far removed from those of the major industrial actors. Faced with these difficulties, the global ecosystem was struggling to become a reality, and the territory became the ideal candidate to unblock the situation.

A study of the discussions and conflicts that have animated the members of the NFC ecosystem for 12 years (Malherbe 2014) enables us to draw four lessons from the interactions between the local level of action, bounded by a territory, and the global level of action that contributes to the emergence of a global ecosystem – and thus to understand how each level in turn influences the other.

4.4.1. *Lesson no. 1: relying on the territory to integrate a global ecosystem*

The emergence of the NFC ecosystem was driven by two semiconductor giants, Philips and Sony, in the early 2000s. At the time, these two actors dominated the market for cards used for payment and transportation. Their aim was to develop a common communication standard that would enable contactless use of cards and also support this technology with other media. Transforming the cellphone into a "Swiss army knife" that replaced all the plastic cards used in our daily activities quickly became an obvious choice. Actors from a wide range of industries (telephone manufacturers, SIM card makers, semiconductor manufacturers, cellphone operators) decided to combine their interests within the NFC ecosystem.

However, behind this common objective of developing the technical foundations needed to implement contactless services using a telephone, lay a more complex reality. The implementation of certain services required the management and storage of the service user's personal data (e.g. bank details) and/or data with a monetary value (e.g. a ticket to an event). Two distinct visions of how to create value therefore emerged and coexisted initially. The various members of the emerging ecosystem then coordinated their actions around one vision or the other, depending on whether or not they adhered to the structure of the value proposition associated with that vision.

In parallel with the discussions and actions taking place on a global scale, two multinationals with R&D teams in Normandy – NXP and Orange – created a regional dynamic around NFC technology. A group of start-ups, SMEs and higher education establishments shared strong expertise in secure electronic transactions, which, coupled with their short physical distance, encouraged them to join the two multinationals in investigating the opportunities offered by the technology.

This first chapter in the life of the NFC ecosystem feeds our first lesson. In the technological and digital fields, many ecosystems are built on a very large scale, rapidly extending beyond the borders of a single country, under the impetus of one or a few multinationals; this is very often as a result of standardization initiatives. Sharing a common goal and defining a collective vision are then necessary to federate actors around a new idea that will become an innovative value proposition. The members of the ecosystem are then linked by a proximity based on similarity, which means they share the same representation of the value proposition and the role played by each to bring it to fruition. This construction on a global scale does not exclude the possibility for "smaller" actors, who traditionally operate on local markets, to integrate these vast ecosystems. Let us not forget that the key to an ecosystem's success lies in its attractiveness, an attractiveness sustained by the proliferation of niche actors.

In other words, all new actors are welcome, but this is not self-evident. In order to support the integration of local actors into a global ecosystem, we need to activate relationships within the territory. In particular, this requires the presence in the territory of a number of multinationals, which help to create the ecosystem and act as a bridge between local actors and the ecosystem. Alongside the logic of similarity, it is the geographical proximity between the members of a territory that enable local actors to integrate a global ecosystem.

4.4.2. *Lesson no. 2: emancipating yourself from the territory to become an actor in the global dynamic*

As members of the NFC ecosystem experimented with the first services with users, they realized that the coexistence of two visions was no longer viable. Therefore, convinced that they were the legitimate leaders of the ecosystem, mobile operators proclaimed the superiority of their vision. This announcement had paradoxical effects. On the one hand, it set out a clear trajectory that enabled many actors to align their efforts (notably service providers and application developers). Collective initiatives such as experiments and working groups proliferated, and local actors gradually emancipated themselves from their territory. Actions were no longer solely carried out by members of the territory on the territory. Normandy organizations became involved in national and international projects. Their work was disseminated at conferences, consortia and associations dedicated to NFC technology and mobile services.

On the other hand, the choice of one vision to the detriment of the other left many people unhappy. Mainly, handset manufacturers were the big losers, and they decided to limit their efforts to develop compatible phones. Despite the tensions, the NFC ecosystem grew and was enriched by complementary innovations, thanks to the contributions of local actors and their ambitions to contribute to the development of the ecosystem beyond their territory.

A second lesson can be drawn from our observation of the proliferation of initiatives crossing local borders, facilitating transfers between the local territory and the global ecosystem. To grow the community, ecosystem members need to stabilize their value proposition around a single vision. This situation is therefore conducive to the development of networks of actors in various forms (e.g. working groups, trade associations, collaborative projects) that reflect a closeness between actors, based on a logic of belonging. These networks support the permeability of territorial boundaries. New perspectives open up for local actors, who emancipate themselves from the territory to become actors in the global dynamic.

4.4.3. *Lesson no. 3: empowering territories to overcome conflict*

Time passed, conflicts persisted and the ecosystem was still in the experimental stage. Given these facts, the self-proclaimed leadership of the mobile operators became more questionable, and the members of the ecosystem had massively undertaken to find alternatives to the structure of the value proposition pushed by the operators. Different ecosystem strategies were gradually taking shape. Primarily, service providers (financial institutions, transport authorities, retail chains) relied on their trade associations to stimulate the use of other technologies (Internet and QR Code to replace NFC) or other storage solutions (SD card to replace the SIM card), or more simply to maintain the use of plastic cards, rather than phones. After a few years of effort in the same direction, the NFC ecosystem went backwards and returned to a situation wherein several visions coexisted[14].

Faced with so much vagueness, the actors in Normandy decided to refocus their efforts on their territory, in order to offer products on their own scale, and thus create a local ecosystem. The presence of a cellphone

14 To deepen their understanding of the different technological alternatives negotiated by the actors and the influence tactics mobilized, the reader can consult the article by Malherbe and Simon (2021).

operator (Orange) in the region naturally led them to align their actions with the vision that was being challenged by members of the NFC ecosystem. Indeed, rather than enter into sterile debates that would penalize the emergence of services, the Normandy actors preferred to capitalize on previous developments to ensure that "contactless" mobile services became a commercial reality as quickly as possible. This territorial focus was also supported by the French government's policy of encouraging local institutions to become the driving force behind the launch of local NFC mobile services. This is how private and public actors came together to create the first services.

Some ecosystems become a battleground for dominant actors who are unable to align their interests. As a result, the ecosystem comes to a standstill and fails to become a commercial reality. However, this situation should not be seen as a failure for local actors. Armed with the experience accumulated in the ecosystem, and thanks to local incentives, they are then able to detach themselves from global discussions and continue to autonomously build a regional ecosystem on a territorial scale. Our third lesson therefore argues in favor of emancipating the territory from the ecosystem, so as not to get bogged down in conflicts that seriously threaten the materialization of the value proposition. The logic of belonging is thus reinforced by the geographical proximity of the actors.

4.4.4. *Lesson no. 4: not being blinded by local success*

For five years, the territorial dynamic that had taken hold in Normandy had enabled us to develop and, above all, offer users a number of services accessible from their cellphones. However, the story came to an abrupt halt in the mid-2010s. After withdrawing from the territory, the actors were swept away by the local craze, which grew stronger by the day. Blinded by this enthusiasm, the actors failed to take into account the profound changes taking place in the ecosystem. Indeed, the 2010s marked a major turning point in the history of mobile telephony, with the rapid domination of a handful of giants (Apple, Google, Windows), who revolutionized phone usage. They offered new technological alternatives for "contactless" mobile services, wiping out the negotiations that had animated the NFC ecosystem for a dozen years. Weakened by several conflicts, the latter was unable to build a sufficiently robust foundation to cope with the arrival of the giants, and the value proposition finally emerged around a structure different from that envisaged by the mobile operators.

We conclude with this fourth lesson. Ecosystems are dynamic objects whose existence is influenced by changes taking place within the industries of their members, as well as externally. As a result, the structure of the value proposition is bound to evolve more or less radically over time. It is therefore essential for local actors to keep a constant eye on these developments, and to integrate them rapidly into their actions. The territory cannot operate in a vacuum, and its members must remain aware that any local success may be short-lived. Otherwise, their efforts will be wasted.

4.5. Conclusion

What lessons can be drawn from these two case studies, bearing in mind that our ambition here is not to close a debate between the intersecting dynamics of territories and ecosystems? First, the territory is undoubtedly a powerful asset when it comes to energizing an ecosystem. In order to do so, it has several mechanisms at its disposal: the development of shared projects, the sharing of values and representations by stakeholders in the area concerned, and the writing or rewriting of a common history.

However, the relationship between territory and ecosystem is not a simple one. Put another way, territorializing an ecosystem has both advantages and disadvantages. In particular, it can lock actors into a form of "territorial myopia".

Finally, territory is not a permanent ideal. It is important for the ecosystem to be able to navigate between innovations within the territory and innovations beyond its borders, in line with local and global technological and economic dynamics.

4.6. References

Adner, R. (2017). Ecosystem as structure: An actionable construct for strategy. *Journal of Management*, 43(1), 39–58.

Adner, R. (2021). *Winning the Right Game: How to Disrupt, Defend, and Deliver in a Changing World*. MIT Press, Cambridge.

Autio, E. and Thomas, L.D. (2020). Value co-creation in ecosystems: Insights and research promise from three disciplinary perspectives. In *Handbook of Digital Innovation*, Nambisan, S., Lyytinen, K., Yoo, Y. (eds). Edward Elgar Publishing, Cheltenham.

Boschma, R.A. (2005). Proximity and innovation: A critical assessment. *Regional Studies*, 39, 31–56.

CESR de Basse-Normandie (2002). La filière cidricole en Basse-Normandie. CESR.

Cusumano, M.A., Gawer, A., Yoffie, D.B. (2019). *The Business of Platforms: Strategy in the Age of Digital Competition, Innovation, and Power*. Harper Business, New York.

Detchenique, G. (2012). Les dynamiques de régénération territorialisées : le cas de la filière cidricole. PhD Thesis, Université de Caen, Caen.

Detchenique, G. and Joffre, P. (2012). Un essai de rupture avorté : le cas Val de Vire. *Gestion 2000*, 29(1), 71–85.

Jacobides, M.G., Cennamo, C., Gawer, A. (2018). Towards a theory of ecosystems. *Strategic Management Journal*, 39(8), 2255–2276.

Malherbe, M. (2014). La trajectoire d'innovation de la naissance d'un écosystème d'affaires : une approche multiniveaux. PhD Thesis, Université de Caen, Caen.

Malherbe, M. and Simon, F. (2021). Near-field communication (NFC) technology emergence: One or several technological paths? *Journal of Innovation Economics & Management*, 2(35), 151–185.

Malherbe, M. and Tellier, A. (2022). Explaining the nonalignment of ecosystem partners: A structuralist approach. *Strategic Organization*. doi: 10.1177/14761270221084224.

Moore, J.F. (1996). *The Death of Competition: Leadership and Strategy in the Age of Business Ecosystems*. John Wiley & Sons, Hoboken.

Rallet, A. and Torre, A. (2004). Proximité et localisation. *Économie rurale*, 280, 25–41.

Saxenian, A. (1996). *Regional Advantages. Cultures and Competition in Silicon Valley and Route 128*. Harvard University Press, Cambridge.

Torre, A. (2008). On the role played by temporary geographical proximity in knowledge transmission. *Regional Studies*, 42(6), 869–889.

XERFI (2009). *Marché du cidre : analyse du marché, prévisions 2010, forces en présence*.

5

Reconciling Individual and Collective Territorial Dynamics

5.1. Introduction

The question regarding the creation, development and sustainability of territorial dynamics remains largely unexplored, even if they are at the heart of many analyses. Indeed, territorial development is a major issue at the crossroads of economic, social and, more broadly, political questions. The notions and concepts developed (localized production system, district, ecosystem, etc.) have provided tools for analyzing these development issues, even if they sometimes cover different realities. The focal point of the various approaches is the development of the territory and its economy, in a relatively macro vision, where the territory is the central *quid* of analysis. What about the role of companies in these reflections on territorial development? The entrepreneurial approach, on the other hand, attempts to put the question of the company and the entrepreneur back at the center of the analysis: development of the territory and development of the company appear to be closely linked. Entrepreneurship approaches attempt to put the question of companies and entrepreneurs back at the heart of the territory. From this perspective, a territory's development depends on its businesses and entrepreneurs. In order to develop more effective frameworks for understanding and action, we need to consider the dynamics of the territory itself, as well as those of the companies.

Chapter written by Colette FOURCADE, Stéphanie LOUP and Christophe LEYRONAS.

While the entrepreneurial dimension is fundamental to the analysis of collective dynamics, the role of the entrepreneur is nevertheless insufficiently taken into account. Therefore, how can we better integrate the entrepreneurial dimension into the analysis and modeling of territorial dynamics?

The resource-based view (RBV) focuses on the "company" level, while considering exchanges between companies and their ecosystem. It pays particular attention to resources, whether internal and/or external, when analyzing company development. In this way, the development of companies and territories highlights the issue of resources in the broadest sense, through approaches to social and relational capital, and externalities. Companies involved in this ecosystem would be able to access regional resources to build up part of their resource portfolio.

More generally, entrepreneurship is linked to the question of resources. It enriches "traditional" approaches to territorial development. How, then, can we address the issue of development in a global approach that articulates different levels of analysis and seeks to reconcile individual entrepreneurial logics with territorial dynamics? The challenge lies in the way resources are perceived, mobilized and integrated by entrepreneurs. This approach goes beyond resources alone, and also addresses the ability to mobilize, value and integrate them. Therefore, how do entrepreneurial and territorial logics interact to affect resources and capabilities?

These different questions raise how resources and capabilities are developed at the level of the territory and companies, and also the interactions between companies and the territory. Taking into account the interaction effects between individual entrepreneurial dynamics and collective territorial dynamics requires an analysis of the process through which skills and resources are produced at different levels, and between levels. A detailed understanding of the value-creation process should therefore lead us to rethink territorial development policies, taking into account the dimension of resources and capabilities. To this end, the development of an analysis grid centered on resources and capacities at different levels would enable us to take stock of the dynamics at play, and identify the possible logics of action for companies and territories.

With this in mind, after recalling the notions of resources and capacities, and the need for a global approach that integrates the different levels, we propose an analysis grid. This will be applied to a case study on the artisans situated in Pézenas, a town in southern France. Based on the elements gathered, we will highlight the various dynamics using the proposed grid, and identify possible actions to enable the various actors to change the situation in order to reconcile individual entrepreneurial dynamics and collective territorial dynamics.

5.2. Resource analysis at the center of entrepreneurial and collective dynamics

To understand the dynamics of individual entrepreneurship and territorial collective dynamics, we need to look at the resources mobilized in companies' portfolios, from both the company and the territory. In order to do this, we propose to cross-reference the resource-based approach with the individual strategies and collective dynamics in a multi-level analysis.

5.2.1. *The importance of resources*

Our main theoretical anchor is the resource-based view (RBV). Resources are an important topic in the field of entrepreneurship, insofar as managers of very small enterprises (VSEs) are confronted with the question of resource scarcity.

> The resource-based view (RBV) approach was born in the mid-1980s and underwent significant development in the 1990s. It is a classic in corporate strategy, and tackles the question of how to maintain a sustainable competitive advantage using a resource- and capability-based approach, focusing on the dynamics within the company.

Box 5.1. *Origin of the resource-based view (RBV) approach*

RBV argues that the firm can be conceived as a bouquet of resources, and that sustainable competitive advantage can be achieved by firms capable of mobilizing and combining so-called "strategic" resources because they have VRIN characteristics: valuable, rare, inimitable and non-substitutable. In the case of VSEs, where the notion of competition is different in view of the positioning, strategies and postures implemented, we prefer the term value proposition, more in line with RBV, than that of competitive advantage.

Many RBV authors have, however, introduced the idea that resources – specific assets, as well as human and organizational ones – can come from the company's environment (Barney 1991); this is obtained, in particular, through interactions with other companies or actors, or being internal to the company. These can be a source of distinctive competence and value creation. Small companies will seek external resources from other companies in their vicinity. By extension, other types of external resources can be obtained by companies operating in the same territory, through the use of intangible resources offered by local institutions, such as a common brand, advertising or communication campaigns.

Finally, the territory in which small businesses are embedded and anchored gives them access to external and collective resources, such as agronomic and geoclimatic resources, as well as history, the reputation of a territory, information, etc. Interaction processes between entrepreneurial organizations (companies) and territorial organizations (institutions and agencies present in a given territory) can develop external resources that each company may – or may not – appropriate to integrate with its own resources. Furthermore the process itself, once organized, becomes a resource.

The resulting portfolio of resources determines the company's specific value proposition. However, far from being a simple question of collecting resources, their value and the way entrepreneurs perceive it impact the "perceived quality" of the portfolio and its possible effects on value creation.

5.2.2. *Resource analysis: relativity and subjectivity*

The characterization of resources, and not just their origin – internal versus external – is an important point for analyzing the resource portfolio. This question relates to two points in particular, namely the value of resources and the way in which they are collectively perceived.

The question of resources itself raises the question of the value of resources in a non-essentialist conception (see Box 5.2). Critics of the VRIN characteristics of resources invite us to take into account all types of resources, especially the more "ordinary" ones. Beyond strategic resources, ordinary, performance-neutral resources, or even "negative resources" (Weppe et al. 2013), should be considered, even though the latter category might appear unfavorable in terms of the ideal of seeking competitive advantage or value creation. Under these conditions, an a priori categorization of resources seems impossible, and all must be considered.

> The essentialist conception of resources means considering those that meet the VRIN characteristics: valuable, rare, inimitable and non-substitutable. These resources are made up of specific assets, both tangible and intangible, as well as human and organizational. These may be internal to the company, or come from its environment The subjectivist approach criticizes the "objective" character of RBV resources. It takes into account the entrepreneur's role in evaluating a given resource, by integrating their personal knowledge and skills. A given resource will be "subjectivized" by the differentiated assessment, dependent on the entrepreneur's profile. The place and weight of a resource in the company's portfolio will thus differ from one company to another.

Box 5.2. *Non-essentialist conception of resources*

Other approaches, based on the work of Schumpeter (1934), Penrose (1959) and, more recently, the subjectivist current of entrepreneurship (Foss et al. 2008), respond to certain criticisms of the RBV approach and emphasize the role of the entrepreneur and their ability to acquire and combine the right resources (Sirmon et al. 2007). This subjective conception of the resource seems entirely consistent with the central and major role of the entrepreneur when it comes to small firms. Categorization could be achieved by integrating the entrepreneur's point of view, with regards to their profile, career path, project, etc., in line with the work of Shane and Venkataraman (2000), which highlights individual dimensions – in the sense of cognitive abilities – as playing a key role in opportunity recognition and, more broadly, value creation. Consequently, the "objective" character of resources in the RBV approach, which leaves no room for the "subjectivity of knowledge and the interpretation of the environment by entrepreneurs"[1] (Weppe et al. 2013, p. 45), must be called into question. A subjective approach to resources should therefore be considered (Foss and Ishikawa 2007), involving entrepreneurs' knowledge and beliefs.

A resource would therefore be "subjectivized" by the entrepreneur's perception of it. The same resource would not have the same value for different entrepreneurs; hence, the subjective nature of the resource. The

1 Authors' translation.

entrepreneur's central role in strategic decision-making means that they must integrate the company's objective, operational resources, as well as subjective, more personal ones. From this subjective perspective, we can return to the tripartite classification of resources operated by Weppe et al. (2013). A resource considered uninteresting (or negative) by the entrepreneur of one company may be perceived as ordinary in the "bouquet of resources" characteristic of another small company, or strategic for the latter. In this way, the entrepreneur interprets the potential of each resource in the company's resource portfolio.

If this position holds at the individual level – of each entrepreneur – how can the collective dimension modify (or not) this relativist approach? How can subjective approaches at the individual level be convergent, coherent or divergent at the collective level? The Artificialist school, whose origins lie in the work of Simon (1969), analyzes interactions between individuals with different points of view from a collective perspective, and shows how convergences of subjectivity emerge through intersubjectivity. Davidson (2001) points out that intersubjective relations refer to individual, subjective but coherent points of view.

What framework should be given to the collective? And at what level should this process of construction of intersubjectivity be positioned? The territory seems to be a relevant level because, as Desforges et al. (2012) point out, the whole issue for a territory is to encourage the emergence of individual interests to get involved in the constitution of local collectives. The territory as a level of public action, visibility for customers, identification of companies, support for agronomic–geoclimatic and historical resources is the meeting place of individual and collective logics. In a given territory, the latter can be perceived as a place of emergence of intersubjectivity, defined as the sharing of perceptions of a given resource between the actors of the same collective. This concept is particularly interesting when applied to the perception that companies operating in a given territory would have of specific resources, whether ordinary or strategic, offered by the territorial organization.

5.2.3. *Beyond resources, the importance of capacity*

The notion of dynamic capabilities emerged in the 1990s. The authors' objective was to seek a new paradigm to explain how firms build and maintain competitive advantage (Teece and Dosi 1994). Although Teece and

Dosi's analysis originally focused on multinational firms operating in globalized markets, with a high level of technological change, it could easily be adapted to the case of small firms operating in sectors described as moderately dynamic.

The authors do not agree on the positioning of the concept of dynamic capability within the resource-based approach. Some believe that an understanding of dynamic capabilities enhances RBV theory. Others argue that dynamic capabilities are more than a simple addition to RBV. The resource-competence approach concerns the operational capabilities that support technical skills. Some authors refer to these as ordinary capabilities. Dynamic capabilities, on the other hand, are linked to management's ability to seize opportunities and reconfigure assets.

Dynamic capabilities are defined at three levels (Teece 2007, 2012). These are sensing, seizing, transforming: detecting and formalizing opportunities and threats; mobilizing resources to address the opportunity; configuring and reconfiguring resources. These three levels are interlinked and interdependent. An estimate of a company's dynamic capabilities can be based on two criteria: the ability to do and the ability to evolve. The second criterion appears the most important: dynamic capabilities imply an ability to go beyond mere adaptation to the environment, to achieve a capacity to reconfigure assets and organizational structures with a view to developing, adapting or modifying its value proposition.

Although dynamic capabilities have often been described in very general terms, they can be understood as specific, identifiable processes (Eisenhardt and Martin 2000). Some integrate resources: for example, in small companies, strategic decision-making is the result of a process in which the manager combines their functional and personal expertise with their intrinsic knowledge of their sector of activity. In this case, the dynamic capability results from the combination of external resources (knowledge of the business sector) and resources internal to the company, or even personal resources (the manager's expertise). Other dynamic capabilities concern the ability to continuously reconfigure resources within the company.

In this way, we can distinguish between so-called ordinary capabilities, which enable a value proposition to be maintained through the mobilization of resources, and dynamic capabilities, which renew the value proposition. If every resource does not have the same "value" for all entrepreneurs, its use may give rise to an ordinary or dynamic capability. The weight of a given resource in a small company's portfolio is determined in part by the entrepreneur's subjective assessment of it.

Ordinary versus strategic resources: common, non-scarce resources that do not enable the development of a competitive advantage and are therefore neutral in terms of performance, as opposed to strategic resources, which are scarce and make a positive contribution to sustainable performance.

Objective versus subjective resources: in the first case, the attributes and use of resources derive from their characteristics; in the second, entrepreneurs interpret them according to their profiles, experiences and environment.

Ordinary versus dynamic capabilities: a capability is a particular combination of resources and skills that enables a company to achieve its strategic objectives. Ordinary capabilities enable a company to solve the problems posed by its day-to-day activities. To respond to rapid and/or unpredictable changes, higher-level capabilities are required. Dynamic capabilities enable internal and external skills to be integrated, built up and reconfigured to cope with change.

Box 5.3. *Definitions for the different types of resources and capacities*

In the case of locally embedded companies, processes of alliance or cooperation can lead to capabilities, enabling the company to acquire and integrate external resources. Reconfiguration can then take place through innovation in the broadest sense, bricolage and serendipitous, as well as through collaboration with other companies. Here, we return to the notion of collective dynamics and territorial dynamics, which is the subject of our discussion. Processes of cooperation and coopetition enable small businesses to refocus on their core competencies through the acquisition or mobilization of external resources. In the artisanal sector, for example, the core business is determined by core competencies. Cooperation and pooling enable the entrepreneur (and possibly their staff) to "save" time and skills, so that they can concentrate on developing the company's value.

The ability to forge links with (and within) a territory has an impact on a company's ability to identify, access and mobilize external resources. A company's territorial roots provide it with access to a range of territorial resources. This can provide the company with systemic resources (De Oliveira Wilk and Fensterseifer 2003).

In the case of VSE collectives, the attractiveness of the resource and the perception of its value appear at the heart of the dynamics and relationships between companies, as well as in relation to the territory in which they are located. Furthermore, collective resource co-construction processes could be considered as capabilities.

5.2.4. *A proposed grid analysis*

The elements mentioned above highlight the need for an approach that integrates different levels of analysis, companies/entrepreneurs and the territory, and their interactions. In addition, the question of resources, whatever their origin, raises the question of how they can be mobilized, and therefore of the ordinary and dynamic capacities of both companies and the territory.

The structure of the grid is based on a subjectivist approach to territorial resources, combining the individual viewpoint of the entrepreneur with the collective viewpoint of all the companies in the territory. On the one hand, a strong/weak division is made according to the estimation of value as perceived by the company. On the other hand, the collective perception of the value of territorial resources by all companies in the territory is assessed through strong or weak intersubjectivity.

The concept of intersubjectivity takes into account the convergence or, conversely, the divergence between individualized assessments of the value of territorial resources by the companies present on the territory. A strong intersubjectivity means that the perceived value of these resources by all companies is similar. Conversely, low intersubjectivity means that companies perceive the same perceived value very differently.

Based on these elements, the analysis grid led to the development of four case studies, distinguishing: the status of the resource, the effect on the company's capabilities, the effect on the territory's capabilities. In the grid, ordinary capacities are denoted as OC and dynamic capacities as DC.

Secondly, it is possible to consider the actions taken at company and/or territorial level to improve the effect on the various capabilities.

		The collective viewpoint of local companies	
		Strong intersubjectivity	**Weak intersubjectivity**[2]
The entrepreneur's point of view	**A high perceived value of territorial resources**	*Case study 1* – Resource status: consistency of entrepreneurial perceptions. High perceived value. – Effect on the company: - impact on ordinary capabilities (OC), mobilized for day-to-day management; - no effect on dynamic capabilities s (DC): no differentiating factor. – Effect on the territory: impact on OC and DC: the resource enables the territory to strengthen and differentiate itself from other territories.	*Case study 2* – Resource status: divergent entrepreneurial perceptions. No consensus on the value of the resource. – Effect on the company: impact on DCs, as resources are mobilized as an element of uniqueness. – Effect on the territory: - impact on OC, as some companies use the resource; maintenance of resource value; - impact on DCs: differentiating effect induced by companies.
The entrepreneur's point of view	**A low perceived value of territorial resources**	*Case study 3* – Resource status: consistency of entrepreneurial perceptions. Low perceived value. – Effect on the company: indirect effect, possible emergence of dyadic inter-company links. – Effect on the territory: - no direct effect; - differentiated effects.	*Case study 4* – Resource status: diverging entrepreneurial perceptions. – Effect on the company: divergent impacts. – Effect on the territory: - impact on OC, as some companies use the resource; - maintaining the value of the resource; - impact on DCs: differentiating effects.

Table 5.1. *Proposed analysis grid*

2 Measuring intersubjectivity is a way of understanding the consensus that exists at the collective level. This can be done from a simple quantitative point of view in terms of the number of companies. More refined measures could weight this by company size, or by mobilizing social network analysis tools, according to their degree of centrality in the graph of relationships.

5.3. Presenting the case studies

In order to understand how individual entrepreneurial logics can be reconciled with collective territorial dynamics, we have chosen to focus on the Pézenas territory, which has been characterized by the presence of artisans for over half a century.

5.3.1. *Characteristics of the Pézenas case study*

In the art and craft sector, the majority of small business owners work independently. Within the framework of development initiatives based on the crafts, artisans are called upon to collaborate with their peers, whether within a business logic (entrepreneurial) or a territorial logic via the constitution of a *terroir* and/or the use of a territorial resource (agro-geoclimatic, know-how, myth or history), or even a collective resource to benefit from agglomeration effects – when they are set up in a town or district. Here, we find a territorial logic with a dual dynamic: entrepreneurial and territorial. This translates into the creation of collective actions that are often territorialized, given the importance attached to arts and crafts in terms of local development.

In the case of Pézenas, the local development dynamic based on arts and crafts is underpinned by a long tradition and significant architectural heritage. There are two noteworthy aspects to the situation of artisans in Pézenas:

– In the diversity of the trades present: while traditional arts and crafts are grouped together by district or town, the logic is attached to a particular trade, and the dynamic is often driven by a larger company than others working with smaller workshops. Proximity to suppliers and/or customers explains location. Glassmaking, earthenware, pottery, knives, etc., bear witness to this logic of territorial concentration. Since the 1960s, Pézenas has been home to a diverse range of artisans: ironmongers, jewelers, cabinet-makers, ceramists and others. Its constitution therefore eludes the logic of concentration around a single activity.

– In terms of territorial resources: while Pézenas benefits from its historical and tourist assets, it does not have any typical agro-geoclimatic resources and/or know-how specific to arts and crafts within its territory. Pézenas has a rich architectural heritage, having been a royal town since the 13th century, and a trading center for fairs in the 18th century. The town also boasts an artistic and cultural interest, inherited from the presence of artists who left their mark on their era, and represented today by the various festivals and events organized throughout the year. Its location, close to Mediterranean seaside resorts, at the junction of two major road transport routes, has long made it an essential crossroads.

5.3.2. *The history of Pézenas: between business dynamics and territorial dynamics*

Pézenas' arts and crafts scene has developed in three phases.

5.3.2.1. *Phase 1: artisans and shopkeepers join forces to revitalize the town*

The creation of an arts and crafts cluster dates back to the 1960s. A group of shopkeepers, artisans and community leaders decided to revitalize the historic center. From May 1968 onwards, this initial initiative was reinforced by the arrival of new designers, as well as by the installation of souvenir stores and resale outlets for mediocre-quality handicrafts.

5.3.2.2. *Phase 2: institutional dynamics to boost tourism and cultural activity*

After a period of inactivity, the 1980s saw the government and the region take steps to promote local development initiatives, based on the resurgence of an industry or tradition. Since the 1990s and 2000s, a number of institutional initiatives have been launched. This development is part of a regional scheme involving partnerships between local actors. In 1996, Pézenas joined the Ville et Métiers d'Art association, created on the initiative of municipal councilors "anxious to promote the richness and diversity of arts and crafts in their town"[3]. The project focuses on six areas of action: welcoming businesses, providing information and promoting the arts and crafts, preserving know-how, promoting tourism, raising awareness among schoolchildren, and training (initial and continuing). These initiatives are designed to foster economic development, by providing a forum for exchange and concertation with artisans. The municipality set up a dispersed business incubator and created a third-party space (the Maison des métiers

3 The Ville et Métiers d'Art network brings together 106 local authorities (metropolises, communities of communes, medium-sized towns and small communes). This now represents 610 municipalities. The members of the Ville et Métiers d'Art association share the same policy: to encourage the development and transmission of exceptional skills.

d'art). Designed by Ateliers d'Art de France, a leading association in the national arts and crafts sector, the third-location facility was inaugurated in 1994[4].

5.3.2.3. *Phase 3: the importance of artisans' associations in defending their activity*

The "*Association des Créateurs et Fabricants du Piscénois*", an association dedicated to arts and crafts, counts around 30 of the 60 or so artisans in Pézenas and nearby villages. Other managers who do not meet the association's selection criteria, particularly in terms of creation, are members of another association with a broader remit that brings together retailers, artisans and industrialists in Pézenas. Some artisans are members of several associations. Several events are organized by the various associations. The most popular of these is the night-time opening of stores organized by the oldest of the associations.

These dynamic associations have received substantial support from the municipality. This has led to a form of institutionalization of the artisans' collective project. Some artisans feel that the focus is solely on tourism and does not sufficiently promote their artisanal skills. In response, new groups of artisans have formed associations and are carrying out new actions.

Whatever the initiatives, the project has always been supported by the territory's community, whose development is largely based on tourism. They reflect a genuine, long-term policy of enhancing the tourist value of the region's heritage. This is the result of a combination of public and private initiatives.

5.4. Deciphering individual entrepreneurial logics and collective territorial dynamics

Studying the case of Pézenas over a long period of time enables us to identify the effects on the capacities of companies and the territory, as well as to perceive changes in situations. The analysis grid is based on the various materials gathered during the in-depth study of several companies. This will be illustrated by actual situations identified during the survey. Each of the

4 Ateliers d'Art de France is the trade association representing the art professions. It brings together over 6,000 artisans, material artists and art manufacturers, as well as over 95 associations.

cases in the grid corresponds to one or more companies in the Pézenas region. We present the main characteristics of each of the four cases identified on the basis of company data.

5.4.1. *Effects on business and territory capacities*

The proposed grid allows us to cross-reference the entrepreneur's perception of the value of territorial resources with the intersubjectivity of the perception of the value of the resource retained here. We consider intersubjectivity to be strong if the majority of entrepreneurs share the same conception of the resource. Weak intersubjectivity refers to the case where there is little consensus on the value of the resource. Four case studies can be identified.

5.4.1.1. *Case study 1: strong perceived value of territorial resources and strong intersubjectivity*

The reputation and geographical position of Pézenas, the proximity effect of the stalls and their attractive rates in terms of communal leases, etc., are examples of territorial resources perceived by all artisans as having a strong value.

The region's reputation and geographical position attract a clientele of tourists and enthusiasts. While they ensure commercial activity for local businesses, they do not allow for the development of dynamic capacities. The "stall" resource has a commercial impact because it improves visibility and also affects the level of charges, but it does not modify the artisan's value proposition. Resources have an effect on the market, in terms of attracting customers, but do not affect the production of artisanal businesses. In this sense, they only impact the company's ordinary capabilities.

At a territorial level, the agglomeration effect of companies has an impact on the territory's ordinary capacities, through its attractiveness to tourists and new artisans wishing to benefit from the resources mentioned above. In addition, by attracting different profiles of artisans and new institutions, such as *Ateliers d'Art de France*, the territory differentiates itself from other territories and also develops its dynamic capacities.

5.4.1.2. *Case study 2: high perceived value of territorial resources and low intersubjectivity*

The presence of *Ateliers d'Art de France* is valued differently by artisans. While some perceive this resource as important to their activity, others are far removed from the interest of this organization. Those who mobilize this resource consider that it generates dynamic capabilities, as it has an impact on their company's value proposition by developing skills transfers, visibility actions and recognition vis-à-vis peers and art amateurs. The implementation of a third-living space also encourages the development of dynamic capabilities by enhancing relationships and exchanges between companies.

The visibility given to the 400th anniversary of Molière's birth – one of France's greatest playwrights – was not seized by everyone in the same way. While some simply decorated their stores or productions, mobilizing ordinary skills, others took advantage of this opportunity to integrate the history of Pézenas into their portfolio of resources, developing dynamic skills in the process.

At a territory level, the use of these resources, even if limited to a few local businesses, nevertheless helps to maintain and develop their value, thus reinforcing the territory's ordinary capacities. The two examples of resources mentioned above increase the territory's reputation and attractiveness. As in case study 1, they also have an effect on the territory's dynamic capacities. Enhancing the value of a symbolic actor in the town's history, such as Molière, and/or encouraging the presence of a new actor, the *Ateliers d'Art de France*, strengthens the territory's resources available to existing businesses and helps to distinguish Pézenas from other territories.

5.4.1.3. *Case study 3: low perceived value of territorial resources and high intersubjectivity*

In this case, the company does not mobilize any of the territory's resources at its disposal. The resources have no direct effect on the company's activity. As it does not integrate them, it cannot develop ordinary or dynamic capacities directly linked to the territory. The consensus established around the low value of territorial resources does not allow the territory to directly develop capabilities.

Nevertheless, in this situation, beyond the direct effects, the Pézenas case highlights the emergence of indirect effects. Inter-company business or geographical proximity, stimulated by territorial initiatives, can generate dyadic or collective links. The resources exchanged through these links and/or newly created can mobilize ordinary and/or dynamic capacities on the part of the companies involved, by reconfiguring their resource portfolio or redefining their value proposition. The identification of such inter-company cooperation has highlighted its importance in the development of their activities. Through certain actions, such as support for events or associations of artisans, the territory is helping to develop these exchanges, although it is not necessarily aware of them, nor does it perceive the indirect effects in terms of capacity.

Indeed, these relationships have an effect on the resource portfolio and capabilities of companies. The creation of the Métiers d'art cluster in Pézenas in the 1960s illustrates this state of affairs: territorial resources were perceived as being of low value by the companies (distance from seaside areas, poor town center, lack of dynamism), but the strong intersubjectivity – on the low value of territorial resources – prompted them to look for a solution to economically revitalize a dormant town center. An association was set up, which had an effect on the ordinary and dynamic capacities of the participating companies. The arrival of new artisans and the reputation created around the arts and crafts enabled the territory to increase its attractiveness to tourists and businesses alike, and to differentiate itself from other artisanal villages. The territory, in the sense of an institution, is thus developing ordinary and dynamic capacities.

5.4.1.4. *Case study 4: low perceived value of territorial resources and low intersubjectivity*

If a given company does not mobilize any of the territorial resources at its disposal, and therefore does not develop any ordinary or dynamic capacity linked to the territory, the same is not true for all companies in the territory. Some recognize the value of territorial resources, while others ignore them. For companies that do not recognize the value of local resources, the search for external resources necessary to their activity and development leads them to seek links with other companies. The development of these relationships, whatever their geographical location, has an effect on the company's portfolio of resources and capabilities. If these companies are located outside the company's territory, the capabilities developed will not be linked to the territory, but more often to specific business lines. The development of innovations in techniques, know-how, commercial approaches, etc., has an impact on the ordinary and dynamic capabilities of companies. However, their possible spread remains limited, as the companies involved in these relationships are often more outward-looking than inward-looking.

On the other hand, if the companies are geographically close, the links developed may give rise to the emergence of ordinary and/or dynamic capabilities, or even lead in time, by isomorphism, to a diffusion to other companies in the territory and recognition of these locally embedded resources. However, this second possibility remains more limited.

The consensus established around the low value of territorial resources does not allow the territory to develop capabilities directly. As in case study 2, differences in perception at the company level could lead the territory to work towards a more global recognition of the value of the resources it makes available to companies. The experiences of the 1990s, and membership of the *Ville et Métiers d'Art* association, underline the development of the territory's ordinary and dynamic capabilities.

The four case studies identified in the analysis grid make it possible to identify situations and actions that differ from one case to another. The elements presented above enabled us to identify the actions of territorial companies and institutions that have an impact on the perceived value of the resource, on intersubjectivity, and on the capacities of companies and the territory. Logics of intention and action allow us to understand the grid in dynamic terms and to envisage actions to be taken, which will now be described in detail.

5.4.2. *A dynamic approach*

Although the grid appears static at first glance, the situations observed were influenced by the logic of action, and sometimes intention, of the various actors in the territory. Therefore, actions implemented by the territory may have altered companies' perceptions of value, just as actions taken by companies may have had an effect on resources and capacities in the territory. This observation opens up the possibility for the various actors involved to reflect on the scope for strengthening resources and capabilities. That said, it shows that the effects of each must be taken into account in their interactive dimension, and that ambivalent effects may emerge. Indeed, an increase in perceived value or intersubjectivity is not necessarily positive. As with externalities, negative effects also arise. A fine-tuning of actions between too much and too little should therefore be considered.

5.4.2.1. *The transition from case study 3 to case study 4*

The history of the Pézenas case highlights the dynamic that exists between these two cases. While the entrepreneurial logic of a few actors is at the origin of the territorial dynamic, the institutionalization of the approach may have limited the dyadic and/or collective relationships between entrepreneurs and thus restricted the development of capacities for companies.

The efforts made by the collective action of entrepreneurs and the territory enabled some companies to consider the territorial resource as valuable within their resource portfolio. While this dynamic may initially be of interest to the territory in developing territorial dynamics, it can be limiting over time for individual entrepreneurial logics and ultimately impact on territorial dynamics.

5.4.2.2. *Obverse and reverse of case study 2 and case study 4*

In both cases, the consensus on the value of the territorial resource was not established. While some companies include the territorial resource in their portfolio of resources, others shun it. Comparing the two cases highlights the importance of the entrepreneur's perception and action within the territorial dynamic. Dynamics at resource level do not necessarily affect dynamic capabilities. For example, when two companies develop a joint project, based on a logic of additive resources, at the end of the collaboration they would not necessarily have developed more resources. There are effects on ordinary capabilities, but not necessarily on dynamic capabilities, and yet this is not without interest for the development of companies.

The territory will be taking steps to increase the recognition of the resources available to businesses: encouraging the arrival of *Ateliers d'Art de France*, setting up "third parties" and loaning workshops to encourage new artisans to set up shop. This situation encourages the territory to develop ordinary, dynamic capabilities.

5.4.2.3. *The controversy between case study 1 and case study 2*

In a four-box grid, the most favorable situation is usually the one where the strong meets the strong. However, in the case of a reconciliation between individual entrepreneurial logics and territorial dynamics, this is not the case.

The implementation of territory-based strategies of singularity requires that there be no consensus on the value of the territorial resource. In the case studies, the companies are very diverse in terms of their trades, so the shared territorial resource is not linked to agronomic–geoclimatic resources or specific know-how. Even if it is situated at the level of myths and histories, the different trades mean that it is exploited in very different ways, thus distancing the notion of consensus.

Even if, through its actions, the territory seeks to reinforce consensus on the value of the resources made available, such as the reputation of Pézenas or the valorization of a historical figure, the sharing of a perceived value of the territorial resource is achieved on resources that could qualify as operational; that is, facilitating communication or the arrival of customers. Here, the consensus on the value of a territorial resource is limited to its operational, rather than strategic, nature.

5.5. Conclusion

Historically, artisans have grouped together in neighborhoods or towns. The proliferation of tourist routes, clusters and artisanal districts bears witness to this interest, and to the importance of both territories and the collectives that are partly associated with them. The development and/or mobilization of resources are in part linked to the collective and the territory. However, the different experiences reveal situations that are, to say the least, disparate, many of which point to the relative failure of these policies. Now more than ever, we need to understand the reasons for these failures, as well as the strong points that could structure and renew our approaches.

It is therefore essential to develop diagnostic and decision-making tools that will enable us to consider the development of both territories and businesses. The elements developed here underline the need for an approach that integrates both the question of companies and the territory, and the effects of interaction. In addition, a focus on resources and capabilities enables us to concentrate on a strong axis in questions of development and value creation.

Based on this tool, three points need to be addressed: the use value of such a grid, the mobilization of the grid and its implications for development policies.

The grid's contributions: first and foremost, the proposed grid puts the entrepreneur and their perceptions back at the heart of the analysis of territorial dynamics. The territory, for its part, is no longer considered as a simple organization of means, but as the holder of specific resources made available to companies in order to build up their resource portfolio. The identification of the ordinary and dynamic capacities of companies and the territory enables us to understand how individual entrepreneurial logics and collective territorial dynamics can be reconciled. Secondly, as a management tool, the grid helps us to understand complex processes by reducing complexity and shedding new light on phenomena. Derived from an analysis of the literature, it enables us to duplicate reality and establish structuring properties for different situations. Applied to a specific case, it suggests courses of action to reconcile individual entrepreneurial dynamics with collective territorial dynamics.

Mobilizing the grid: from a methodological point of view, we can suggest two ways of mobilizing this tool. The first is to identify the resources cited by the actors, even if their perceptions differ, in order to retain only those most frequently cited. The resources thus identified will be analyzed in the light of the grid. The second, more exhaustive approach, consists of identifying territorial resources and, for each of them, analyzing the perceived value between companies and identifying the position of the company portfolio in terms of intersubjectivity and value. The synthesis then enables the grid to be mobilized for analysis.

Involvement in local development policies: at first glance, local development policies can be seen as a simple organization of resources, enabling local companies to share and mobilize them individually as required. However, the reality is more complex. The notion of intersubjectivity and the impact on capacity development suggests that these policies cannot be reduced to a mere question of means. By producing a common good, which companies choose to mobilize, or not, or to varying degrees, policies have an impact on the resources and capabilities of companies and the territory. Looking at the impact of local development policies without considering the resources and capacities of companies and the territory as a whole does not allow us to consider all the dynamics at work. The existence of ambivalent effects, of direct and indirect effects, complicates the reality of expected actions. It is therefore necessary to take into account the effects of interaction when analyzing the dynamics between entrepreneurial and territorial logics, as well as the effects of the intersubjectivity of territorial resources. At the company level, we have seen that territorial resources have an effect on ordinary capabilities, but their homogeneity/convergence linked to the development of intersubjectivity can limit the dynamic capabilities of companies. In this case, companies will struggle to develop singularity strategies.

At the territorial level, intersubjectivity strengthens the attractiveness of the territory, by giving consensus to the perceived value of territorial resources. However, if the attraction effect is only applied to companies with identical profiles, this develops ordinary capabilities but limits their dynamic capabilities. Conversely, the development of dynamic capabilities at the company level through inter-company cooperation can enhance a territory's image and attractiveness, by developing new resources embedded locally and/or through an agglomeration effect, thus enabling territories to attract new entrepreneurial profiles and strengthen their own dynamic capabilities. Depending on the case identified in the grid, the territory, as an institution through the policies it implements, may have an interest in playing on the perception of the value of targeted territorial resources for just a few companies, or on the consensus of value by seeking intersubjectivity.

The grid highlights the interweaving of entrepreneurial and territorial logics. Local development policies could strive to overcome the interweaving of these logics, aiming for their convergence towards a territorial entrepreneurial logic.

5.6. References

Barney, J. (2001). Is the resource-based "view" a useful perspective for strategic management research? Yes. *Academic of Management Review*, 2(1), 41–56.

Casanova, S., Messeghem, K., Sammut, S. (2019). Idéaltype de l'émergence collective des opportunités d'affaires sous l'angle intersubjectif. *Management International*, 23(3), 106–117.

Davidson, D. (2001). *Subjective, Intersubjective, Objective*, volume 3. Oxford University Press, Oxford.

De Oliveira Wilk, E. and Fensterseifer, J.E. (2003). Use of resource-based view in industrial cluster strategic analysis. *International Journal of Operations & Production Management*, 23(9), 995–1009.

Desforges, M., Gilli, F., Cordoba, V. (2012). Territoires et innovation – Synthèse. *Travaux en ligne*, 9.

Dosi, G. and Teece, D.J. (1994). Preface: Dynamic capabilities. *Industrial and Corporate Change*, 3(3), 537–537.

Eisenhardt, K.M. (1989). Making fast strategic decisions in high-velocity environments. *Academy of Management Journal*, 32(3), 543–576.

Eisenhardt, K.M. and Martin, J.A. (2000). Dynamic capabilities: What are they? *Strategic Management Journal*, 21(10/11), 1105–1121.

Foss, N.J. and Ishikawa, I. (2007). Towards a dynamic resource-based view: Insights from Austrian capital and entrepreneurship theory. *Organization Studies*, 28(5), 749–772.

Foss, N.J., Klein, P.G., Kor, Y.Y., Mahoney, J.T. (2008). Entrepreneurship, subjectivism, and the resource-based view: Toward a new synthesis. *Strategic Entrepreneurship Journal*, 2(1), 73–94.

Penrose, E.T. (1959). *The Theory of the Growth of the Firm*, 3rd edition. Oxford University Press, Oxford.

Schumpeter, J.A. (1934). *Theory of Economic Development: An Inquiry into Profits, Capital, Credit, Interest, and the Business Cycle*. Harvard University Press, Cambridge, MA.

Shane, S. and Venkataraman, S. (2000). The promise of entrepreneurship as a field of research. *Academy of Management Review*, 25(1), 217–226.

Simon, H.A. (1969). *The Science of the Artificial Cambridge*. MIT Press, Cambridge.

Sirmon, D.G. and Hitt, M.A. (2009). Contingencies within dynamic managerial capabilities: Interdependent effects of resource investment and deployment on firm performance. *Strategic Management Journal*, 30(13), 1375–1394.

Sirmon, D.G., Hitt, M.A., Ireland, R.D. (2007). Managing firm resources in dynamic environments to create value: Looking inside the black box. *Academy of Management Review*, 32(1), 273–292.

Teece, D.J. (2007). Explicating dynamic capabilities: The nature and microfoundations of (sustainable) enterprise performance. *Strategic Management Journal*, 28(13), 1319–1350.

Teece, D.J. (2012). Dynamic capabilities: Routine versus entrepreneurial action. *Journal of Management Studies*, 49(8), 1395–1401.

Teece, D.J. and Dosi, G. (1994). Preface: Dynamic capabilities. *Industrial and Corporate Change*, 3(3), 537.

Teece, D.J. and Pisano, G. (1994). The dynamic capabilities of firms: An introduction. *Industrial and Corporate Change*, 3(3), 537–556.

Weppe, X., Warnier, V., Lecocq, X. (2013). Ressources stratégiques, ressources ordinaires et ressources négatives. *Revue française de gestion*, 5, 43–63.

6

Supporting Social Innovation Within Territories

6.1. Introduction

This chapter explores the links forged between the social and solidarity economy (SSE)[1] sector and public sector actors, particularly when the latter initiate "institutionalization processes" for social innovation, leading to its integration into public policy. Through confrontation with their environment, the actors behind social innovations help to build new relationships with the state and their institutional environment, shaping new rules and norms, and thus helping to chart "new institutional paths" (Klein et al. 2016a, p. 3). Drawing on local resources and involving a wide range of actors (institutions, businesses, users, etc.) in the development and appropriation of a social innovation, project leaders participate in the construction of a network that proves to be a stakeholder in a dynamic of social transformation in the territory.

Since France's most recent decentralization laws[2], SSE companies have benefited from new support from local authorities such as cities and regions. Through economic development programs, these public actors are helping to

Chapter written by Yamina VIERGE and Nathalie RAULET-CROSET.

1 SSE refers to a wide range of economic activities that aim to prioritize social profitability instead of purely financial profits. SSE organizations are driven by common principles, such as solidarity, the primacy of people over capital, democratic and participative governance and the pursuit of social and environmental objectives.

2 The NOTRe law, Law No. 2015-991 of August 7, 2015, on the new territorial organization of the Republic, strengthens the powers of cities and regions in terms of economic development.

foster the emergence, dissemination and even integration into public action of the social innovations they have helped to bring about. This is a recent development in public policy, and it is interesting to examine its effects on the evolution of territories.

The aim of this chapter is to study such institutionalization processes on the scale of a territory, the Toulouse metropolitan area, and highlight the factors that can encourage them. The case of one social innovation project will be analyzed, that of the *E-Hé* company, which is developing the "Flâneuse"[3], an inclusive walking frame for people with reduced autonomy in public establishments. Relying on various public support schemes run by the Occitanie Region and Toulouse Métropole, it interacts with these two public actors. Through this project owner's story, we aim to identify the processes by which these interactions can contribute to the construction of territorial public policies that bring about social transformations based on the SSE.

The first part (see section 6.2) of this chapter will be devoted to the presentation of the main concepts and the articulation of the research questions. After a methodological review, the second part (see section 6.3) will be devoted to the background context of the case study and a presentation of the main public actors supporting social innovation in the Toulouse metropolitan area. The third part (see section 6.4) will present the story of a social innovation company, and in particular the stages of its support through the various schemes. Finally, the presentation of the results and discussion will lead to a number of questions on the effects of public policies to support social innovation on social transformations and territorial construction.

6.2. The process of institutionalizing social innovation

Social innovation has a strong presence in the social economy sector. How can these often localized, emerging initiatives become an integral part of public action? To answer this question, we draw on a variety of theoretical approaches. Analytical frameworks relating to social innovation and its institutionalization are presented in the first part. Second, the reflections of various authors on entrepreneurial support shed light on the role that intermediary organizations can play in the territory, through the

3 This refers to the French word "flânerie", which is the act of taking a leisurely stroll.

prism of Cohendet et al.'s (2010) analysis of the articulation between middleground and upperground.

6.2.1. *Social innovation in the SSE sector and its institutionalization*

Following Bouchard et al. (2015), social innovation, in the context of the social/solidarity-based economy, can be considered as "an intervention initiated by social actors to respond to an aspiration, meet a need, provide a solution or take advantage of an opportunity for action in order to modify social relations, transform a framework for action or propose new cultural orientations"[4] (Bouchard et al. 2015, p. 9).

Two antagonistic visions of social innovation coexist: a dominant conception, the so-called "weak" approach, and a radical conception, the "strong" approach. They "constitute two poles from which it is possible to establish a continuum of practices" (Fraisse, quoted by Juan et al. (2020, p. 66)). The innovations promoted by SSE actors fall into these two types of approach. They either follow an entrepreneurial and philanthropic approach and remain embedded in the so-called functionalist market economy, in which case the innovation is "weak", or they carry a strong innovation objective, namely social transformation based on changes in practices and representations (Besançon and Chochoy 2015). Whether actors mobilize one approach or the other, social innovation can be the object of institutionalization processes (Klein et al. 2016a), but with a more or less transformative objective. The institutionalization of social innovation is understood as a process of recognition and appropriation of social innovation by the actors in a system, leading to the adoption by all these actors of new practices, norms and rules.

SSE organizations, which can carry a strong dimension of rupture and transformation, have been at the origin of processes to institutionalize innovations since the 2000s, as shown by Richez-Battesti and Vallade (2017). Initiatives are being taken to promote the institutionalization of social innovations from the SSE. In this way, SSE organizations interact with territorial public support and accompaniment policies initiated and piloted by public actors, in particular local authorities. The latter respond to a specific social order and can exert pressure to conform. This pressure to

4 Authors' translation.

conform is likely to conflict with the conditions conducive to the emergence of social innovation in its dimension of breaking with and challenging conventional systems.

These initiatives to institutionalize social innovation include, for example, the creation of TCEC[5] (Territorial Clusters for Economic Cooperation) from 2009 onwards (Fraisse 2017). The adoption of the SSE law in July 2014 also represents a major step in the institutionalization of social innovation and the SSE sector, by proposing a definition and regulatory framework. Public policies in support of social innovation are now backed by this regulatory framework and are translated into territorial economic development plans. These plans now include strategic orientations specific to the SSE sector. To implement these guidelines, local authorities have set up services dedicated to the emergence and support of social innovation, and run support systems for the creation and development of companies in this sector.

As part of these support dispositives for social innovation and the SSE sector, a new social order seems to be emerging as a result of the interactions between SSE actors and public actors. These interactions are leading to the creation of organizations that could be described as "intermediaries", dedicated to implementing public policies in support of the sector.

6.2.2. *"Intermediary" organizations: mechanisms for supporting social innovation in territories*

To encourage the emergence of innovation as a mechanism for local economic development, local authorities are helping to set up organizations dedicated to supporting socially innovative businesses. These include incubators, initiative factories, accelerators and other SSE business incubators. These organizations can be described as "intermediary organizations", by transposing to the organizational level the notion of intermediary institutions, proposed by Sainsaulieu (1983, 2001) and cited by David and Mounier (2021). The intermediary institution is defined as linking separate units in a movement that brings innovation, "conferring a particular legitimacy of transitional creativity and social bonding between actors of change"[6] (Sainsaulieu 2001, p. 133). It seems to us that the notion of intermediary organization could thus be used to qualify organizations created by public authorities, associating SSE actors and drawing on the

5 Translation of PTCE: pôles territoriaux de coopération économique.

6 Authors' translation.

organizational forms of the social economy in order to implement public policies in support of social innovation. These intermediary organizations can be studied through the prism of the support dispositives (Gilbert and Raulet-Croset 2021) they set up, and the supporting actors.

These intermediary organizations promote "the constitution of a space of cooperation between local actors in a logic of proximity"[7]. This space of cooperation integrates various territorial networks involving diversified actors (Besançon and Chochoy 2015, p. 83). These organizations, dedicated to supporting social innovation and accompanying project leaders, play an intermediation role in the territorialized ecosystem. In other words, they link domains or universes that usually ignore each other, mobilize them, add value to them and facilitate the "multiple feedbacks that organize the metropolitan economy and enable the mobilization of heterogeneous resources"[8] (Halbert 2010, p. 75).

6.2.3. *The territory as a middleground, supporting intermediary organizations*

In recent years, entrepreneurial support has undergone a number of changes, opening the door to new systems and entrants: "the development of social entrepreneurship is generating new behaviors, such as the spin-off of support structures, which have as yet been little explored"[9] (Messeghem et al. 2020, pp. 60–61). To observe the impact of these dispositives on the territory, these authors invite us to concentrate on "the coordination of dispositives and the interaction of intermedial ecosystems"[10]. In this context, dispositives are chosen and mobilized by intermediary organizations to act as mechanisms for the implementation of public policy orientations, and in our case, to support social innovation. They are thus incorporated into public policy and play a part in the process of institutionalizing social innovation within territories.

"Intermediary" organizations, as defined, are situated between public authorities, and the talents, the project owners. To analyze the interaction between these actors on different scales, we refer to Cohendet et al.'s (2009) analysis of the notions of middleground, and underground, developed to

7 Authors' translation.
8 Authors' translation.
9 Authors' translation.
10 Authors' translation.

analyze the creativity of cities. Indeed, the creativity of cities would be linked to interactions between formal units (companies, universities, local authorities and administration, etc.) located in the upperground, and informal and creative units (communities, individual talents, informal groups) located in the underground. These interactions take place within an institutional process of development and animation of intermediate platforms that constitutes the middleground (Cohendet et al. 2021b).

In the case studied here, intermediary organizations generate intermediary strata, or middlegrounds, on the territory, linking the upperground where public authorities are located, and the underground from which project leaders emerge (see Figure 6.1). It is in this space that the institutionalization of social innovation can take place, insofar as it is "an institutional process that connects an underground of talented individuals and an upperground made up of formal public and private institutions"[11]. This connection is impelled and organized by a middleground that acts as a link (Le Nadant and Marinos 2020, p. 42).

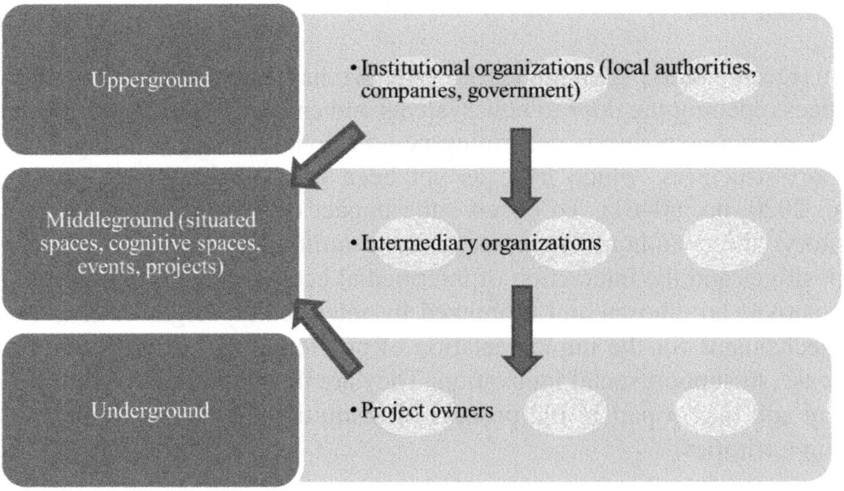

Figure 6.1. *Positioning of actors between upperground, middleground and underground*

Acting as institutional intermediaries, middleground actors participate in transformative movements based on four pillars (Grandadam et al. 2013):

11 Authors' translation.

situated spaces (third place), structuring cognitive spaces (in our case, SSE, social innovation, social entrepreneurship, engaged, etc.), events (e.g. project reviews, sector visibility events, awards ceremonies), projects (e.g. implementing support systems for project leaders, obtaining labels, creating impact assessment). This middleground approach provides a framework for observing all the stakeholders involved in social innovation stemming from the SSE, situating the actors and identifying the phenomena of institutional creation.

In this chapter, we therefore propose to shed light on how an intermediary organization, in a territory, can contribute to the institutionalization of a social innovation, particularly in its participation in the middleground, and by mobilizing the four pillars of transformation according to Grandadam et al. (2013) (see Table 6.1). Our empirical work focuses on the journey of an entrepreneur and their social innovation project, leading them to make this link between upper-, middle- and underground. This approach will highlight the interaction between the intermediary organization and the project owner, as well as the dynamic role of the project owner in the networks.

Situated spaces	Cognitive spaces	Events	Projects
Third places Public establishments open to project leaders => innovation experimentation Business incubators	SSE Social innovation Social utility General interest Committed entrepreneurship Impact assessment Circular economy	Project reviews SSE Month Awards ceremonies Inaugurations of premises and dispositives	Call for projects Creation of impact assessment Obtaining labels (ESS 2024 call for solutions, *Smart City*)

Table 6.1. *The four pillars of transformation (source: Grandadam et al. (2013))*

6.3. Methodology and background

6.3.1. *Methodology*

Our longitudinal study enables us to examine the dynamics of an entrepreneur with a social innovation project, following the stages and conditions of the diffusion and appropriation of its innovation.

The various stakeholders in the local network follow distinct paths, face diverse temporalities and experience evolutions in their arrangements (Bidart and Mendez 2016). In order to situate the issues at stake in the interrelationships within the network of actors, they were placed in a long-term process, and 19 interviews were conducted with 12 people[12].

Analysis of the interviews revealed points of tension and controversy, and how they are at the root of turning points and changes. By observing these areas of conflict, we can identify the mechanisms at work in the process of appropriating social innovations and integrate them into territorial public policies.

6.3.2. *Background: the identification of a key actor in the territory, the Première Brique intermediary organization*

In the Toulouse metropolitan area, a number of intermediary organizations provide support dispositives for the development of the SSE, and for entrepreneurs promoting social innovation. They are made up of various public or private sector organizations that pool resources to achieve a goal of supporting local economic development. Their legal structure and organizational methods are not always clearly defined. As a result, they benefit from flexibility and agility in their operations. *Première Brique* is one such organization.

Created on an experimental basis in January 2014 and officially inaugurated in October 2015, it is co-piloted by a local authority, Toulouse Métropole, and an association, *France Active – MPA Occitanie*. *France Active* is an association of committed entrepreneurs that finances and supports entrepreneurs through various dispositives. The local authority and the association jointly make human and financial resources available to *Première Brique*, and together manage the organization's strategic direction through a close-knit Board of Directors. *Première Brique* is a registered trademark of Toulouse Métropole, while *France Active* supports the structure and its salaried team within the framework of a renewed agreement, co-financed by a grant from the metropolis amounting to 40% of its budget. *Première Brique* is coordinated by a *France Active* employee and

12 Interviews conducted between June 2020 and March 2022 with local authority officials responsible for economic development and SSE, leaders of intermediary organizations (city-based and regional) and project developers.

a Toulouse Métropole territorial officer. The latter is seconded for part of their working time to the Toulouse Métropole economic development department, where they are in charge of the SSE sector.

Première Brique is now based in a third-location facility, *Imaginations Fertiles*, supported by the metropolis, and has expanded its team with the creation of additional positions, bringing the total to six. From the outset, *Première Brique* has run an incubator and obtained the *La Fabrique à Initiatives*[13] label. The two coordinators assert their attachment to the SSE sector and to social innovation, and adopt a posture close to that of social entrepreneurs, broadening the range of interventions and positioning *Première Brique* as a social innovation enterprise.

In 2020, to celebrate its 5th anniversary, *Première Brique* began work on impact assessment with the support of an agency specializing in social innovation, *Ellyx*. The results of this work are presented in a publication that presents the impacts obtained in five areas (political, economic, social, individual and environmental), and promotes social innovation and the SSE. The health crisis prevented the public event planned for this occasion from taking place. In April 2021, *Première Brique* added a business accelerator to its range of services to support the establishment of exogenous social enterprises wishing to join the metropolitan area in a dynamic of spin-off and scaling-up of their project.

Première Brique plays a central role in coordinating the network of public and private actors involved in supporting social innovation, by taking action to structure a local ecosystem and build a support chain. The aim is to cover the various stages in the life of the companies and supported projects, through the complementarity of dedicated public and private dispositives and through the organization of their interactions with a fairly broad panel of locally implanted economic actors, and in particular the involvement of the territory's major corporations.

Finally, a new institutional actor is participating in the evolution of the local network supporting social innovation in the metropolis. Indeed, as of September 2021, the Occitanie Region has been setting up a new intermediary organization within the territory (*Cité+*). It is accommodated as a new third service – *La Cité* – and runs a new social innovation incubator.

13 *La Fabrique à Initiatives* is a system created by *Avise* in 2010, which makes it possible to design innovative solutions that are useful for the territories.

6.4. The *E-Hé* company at a glance

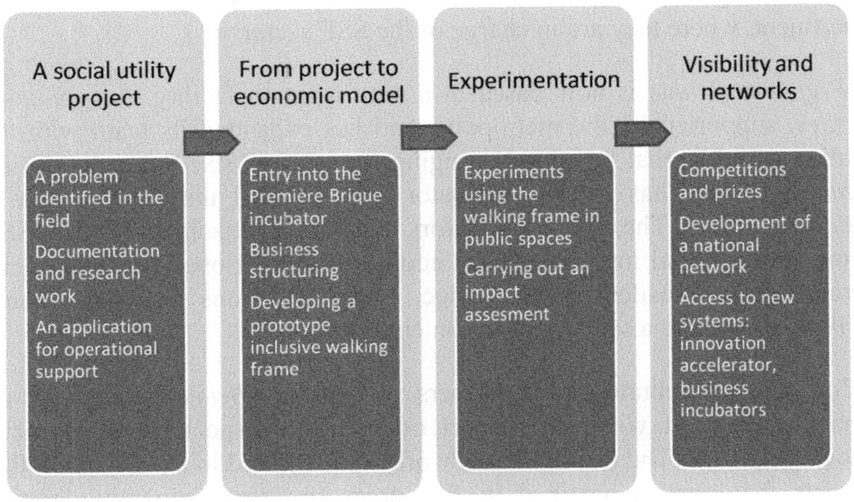

Figure 6.2. *Different stages of the* E-Hé *journey*

Our analysis focuses on the interaction between the intermediary organization *Première Brique*, and a project initiator, the *E-Hé* company, at the origin of a social innovation. In this section, we retrace the path and process of institutionalization of this innovation. Supported from the outset by *Première Brique*, the company followed a path that brought it into contact with numerous local actors and enabled it to benefit from a variety of support dispositives. The following narrative reconstructs the various phases we have identified in the institutionalization process.

6.4.1. *From the outset, a social utility project: from idea to project*

Founded by a brother and sister from Toulouse, *E-Hé* aims to combat the isolation and stigmatization of people losing their autonomy by creating inclusive mobility aids. He is a designer; she comes from the personal care sector and has participated in the fight against mistreatment of the elderly and disabled. Based on a personal experience, they began imagining the project in 2016:

> Our encounter with the project is based on the environment we make available to people losing their independence. And that's what gave rise to the foundation of the project and what we're developing today[14] (Director 1).

In June 2017, they both put an end to their respective professional activities to devote themselves entirely to the project, having, they say, evaluated the risks involved and the level of commitment required. Having no skills or experience as entrepreneurs, they set out to find support, and made the rounds of Toulouse's entrepreneurial support structures (see Table 6.2). In October 2017, *Première Brique* opened its 2018–2019 call for projects, covering several themes including "*Enfin vieux, vivre heureux!*"[15] to discover and support silver economy projects. The two founders then drew on a sociological survey carried out by researchers from Scool, a Toulouse-based humanities research cooperative. The study focused on maintaining the autonomy of the elderly. The investigation into the lifestyles of the elderly involved designers, a Toulouse-based third-living space, *Imaginations Fertiles* and *Fablab Makers* (France's oldest Fablab). It revealed that some people facing a loss of mobility develop strategies to circumvent the use of a walker, and highlighted the mechanisms by which these people are excluded from cultural spaces such as museums, or from certain administrations when access conditions are not appropriate:

> So little by little, we cut ourselves off from these visits because we knew we were going to be too tired and didn't want to be a burden on others. And so, we start to isolate ourselves[16] (Director 1).

At the end of 2017, the two entrepreneurs were selected to join the *Première Brique* incubator with a first project. The aim was to provide medicalized solutions for people with loss of autonomy and mobility by creating non-stigmatizing objects. The idea was to mobilize the "design for all" approach, which is linked to the notion of "universal design" in the United Nations Convention on the Rights of Persons with Disabilities. The aim was to change the way society looks at loss of autonomy.

14 Authors' translation.
15 Translation: "Finally old, live happily".
16 Authors' translation.

6.4.2. *From project to business model: support from Première Brique*

The 18-month support provided by the *Première Brique* incubator comprises an initial nine-month phase, during which project leaders take part in weekly group workshops to tackle all the issues involved in building a project: drawing up a business plan, measuring the social impact of economic and strategic plans. These workshops include meetings with experts in the various fields explored. For the managers, this initial period of support by the incubator was the first step in moving from idea to project, based on the contribution of expertise and skills:

> Within 9 months we went from this idea to "OK, we have an entrepreneurial project with its business model"[17] (Director 1).

Première Brique selects around 10 candidates each year who will join the incubator. Projects are selected based on their ability to:

> Bring about systemic change […] come and change the paradigms on a specific subject. […] We are really interested in projects that are embryonic […], the idea is that we do not hesitate to question the projects or solutions that are proposed by project leaders. They arrive and we completely deconstruct their solution. We are really in a process of innovation, that is to say we are reopening all the fields, we are going to re-question the problem, and starting from the problem which is re-questioned with a lot of participatory approaches, collaborative […][18] (*Première Brique* Project Manager 1).

The creation of an inclusive mobility assistance tool is based on usage design, promoting co-construction within a collective and bringing together makers, designers and various stakeholders concerned by the issue, including potential users. This co-construction approach involves a usage laboratory, the *Living Lab l'Étape*, based in Lattes near Montpellier, which participates in the construction of the working method: six workshop sessions bring together people who are directly concerned (elderly and/or losing mobility) and professionals (physiotherapists, occupational therapists, geriatricians). Drawing on usage design, the proposal for a mobility aid was developed

17 Authors' translation.
18 Authors' translation.

within this collective framework, leading to the production of a first prototype of the "Flâneuse".

This "design for all" approach, introduced by the project leader (a professional designer) and promoted by the *Première Brique* incubator, involves working first and foremost on the basis of usage, involving stakeholders upstream of product design. During this period, the entrepreneurs will identify a need: establishments open to the public are subject to regulations guaranteeing access to public establishments for people with disabilities, including those facing a loss of mobility. However, these establishments have no solution to meet this need, "in any case, no acceptable solution"[19], says an *E-Hé* manager. Work is therefore underway with certain establishments to examine the conditions under which they would be willing to adopt a solution: the provision of an inclusive walking frame, the "Flâneuse". This is the first stage in identifying the potential market. The *Première Brique* incubator will support these initiatives until July 2019, marking the end of this first phase of support.

6.4.3. *Entering the experimental phase*

E-Hé joined the *Smart City* program (Toulouse Métropole's master plan for "building tomorrow's intelligent city with citizens") with a first prototype of the "Flâneuse", an inclusive walking frame for different uses and users. Entrepreneurs will be able to experiment with the use of the first prototypes in various cultural establishments open to the public (the *mediatheque*, the *Cité de l'espace*, the *Basilique Saint-Sernin* and the *Convent des Jacobins*). Toulouse Métropole organizes contacts between project promoters and the local authority's establishments, and takes charge of some of the logistical aspects of the experiments in the establishments:

> They were also very adept and benevolent in the context of Covid, because even though there were periods of closure, we were still able to experiment when they reopened, with all the uncertainties they had. They were receptive across the board, and I think that's one of the keys to our success[20] (Director 2).

However, the *Smart City* scheme was not initially very open to social innovation projects, due to the associative status of most of the project

19 Authors' translation.
20 Authors' translation.

leaders. *Première Brique*, the city's SSE officer and the elected representative, then began lobbying the local authority, drawing on the European definition of a company and the relevance of SSE projects to *Smart City*'s objectives. This institutional work culminated in a deliberation in April 2019, opening access to associations, recognizing them as companies. They now account for more than half of the experimentation projects carried out under this scheme supported by the metropolis.

This new stage of the project involves working with the *Ellyx* agency (Scoop of expertise in social innovation, based in Bordeaux) to develop a social impact assessment tool based on the method and indicators defined by *Avise* (engineering agency dedicated to SSE companies) and carried out by *France Active* in 2019 to assess the performance of the local SSE support scheme (DLA). This measure was financed by the Occitanie Region and the *Banque publique d'investissement*. This impact assessment is envisioned by the entrepreneur as:

> [...] a tool for enhancing the value of the project, and it enabled us to see where we are in relation to certain aspects, so that we can report back to our customers. [...] It's something we promote to certain partners[21] (Director 1).

The use of this approach and the choice of a service provider specialized in the SSE sector have created new links with the public sector. Indeed, Toulouse Métropole has already used this agency to measure the impact of the SSE companies supported by its dispositives, in order to highlight the importance of *Première Brique*'s support for innovative companies and its contribution to the territory in terms of well-being and concerning the environment, over and above strictly economic results. This impact assessment, carried out on the scale of *Première Brique* to highlight its contribution to the territory, is intended as a means of recognition by the community and the metropolitan economic ecosystem.

The directors of *E-Hé*, while defining themselves as part of the economy of solidarity, structured themselves into a simplified joint-stock company in October 2018. Their starting point was the project's financing needs, and in particular the need to raise funds to move on to the industrialization and marketing phase of the "Flâneuse". They feel that this status is better suited to discussions with various economic actors, and offers greater guarantees in

21 Authors' translation.

terms of economic profitability. It is also a status that enables the two entrepreneurs to retain control over the personal investment they have made in the project:

> When you're an accredited company in the social economy, the return on investment isn't just financial. And in fact, as a result, you have access to certain solidarity-based investments which, for some project leaders, can seem [...] scary because they say to themselves: I won't have access to traditional financing, such as angel investors, etc.[22] (*Première Brique* Project Manager 2).

The intermediary organization understands the project owner's problem, but regrets this strategic choice. As far as *Première Brique* is concerned, public procurement conditions are evolving to integrate social and environmental criteria supported by the SSE. As a result, certain public procurement contracts will become more difficult to access for companies that do not hold the *ESUS*[23] accreditation.

6.4.4. *A strategy of visibility, network building and institutional adaptation*

The fact that the business is based in the territory means that more people can meet up and join the project, as it facilitates local exchanges. In addition, through a strategy of visibility, the project owner will develop their own network at a national scale:

> I would say that shared territorial roots is a facilitator for developing social innovations because we also share the same background. In today's world this could become a challenge, but I feel that in the context of development, it's an effective mechanism, yes[24] (Manager 1).

With this in mind, *E-Hé* competed for a number of awards, enabling it to expand its support base and network. In December 2020, the company won the call for solutions 2021 (a group of eight innovation accelerators) and joined a national network of social entrepreneurs (the *Ashoka Fellows*).

22 Authors' translation.

23 Proposed translation of ESUS: *Entreprise Solidaire d'Utilité Sociale*, as "Solidarity Enterprise of Social Utility".

24 Authors' translation.

Première Brique is a stakeholder in this national scheme, and renewed its support for *E-Hé* for a further year. At the end of 2020, *E-Hé* was also selected as a laureate of the *Entreprendre Garonne-Occitanie Reseau*, a private intermediary organization run by a federation of associations of company directors committed to job creation through support for economic development.

In January 2021, the company joined the Toulouse Métropole incubator, receiving support from the French chamber of commerce and industry (*CCI*) and *Nubbo*, a technological innovation accelerator supported by the Occitanie Region. In February 2021, *E-Hé* was also the winner of the *Viva Lab* prize, an accelerator run by the *Caisse nationale d'assurance vieillesse* (CNAV), in which France Active (*Première Brique*'s co-pilot) is a stakeholder. In 2021, *E-Hé* was the winner of the *Charles Foix – Silver Valley* grant, which rewards innovative projects for the autonomy of seniors, and gains access to the *Silver Valley* support fund, as well as the support of *Grand Orly*. In March 2021, *E-Hé* also won the Toulouse Métropole Innovation Challenge on the theme of "Getting around in the city of tomorrow"[25]. This distinction gives *E-Hé* access to public contracts. In September 2021, *E-Hé* won first prize in the technological innovation category of the Start-up Contest at the *Salon international des musées (SITEM)*. This trade show brings together professionals involved in equipping museums and promoting their innovation; yet another recognition by public actors.

6.5. The end of the project: first orders and the start of production

Toulouse Métropole placed its first order for "Flâneuses" in July 2021. Production of the "Flâneuses" began in November–December 2021. *Milc*, a company based in the Pyrenees, was chosen for production. This scoop company is itself committed to localizing production and reducing its environmental impact. The *Caisse nationale de solidarité pour l'autonomie* ordered 54 "Flâneuses". The project continued with the introduction of an awareness-raising and training service for staff responsible for welcoming people to the establishments, and a communication campaign aimed at people who are far away from the establishments, to promote access to them:

25 Proposed translation of "*Se déplacer dans la ville de demain*".

> Because they don't have the knowledge that there will be a solution that will enable them to have a pleasant visit for everyone. It's a form of communication that museums don't know how to do today[26] (Director 1).

In December 2021, *Première Brique*'s support as part of the accelerator came to an end. However, *E-Hé*'s managers were aware that the radiance of their project could also have a positive impact on *Première Brique*, and this is seen as a fair return:

> I think they're looking for projects that promote their approach, obviously. Obviously, because we're not the first social innovators. They are. In other words, before we did social innovation, they did it and supported social innovation project owners. The first link in the chain is the incubator, not *E-Hé*[27] (Director 2).

Dates	Milestones
June 2017	The two founders stop their professional activities to devote themselves to the project.
2018	Response to the call for projects and selection for support in the *Première Brique* incubator.
October 2018	Creation of *E-Hé* as a simplified joint-stock company. Development of the business plan and the *La Flâneuse* objective (inclusive walking frame).
July 2019	End of support from the *Première Brique* incubator
December 2020	Winner of the *Ashoka 2021* call for solutions, leading to further support from *Première Brique* as part of an accelerator program. Integration into a Toulouse Métropole business incubator, with support from *Nubbo* (an incubator dedicated to technological innovation).
February 2021	Winner of the *Viva Lab* prize (*Caisse nationale de l'assurance vieillesse, France Active*). Application for the *Charles Foix* grant.
March 2021	Winner of the Challenge innovation – Toulouse Métropole prize as part of the 2020 employment stimulus plan.
May 2021	Winner of the 2021 *Charles Foix* fellowship.

26 Authors' translation.
27 Authors' translation.

September 2021	First Prize in the Start-up Contest (SITEM International Museum Show).
December 2021	"Flâneuses" go into production for the first time. Creation of a research and development manager position. Creation of a sales position planned for the 1st half of 2021. End of support from *Solution 2021 – Ashoka.*

Table 6.2. *Key milestones of the E-Hé company*

E-Hé's managers have a social objective, which is to contribute to the inclusion of people with reduced mobility. They also want to create an industrial tool in the territory that will have an economic impact and create jobs for people who are far from it. Their ambition is to lead a project that will unite people around the values of inclusion, design for all and made in France. It is a social innovation that defends a project of general interest, and the process of institutionalizing this innovation is part of a "strong solidarity" approach.

6.6. Lessons: the institutionalization mechanisms of social innovation

The process of institutionalizing social innovation reveals several dynamics harbored by stakeholders. By focusing on the actions of local authority stakeholders and project leaders, we highlight their different strategies and the tensions arising from the interrelationships involved in the institutionalization process. We can then observe the effects of these tensions on the transformative capacity of social innovation in the territory.

6.6.1. *Strategies and the role of key actors in communities*

In order to better analyze the integration of social innovations into public action, various mechanisms of institutionalization are identified. Certain conditions are identified (see Figure 6.3).

By taking a closer look at one organization, *Première Brique*, and its interaction with a project leader, the *E-Hé* company, we have qualified it as an intermediary organization, since it was set up, on the initiative of public actors, to support the consideration of new economic proposals stemming from social innovations in the territory. This organization fosters links between various actors in the monitoring and support of project leaders. It stimulates the dynamics of change and generates knowledge. Through the creation of support systems for the various stages in the development of entrepreneurial projects, it helps to rally local economic actors around social innovation projects.

Other key actors, particularly within public authorities, are responsible for disseminating and appropriating social innovation. They rely on a foundation of national and European legal and regulatory constraints to push for the integration of social innovation criteria from the SSE into territorial public management and public economic development policies. For example, the metropolitan authority's SSE project manager is involved in drawing up the authority's purchasing procedures, and is participating in the development of the collectivity's relations with its suppliers around the notion of responsible purchasing.

Another example: the Occitanie Region's economic and innovation department has been working on the implementation of an investment financing tool open to "social entrepreneurs", with the aim of not restricting the region's support solely to companies with *ESUS* status, and thus supporting a wider range of companies in a "more virtuous" economic approach.

Actors integrated into communities thus foster the institutionalization of social innovation, by changing not only the rules, but also the systems of meaning within the very organization that they are a part of, through processes that could be described as institutional work in the sense of Lawrence et al. (2009).

6.6.2. *The entrepreneur, a key actor in institutionalization*

The increasing number of responses to calls for projects enables *E-Hé* managers to acquire the skills they need to carry out and manage their projects, build a territorial and national network around them and give visibility to their commercial offering. This requires project leaders to keep a close eye on the market and work hard on each application for these calls for projects, which are subject to a lengthy selection process. This strategy leads to an entanglement of different types of support, but when their multiplication becomes problematic, they indicate that they know how to take the time to have a discussion with the preceding parties to ensure that they complement each other:

> The idea isn't to do the same thing twice with two different people, but to say: if there are two people who can help us, how do we go about questioning them? The basis is collective intelligence, and that's something we rely on a lot [28] (Director 2).

The case study of the *E-Hé* company shows that the support provided by these different organizations has helped the project owner to build a business model that can combine the objective of social utility with that of economic profitability. The first stage of support with the *Première Brique* incubator, which consists of deconstructing and reconstructing the project, is a founding moment that places the company in the field of social innovation. Entrepreneurs are put in touch with a wide network, and then develop their own strategy by consolidating a network of support and allies through applications to calls for projects and competitions, and by winning prizes. This has the effect of raising the profile of the company, enabling the entrepreneurs to build up their network throughout the process, access various support dispositives to help them through the development stages of their entrepreneurial project, and extend their territory of action nationwide.

In the process of building a network, and by promoting their innovation through numerous applications, the entrepreneur will continue to institutionalize their social innovation through a chain of translation: the formulation of a problem (the isolation of people losing their autonomy and the obligation for public establishments to provide access for people with disabilities), involvement (through the design of the solution with stakeholders and the mobilization of systems and actors around the prototype testing phase to validate the relevance of the solution), enrolment of network members through the support of various dispositives that will support the company's development. Finally, mobilization, through the final stage of manufacturing and marketing, is a process which is still underway (Akrich et al. 2006).

28 Authors' translation.

6.6.3. *An institutionalization process carrying a transformative vision*

We have shown that *Première Brique* adopts institutional communication strategies, mobilizing concepts linked to classic economic performance to demonstrate the effectiveness of its project. The organization rebuilds its tools, proposing an evolution in performance indicators, for example, by working on impact assessment. It introduces social and environmental indicators with the aim of legitimizing the SSE sector by demonstrating its efficiency. Through communication within the network and the appropriation of these new tools by the project leaders themselves, *Première Brique* aims to change the way the notion of economic performance is perceived by the region's political and economic actors. This meets an objective of the Occitanie Region, which, through its training programs and its criteria for supporting entrepreneurs (mission-based enterprises, impact enterprises, social entrepreneurs), intends to develop the notion of impact economy, by also reaching out to traditional commercial enterprises.

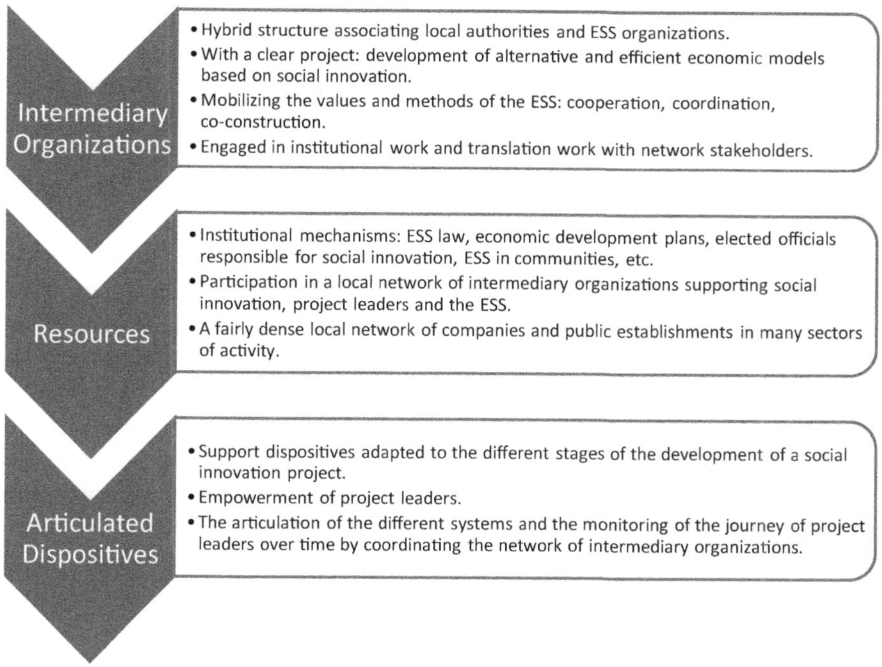

Figure 6.3. *Identification of conditions conducive to the institutionalization of social innovation*

However, not all organizations adopt the same posture when it comes to supporting project leaders. Through the journey of the *E-Hé* company, we observe that *Première Brique* encourages entrepreneurs to appropriate the ideological foundation of the SSE, mobilize the methodologies of social innovation and adopt a legal structure corresponding to the 2014 SSE law. For the region, the posture is different: "status does not make virtue"[29] and the authority favors the notions of impact economy and engaged enterprise, and advocates a broad opening to entrepreneurs, including those who are far from the criteria and objectives of the SSE. These are two approaches to social innovation and the social/solidarity-based economy, supported by two key organizations in the territory, each with its own transformative vision. These two visions are part of the process of institutionalizing social innovation throughout the territory.

6.7. Conclusion

This research takes place in a territory where the local and metropolitan authorities responsible for economic development pay particular attention to the social economy and social innovation. They have established intermediary organizations responsible for fostering the development of social innovation in the territory, through dedicated dispositives. Here, we have analyzed the role of one such organization, *Première Brique*, which is particularly linked to the metropolis. We wondered whether these intermediary organizations, through the dispositives they run, contribute to creating the right conditions for the institutionalization of the social innovations they support. *Première Brique* has the particularity of being strongly attached to the values and standards of the SSE (*ESUS*-compliant structuring of companies, support for systemic transformations of the economy). If we take up the distinction between strong and weak social innovation (Laville in Klein et al. 2014; Laville 2016; Fraisse 2020), presented in section 6.2.1, *Première Brique* seems to us to be more in line with a desire for transformation, associated with strong social innovation. Active in the territory and a pioneer in the institutionalization of social innovation in the SSE sector, this organization is involved in institutional work within Toulouse Métropole.

To analyze this institutional work, we have proposed to consider intermediary organizations as actors located in a middleground (Grandadam

29 Authors' translation.

et al. 2013; Cohendet et al. 2021a, 2021b) and acting as a link between institutions and innovators. They rely on support dispositives for project leaders, which they articulate across the territory, with the ambition of building and coordinating an ecosystem to support social innovation. They are part of a dynamic to renew entrepreneurial support (Messeghem et al. 2020).

These dispositives contribute to the middleground by facilitating complementarity between actors, delimiting the scope of each actor's intervention, organizing the distribution of support for project leaders according to the stage of development of the entrepreneurial project, and constituting a common framework for action. Here, they play a regulatory role within the network, which they help to expand and consolidate by mobilizing different actors in meeting and cooperation forums. Through these dispositives, the intermediary organization encourages project owners to become acculturated to social innovation and the social/solidarity-based economy, and supports the process of transforming the project owner into an entrepreneur. When working in middleground mode, the dispositives are also appropriated by project owners, who thus reduce their dependence on intermediary organizations. They enable them to regulate the pressures to that they are subjected to, by building and expanding their own network and thus their territory, going beyond the local scale and building a hybrid economic model.

In terms of lessons learned, this case study makes it possible first and foremost to characterize the institutionalization processes of social innovation stemming from the SSE, in a metropolitan territory where local authorities encourage support and accompaniment of the sector through the implementation of territorial public policies. The middleground approach thus makes it possible to distinguish the key stakeholders in the institutionalization process and position them in a local network. Each of the three levels plays a role in the process of institutionalizing social innovation on the territory, based on its own interests. Local authorities in the upperground play an important role in terms of economic and social development; intermediary organizations in the middleground, whose role is to energize the local economy, focus on developing a sector – the SSE – and disseminating new business models. Finally, underground entrepreneurs must create a viable, sustainable economic activity that meets the challenge of social utility.

Second, we show that, if the entrepreneur is gradually "acculturated" to the values of social innovation and SSE approaches, they will implement their own strategy within the network and adjust their response to the various external constraints that they must submit to. It refers to an objective of social transformation, and mobilizes the SSE in the construction of its project: co-construction, participative approach through design for all, association of users and establishments concerned, researchers, makers, etc.; elaboration of a measure of social impact, localization of production in particular. However, it also refers to the ideology of a classic capitalist economy in terms of economic performance, fundraising and the distribution of capital within the company. It is subject to contradictory pressures, which it confronts by developing its own partnership logic. In this way, it enlists the support of a wide range of economic actors in its project, helping to institutionalize social innovation.

In conclusion, the middleground, animated by intermediary organizations, represents a level which is particularly important to observe the process of institutionalization of social innovation and the entrepreneurial specificities of social innovation project leaders. Of course, this remains to be explored in greater depth. This process of institutionalization has its own specific features, linked to its roots in the SSE. Further analysis will provide a deeper understanding of this dynamic.

6.8. References

Akrich, M., Callon, M., Latour, B. (2006). *Sociologie de la traduction : textes fondateurs*. École des Mines, Paris.

Besançon, E. and Chochoy, N. (2015). Les marqueurs d'innovation sociale : une approche institutionnaliste. *Revue internationale de l'économie sociale (RECMA)*, 336, 80–93.

Bidart, C. and Mendez, A. (2016). Un système d'analyse qualitative des processus dans les sciences sociales : l'exemple de la mutation d'une organisation. In *Andrew Abbott et l'héritage de l'école de Chicago*, Demazière, D. and Jouvenet, M. (eds). EHESS, Paris, 217–231.

Bouchard, M.J., Evers, A., Fraisse, L. (2015). Concevoir l'innovation sociale dans une perspective de transformation. *Sociologies pratiques*, 31(2), 9–14.

Cohendet, P., Grandadam, D., Simon, L. (2010). The anatomy of the creative city. *Industry and Innovation*, 17(1), 91–111.

Cohendet, P., Grandadam, D., Suire, R. (2021a). Reconsidering the dynamics of local knowledge creation: Middlegrounds and local innovation commons in the case of FabLabs. *Zeitschrift für Wirtschaftsgeographie*, 65(1), 1–11.

Cohendet, P., Simon, L., Mehouachi, C. (2021b). From business ecosystems to ecosystems of innovation: The case of the video game industry in Montréal. *Industry and Innovation*, 28(8), 1046–1076.

David, A. and Mounier, C. (2021). Travailler en mode middleground : collectifs créatifs et institutions intermédiaires. *Management International* [Online]. Available at: https://halshs.archives-ouvertes.fr/halshs-03241596.

Fraisse, L. (2017) Mieux caractériser les TCEC face à un processus rapide d'institutionnalisation. *RECMA*, 343(1), 21–39.

Fraisse, L. (2020) *Janus et l'innovation sociale*. Érès, Paris [Online]. Available at: https://www.cairn.info/load_pdf.php?ID_ARTICLE=ERES_LAVIL_2020_01_0045&download=1.

Gilbert, P. and Raulet-Croset, N. (2021). *Lire le management autrement : le jeu des dispositifs*. EMS, Caen.

Grandadam, D., Cohendet, P., Simon, L. (2013). Places, spaces and the dynamics of creativity: The video game industry in Montreal. *Regional Studies*, 47(10), 1701–1714.

Halbert, L. (2010) *L'avantage métropolitain*. Presses Universitaires de France, Paris.

Juan, M., Laville, J-L., Subirats-Humet, J. (2020). *Du social business à l'économie solidaire : critique de l'innovation sociale*. Erès, Toulouse.

Klein, J.-L., Laville, J.-L., Moulaert, F. (2014). *L'innovation sociale*. Érès, Toulouse.

Klein, J.-L., Camus, A., Jetté, C., Champagne, C., Roy, M. (2016a). *La transformation sociale par l'innovation sociale*. Presses de l'Université du Québec, Quebec.

Klein, J.-L., Pecqueur, B., Koop, K., Soussi, S.A. (eds) (2016b). *L'innovation locale à l'épreuve du global : un défi pour les acteurs*. Presses de l'Université du Québec, Québec.

Laville, J.-L. (2016). *L'économie sociale et solidaire : pratiques, théories, débats*. Le Seuil, Paris.

Lawrence, T.B., Suddaby, R., Leca, B. (2009) *Institutional Work: Actors and Agency in Institutional Studies of Organizations*. Cambridge University Press, Cambridge.

Le Nadant, A.-L. and Marinos, C. (2020). Espaces de coworking et fablabs des villes petites et moyennes : un rôle de middleground ? *Innovation*, 61(1), 41–66.

Messeghem, K., Sammut, S., Temri, L., St-Jean, E. (2020). Les mutations de l'accompagnement entrepreneurial. *Revue française de gestion*, 286(1), 59–67.

Richez-Battesti, N. and Vallade, D. (2017). ESS, territoire et régime de solidarité : l'innovation sociale comme levier pour une "ville solidaire" ? *Management Avenir*, 97(7), 105–127.

Sainsaulieu, R. (2001). *Des sociétés en mouvement : la ressource des institutions intermédiaires*. Desclée de Brouwer, Paris.

7

Tackling Medical Deserts in Rural Territories

7.1. Introduction

The issue of medical desertification, which has been widely reported in the media over the last 10 years or so, is a recurring theme in election campaigns. This attests to the difficulty of finding a satisfactory and lasting response to this essential issue, which, according to the United Nations, is a pillar of sustainable development. Numerous individuals and organizations have alerted us to the importance of this issue, and the urgent need to identify acceptable and viable solutions. In March 2022, the Senate mission on the prospects for territorial planning and territorial cohesion submitted a report on medical deserts. The findings were alarming: "If nothing is done, the worst is yet to come. The prospect of a dark decade in terms of medical demography is a reality[1]." In its report, the mission sets out 32 proposals to address the shortage of town doctors in the territories, focusing on incentives, medical services organization and constraint. While a number of these measures have already been formulated and are well known (development of telemedicine, internships for medical students in under-resourced regions, etc.), others have been added to the list. In particular, it proposes to "involve territorial authorities, who are on the front line" [2] in defining local organizational solutions for the provision of healthcare services. As the mission points out, "basing a policy of

Chapter written by Corinne ROCHETTE.

1 Author's translation.

2 Author's translation.

attractiveness on financial aid alone"[3] is an illusion, as this mechanism is not enough to develop a sustainable healthcare service.

Therefore, the question – how can we guarantee that everyone, regardless of where they live, has access to the care they require for its health? – remains unresolved to this day. This is a key issue at a time when it is estimated that 30% of the French population live in a medical desert; that is, 1.6 million French people forego medical care every year, and waiting times for appointments sometimes exceed several months (over 200 days for an ophthalmologist or gynecologist in some areas). Studies show that situations for which access is difficult result in an increase in hospitalizations, which are costly and could be avoided with better access to healthcare (Gulliford 2002).

This situation feeds territorial inequalities in terms of access to healthcare (Guagliardo 2004) and the feeling of abandonment felt by fellow citizens, to which a response is urgently needed. The United Nations recognizes that healthcare coverage is a pillar of sustainable development and global security. This coverage implies that healthcare facilities are available, accessible, acceptable, appropriate, and offer a good quality (Campbell et al. 2013). As research shows, the availability of local healthcare services for beneficiaries is an important determinant of population health (Mizen et al. 2015). Solving the problem of easy, comfortable access to healthcare for all is a societal and organizational challenge to which the Management Sciences can contribute.

Over the past decade, work in public and healthcare management has nourished a dynamic field of research. A few works (Hunter and Killoran 2004; Ghorob and Bodenheimer 2012) explore this issue. They focus on identifying suitable organizational solutions (Bartoli and Sebai 2015; Giusti et al. 2019). However, the relevance and viability of these organizational solutions remain under addressed. They highlight the value of mobilizing the analytical grids of collective action to think perennial organizational forms.

In the first part of this chapter (see section 7.2), we define the notion of the medical desert, which is still difficult to define, as well as its

3 Author's translation.

determinants. In the second part (see sections 7.3.1 and 7.3.2), we show how collective action is increasingly becoming the only relevant option in this context. Finally, we present two (initiated by the state) organizational arrangements designed to respond collectively to the problems of access to healthcare, and to find new ways to reduce medical deserts (see sections 7.3.3 and 7.3.4). These illustrate current developments.

7.2. The medical desert: a difficult to define object

The notion of medical desertification first appeared in the press in the 1970s. In 1991, a report on a parliamentary session (April 10) mentions "medical desertification". The subject quickly became political, giving rise to administrative reports and government speeches (Véran 2013), and then became a subject for action. The fight against medical deserts asserted itself as a priority for public health policies, with its inclusion on the agenda (Hassenteufel 2011). Parallel to this, and as early as the 1990s, this expression gradually began to take wing amongst the academic community, as evidenced by a quick search on scientific databases using the keywords "medical desert", "healthcare desert" (both singular and plural) and "medical desertification".

The medical desert is both a social (difficulties and inequalities in access to healthcare, Penchansky and Thomas (1981)) and a political object regularly seized upon by citizens and elected representatives demonstrating their discontent – for example, on the occasion of the announcement of the closure of a hospital or service – but more rarely constitutes an object of management.

Authors of Political Science and Political Sociology (Hassenteufel 2011) are interested in the construction and framing of medical deserts as a public problem (Neveu 2017). They investigate the actors and processes leading to the placing on the agenda of the reorganization of primary healthcare as a solution to medical deserts. They look at the stages from the construction of the public problem of a territorialized primary healthcare supply deficit to the implementation of public policies at the local level, via the selection of instruments to implement solutions (Hassenteufel et al. 2020a, 2020b).

7.2.1. *Definition elements*

Over and above the simple use of the term "medical desert", the research carried out sought to better define the concept and, as is the case for any research object, to provide a definition. Initially, the approach adopted was highly spatial (Gesler 1986), with the very term "desert" referring to an uninhabited, hostile space derived from geography. In simple terms, the medical desert was the result of an observation that became apparent in the 2000s: a lack of medical professionals in a given area. This translated into localized deficits in primary healthcare provision, the main explanatory factors being the aging of GPs, reduced medical time and reluctance to settle in certain territories, particularly rural ones (Chevillard et al. 2018; Hassenteufel et al. 2020a). The data produced by the ONDPS[4] helped to capture the reality of this phenomenon. The approach developed, based on medical demography, was largely fed by data produced by organizations such as the DREES[5] and the IRDES[6]. Comparing the figures with the realities on the ground, however, shows how difficult it is to come up with a relevant indicator that accurately reflects this reality.

Indeed, the initial temptation may be to use the territorial density of healthcare professionals as a criterion for identifying a medical desert. Although this simple indicator allows for a rapid identification of problem areas by highlighting inequalities in access to healthcare, it has a significant limitation.

For example, during the period from 1985 to 2004, the average density of doctors in France increased (moreover, much more clearly for specialists than for generalists) (Berland 2005); however, beyond the figures, the distribution of these professionals throughout the territory between those areas with the highest concentration and those with the lowest concentration raises questions. Indeed, correct medical density (as calculated at this stage) can go hand in hand with proven difficulties in accessing healthcare. In order

4 ONDPS: *Observatoire national de la démographie des professions de santé*, the French national observatory of the demography of health professions, created in 2003 following the "Berland report" (Berland and Gausseron 2002).

5 DREES: *Direction de la recherche, des études et de l'évaluation et des statistiques*, the directorate for research, studies and evaluation and statistics.

6 IRDES: *Institut de recherche et documentation en économie de la santé*, the institute for research and documentation in health economics.

to overcome this pitfall, it is appropriate to better understand medical practice using a multifactorial approach (Penchansky and Thomas 1981). The density indicator turns out to be reductive and insufficient to reflect the actual practice of healthcare professionals for several reasons:

– It does not consider the declared volume of activity, but only the number of professionals in an area. Furthermore, this volume of activity is not necessarily time available for consultation. The available data does not allow us to know the workload represented by the activity of each doctor, and therefore, the working time is actually devoted to consultations. Many professionals have two places of practice (independent medical practitioners working in hospitals or in a healthcare center) and do not necessarily practice full time. They also devote a significant amount of time to coordinating healthcare, to their training in administrative follow-up, activities which encroach on consultation time.

– It does not integrate territorial specificities in terms of population type, nor the geography of the area, which is nevertheless not neutral in terms of access to healthcare (see mountain areas). Therefore, the sociodemographic structure of the population must be taken into consideration. An older population has a greater demand for localized healthcare than a population that is on average younger and more mobile. Likewise, an older population places greater demands on healthcare professionals and requires different types of healthcare. Irregularity must also be integrated, as well as the distribution or concentration of housing within a given territory.

– It does not integrate the topography of the territory, which can have a significant impact on access times to healthcare professionals (e.g. mountainous areas).

To overcome these criticisms, experts and studies will seek to refine the definition of medical desert, which, we agree, cannot be understood based solely on the criterion of density of doctors in a territory; the behavior of professionals and patients must also be considered (Guagliardo 2004; Weinhold and Gurtner 2014; Chevillard et al. 2018). The Berland report of 2005 presents two main approaches around the categorization of areas in order to more precisely identify areas in difficulty: a cantonal division (*ONDPS* approach) and the division proposed by health insurance (the *URCAM, CNAMTS, MSA* and *CANAM*) (see Table 7.1). These approaches demonstrate the desire to have a closer reading of the reality of territorial situations in order to act more effectively by integrating the level of activity of professionals and cross-referencing it with healthcare data usage.

	Healthcare on offer	Seeking healthcare
Cantonal division (*ONDPS* approach)	Number of professionals in the canton[7] compared to the population. Average level of activity of professionals practicing in the canton.	Average consumption of healthcare by general practitioners within the canton.
Identification of areas in difficulty and fragile (URCAM, CNAMTS, MSA and CANAM division)	Medical density in the area (density corrected for population flows and age structure). Average activity of general practitioners in the area (consultations + visits). Proportion of medical practitioners performing more than 7,500 consultations in the year. Proportion of doctors over 60 years old.	Consultations and visits for people aged 75 years and over (at this age, low consumption may reflect issues of access to healthcare in the area). Indicators measuring travel outside the area to seek healthcare, in general, and for those over 75 (significant travel may signal issues of access to healthcare in the area).

Table 7.1. *Methodology for targeting areas in difficulty: two main approaches to identifying medical deserts (adapted from Berland (2005))*

In 2012, taking stock of this observation, *DRESS* and *IRDES* proposed a new indicator for measuring spatial accessibility to healthcare: local potential accessibility (LPA). This enriches the classic perceptions regarding the supply of independent general practitioners in France, based on the usual accessibility indicators, such as density by living area or travel time to the nearest doctor (isochronic approach). The calculation of the LPA is based on academic work, particularly international (Luo and Qi 2009). It considers behavioral factors, the level of activity of doctors to measure supply, and the recourse rate differentiated by the age of residents, in order to determine demand.

7 A canton is an administrative division within a country, often used for local government purposes.

This is a local indicator, calculated at the level of each community, and also considering the supply of doctors and the demand in surrounding communities. The measure considers population movements across administrative boundaries. This is a marked behavioral characteristic of individuals in small communities and integrates the possibility for a patient to travel to a nearby community for a consultation. It considers the fact that GPs may practice in several locations (primary and secondary practices), may have a particular mode of practice that does not fall within the scope of primary healthcare (acupuncture, etc.), but may also have chosen a low level of self-employed activity. This calculation nuances the activity rate of general practitioners based on the patient's age: the elderly and children under 5 years are significant consumers of healthcare.

While significant progress has been made in recent years to understand what constitutes a medical desert, the approach still needs to be expanded to include other paramedical professionals (pharmacists, nurses, physiotherapists) who contribute to patient care in a given area. We also need to take a closer look at the presence of healthcare structures (hospitals, clinics, medical-social establishments, etc.) within the territorial analysis grid studied. This is the focus of research into the healthcare pathway (Campbell et al. 1998; Atwal and Caldwell 2002), which is now at the heart of issues concerning the organization and coordination of healthcare professionals (Hald et al. 2021).

Beyond these figures, researchers in Social Sciences are calling for the integration of more qualitative data. The needs of populations within the territories may be quite different from those that can be approached using figures. However, it is clear that areas with a shortage of healthcare services are those with low medical density, a high level of physician activity and a relatively low level of medical consumption. These factors could be indicative of an overload of activity, if doctors find themselves unable to compensate for their low numbers, and ultimately, unable to fully satisfy the needs of the population.

7.2.2. *Factors behind the challenges encountered*

There are many factors behind medical deserts: a planned reduction in the overall supply of healthcare, changes in the behavior of young doctors and changes in the needs and demands of healthcare service users. Here, we will focus on three major factors:

– *The numerus clausus introduced in 1971 was designed to limit the number of prescribers in order to reduce social security costs.* It was also intended to reduce competition, so as to guarantee working professionals a sufficient quantity of work, and to control the number of students in healthcare courses to guarantee quality of training. From 1972 onwards, this led to a gradual reduction in the number of students enrolled in healthcare courses. It reached its lowest point in 1993–1994, with 3,500 places (compared with 8,588 in 1971–1972) and then gradually increased to 9,314 in 2019 (Ministry of Solidarity and Health), before being abandoned in 2020. Given the time it takes to train healthcare professionals, the full impact of the increase in the number of trained professionals will be felt after 2030. Today, strategies to attract healthcare professionals to one territory are quite logically at the expense of others.

– *The transformation of practice patterns is another explanation.* Young doctors are expressing new aspirations in terms of the organization of their professional activity. They want to devote time to their family life and have a social life. On the whole, they have little interest in practicing outpatient medicine, in the way that their predecessors did through home visits. They seek the security of multidisciplinary practice and salaried employment. The decline in private practice is particularly marked in certain specialties, such as gynecology and dermatology (–29%), psychiatry (–27%), otorhinolaryngology (–24%), pediatrics (–20%) and ophthalmology (–20%). For these specialties, it is linked to a large number of retirements that have not been replaced by younger generations, who prefer salaried employment. Added to this is the significant feminization of the medical profession. On January 1, 2021, women accounted for 50% of general practitioners and specialists. They accounted for 58% of salaried doctors. In addition, doctors are more inclined to practice in university towns, so as not to be isolated, and to be close to technical facilities. These factors explain some of the inequalities in medical demographics between departments[8] in the same region, and also pave the way for new organizational forms based on group practice (medical office).

– *A transformation of people's needs.* The overall aging of the population is reflected in an aging patient population, which, as a result of polypathologies, is increasing the demand for healthcare and transforming healthcare methods. Patients are also increasingly attentive to the quality of their healthcare. At the same time, the authorities have adopted a rationale

8 Department is part of a larger administrative structure, typically a region. Departments play a key role in the decentralized administration of the country.

based on a minimum threshold of medical activity. This threshold may correspond to a minimum number of medical consultations or patients and/or a minimum number of practitioners, below which the cooperation and complementarity essential to the practice cannot be envisaged (Berland 2005, p. 23). This leads us to think in terms of localized medical clusters.

One way of responding to the issues outlined is through collective action. Surprisingly, of the 32 proposals in the March 2022 report of the French Senate's Committee on "Territorial Planning and Sustainable Development"[9], only one (Proposition 25[10]) expressly mentions cooperation as a mechanism. A second (Proposition 31) suggests "involving local elected representatives in the local organization of healthcare, with a view to subsidiarity and greater territorial awareness"[11]. This may come as a surprise, given that collective territorial dynamics are an entirely appropriate (albeit incomplete) response, complementing a political response, to the problem of medical deserts; and, beyond that, of unequal access to healthcare.

7.3. Drawing upon local collective action

The situation just described shows that public authorities are finding it difficult to respond to the territorial issue of access to healthcare and to pinpoint specific territorial features in an increasingly complex context. This calls for a shift from a highly centralized model to one more in tune with territorial singularities. In order to achieve this, the State initially opted for deconcentration. Deconcentration of the French administration refers to the delegation of powers and responsibilities from the central government to local administrative authorities or decentralized services. Its aim is to enable a more efficient and tailored management of public affairs at the territorial level. It is gradually opening up a space for initiative, enabling local actors to define (in part) their own health action guidelines.

9 Proposed translation for: *Commission de l'aménagement du territoire et du développement durable*.

10 Proposition 25: simplify the procedures for setting up cooperative medical structures to improve patient care and healthcare pathways, by reducing the administrative constraints involved in drawing up and validating healthcare projects.

11 Author's translation.

7.3.1. *Deconcentration: a territorialization lacking in efficiency*

From the 1990s onwards, this highly concentrated and centralized model evolved in response to the growing complexity of healthcare issues. The health context was marked by the chronicization of numerous pathologies, and an increase in the number of poly-pathological patients linked to an aging population and rising life expectancy. To ensure appropriate care, these situations require the involvement of a wide range of professionals and increasingly high levels of technical expertise due to technological advances in treatment, diagnosis and follow-up (4P medicine[12]). The definition of the problems to be managed and their treatment require the state to mobilize many new actors and experts. We are now entering an area of "collective learning of joint conceptualization"[13] (Crozier and Thoenig 1976; Duran and Thoenig 1996), where all stakeholders must build a common cognitive frame of reference for genuine cooperation to develop. This period saw the accelerated development of healthcare networks, a manifestation of a form of appropriation of collective action.

At the same time (as seen in section 7.2), localized shortages of medical care are appearing (Hassenteufel et al. 2020a, p. 3), and are set to increase. To respond to these problematic situations, the state is discovering, albeit timidly, the advantages of relying on local actors. It is doing so through deconcentration. In 2010, it entrusted Regional Health Agencies (RHAs) with the implementation of Regional Health Policy, through the organization and management of the health and medical-social system. Deconcentration is struggling to respond effectively to problematic territorial situations, despite the existence of territorial relays (regional agencies, departmental directorates). The reason for this is that the territorialization of healthcare is primarily a top-down approach, leaving little room for more local, collective initiatives. The state, powerless to truly regulate the healthcare field (including the liberal part of the healthcare system), is seeking to overcome blockages and find new mechanisms; this is because, after more than 10 years, problems of access to healthcare are persisting, if not amplifying.

The territorialization of healthcare policy, which has been underway for many years, is set to accelerate, with increasingly strong references to the territory in recent legislation (Hospital, Patients, Health and Territory Law of

12 Personalized, preventive, predictive and participatory medicine, known as 4P medicine.
13 Author's translation.

2009[14], Healthcare System Modernization Law of 2016[15], Healthcare System Transformation Law of 2019[16]) and the creation of new organizational frameworks: Territorial Professional Health Communities (TPHC), Territorial Hospital Groupings (THG), CTS[17] "territorial health councils" and PTS[18] "territorial health projects", to name but a few.

These developments mark a shift in public policy perspective. For Peter Hall (1993), change is most often apprehended through two dimensions: that of public policy orientation and that of instruments. In the case of health policy, we can identify a genuine paradigm shift. This can be seen, on the one hand, in the territorialization of the health policy; and, on the other hand, in the creation of new instruments. The emergence of new administrative mechanisms and frameworks is in itself a new instrument.

7.3.2. *From government time to collective time*

It is now accepted that responding to the situation of medical deserts requires mobilizing stakeholders around the issues of equal access and enabling cooperation and its development. The centralized, bureaucratic management of public action that has prevailed since the 1960s has led to an overhanging vision of territorial issues, particularly in the healthcare field. It is also criticized for being insufficiently adapted to territory conditions. Even if the state's orientations are implemented locally by decentralized services (the Regional Health Agencies created in 2010), it is the state that defines and steers policies.

Therefore, in the end, the question on how to adapt national policies to local realities remains unanswered (Thoenig 2005). Although civil servants and elected representatives translate these top-down public policies into action, they have virtually no room to maneuver. In the final analysis, they ensure the integration of territories into the national framework. This observation illustrates Duran and Thoenig's (1996) model of the institutionalization of collective action, a model on which Cazin (2017)

14 Proposed translation for: *Hôpital, patients, santé et territoire loi de 2009.*

15 Proposed translation for: *Loi de modernisation du système de santé de 2016.*

16 Proposed translation for: *loi de transformation du système de santé de 2019.*

17 Proposed translation for *CTS: conseils territoriaux de santé.*

18 Proposed translation for *PTS: projets territoriaux de santé.*

bases his definition of the forms of governmentality [19] (Lemke 2015) regarding hospital policies. Among the three forms of governmentality, one of these, the stimulation of collective exploration, provides an interesting key to the territorialization of healthcare supply actions. The "stimulation of collective exploration" [20] is based on a model of action (exploratory cooperation action model) structured around a collective formulation of problems and co-construction of the politics being pursued (Aggeri 2017).

For example, Article 51 is a good illustration of how this principle can be put into practice. Article 51 of the "Social Security Financing Act of 2018"[21] introduces a mechanism for experimenting with new healthcare organizations with novel financing methods. The aim of these experiments must be to develop pathway coordination and inter-professional cooperation to decompartmentalize the healthcare system. They particularly focus on access to healthcare, the structuring of outpatient care and the coordination of healthcare pathways.

Between the possibility offered by Article 51 of imagining new organizational forms, and the prescribed and constrained framework, lie new mechanisms designed to offer, within a "light" framework, the initiative for new territorial collective actions, as well as collaborative approaches designed to imagine new modes of action in the service of people's health.

Cazin (2017, p. 224) defines the performance of "stimulating collective exploration" in the hospital field as "equal access to healthcare thanks to exhaustive territorial coverage"[22]. Performance defined in this way provides a perfectly applicable analytical framework for understanding the collective dynamics at work in the (rather rural) territories we are interested in here. Ultimately, these developments mark a shift in healthcare policy and in the way we think about action.

---

19 The term governmentality was coined by Michel Foucault in 1978. The term is a neologism derived from the terms "government" and "rationality". The former refers to governing people's conduct through positive means (usually voluntary participation), rather than through disciplinary power. "Government" refers to conduct or activity designed to shape, guide or influence people's conduct. Rationality, on the contrary, refers to clear thinking about how things are or should be (adapted from *Encyclopædia Universalis*).

20 Author's translation.

21 Proposed translation for: *loi de financement de la Sécurité sociale de 2018*.

22 Author's translation.

7.3.2.1. *Illustration of two examples of territorialized action plans*

We illustrate these territorialized and collaborative approaches by analyzing two cases based on available secondary data. To read the first case, we use the analytical grid of the proximity school. This deploys a "grammar" that reveals what connects actors (Torre and Talbot 2018). While space is a central element of this approach, which is more topical than ever at a time when we are talking about territorial fractures, the work of the proximity school renews the notion of space by exploring the non-spatial dimensions of proximity (Boschma 2005). In this way, cognitive, social, institutional and organizational proximities enrich the reading of the links between territory and actors, and enable the establishment of perennial collective action, as we will see in the second case. In work, using this analytical grid, it emerges that collaboration between stakeholders in a given territory is largely based on the articulation of different proximities and above all on a shared vision that enables collective action to take root.

7.3.3. *Territorial Professional Health Communities (TPHCs): the case of the South Toulouse TPHC*[23]

7.3.3.1. *Using the TPHC to decompartmentalize and coordinate*

The TPHC is a measure of the "*Ma santé 2022*"[24] healthcare system transformation plan. Its aim is to decompartmentalize and reorganize the healthcare system. It is made up of a group of healthcare actors (self-employed or salaried healthcare professionals, healthcare establishments, prevention or health promotion actors, medico-social and social establishments and services, etc.) who wish to coordinate their efforts in a given area, in response to one or more health issues they have identified in advance. The professionals then draw up a health project, which is then contracted with the Regional Health Agency (RHA).

7.3.3.2. *From the outset, an initiative by a handful of actors*

In 2019, in the "Sud Toulousain" rural territory, a project team made up of four healthcare professionals (doctor, pharmacist, physiotherapist, nurse), who know each other, submitted a letter of intent. Through this act, they

23 See: https://www.cptsdusudtoulousain.org/la-construction-de-notre-projet/.

24 Translation: My Health 2022.

expressed their desire to mobilize territory actors around a project designed to strengthen the healthcare services on offer. The four began by interviewing 50 healthcare professionals representing 10 professions. Their aim was to identify the level of knowledge that the professionals questioned had of the TPHC and their willingness to join the project. The results were revealing: less than 5% of professionals were aware of the TPHC principle and less than 5% wished to participate in the operational team. This illustrated the difficulty of creating a collective territorial dynamic. After two meetings with the *URPS*[25] delegate director (the doctor in charge of TPHC deployment), the project group selected a geographically large territory to inform as many professionals as possible about the 2016 Health Law and the benefits to the scheme. During this phase, they obtained the consent of professionals to participate, and succeeded in defining a territory of intervention, with the added benefit of visibility on current projects. They affirmed their desire to "coordinate and help each other with their respective projects"[26]. This step created a cognitive (a shared knowledge base) and social (creating or reactivating personal ties) proximity that formed the foundation on which solid collaboration can develop.

7.3.3.3. *Communicating and getting to know one another*

The project team develops intense communication using all the channels at their disposal (information meetings, telephone exchanges, emails, working lunches, etc.) in order to inform (cognitive proximity) and motivate other professionals sharing the same vision of their responsibility as healthcare actors (institutional proximity). Actors wishing to participate sign an agreement in principle. Two axes of collaboration are then identified collectively: the first concerns actual and routine collaboration; the second concerns projects currently under development.

The first is that of the natural territory, that of professionals who know each other and are used to seeing one another and working together (cognitive, social, institutional and organizational proximity). This collaboration relies on secondary resources (on-call medical centers, emergency services, specialist correspondents, private and public hospital structures, a wide range of medical and medico-social care services),

25 Proposed translation of *URPS: Union régionale des professions de santé*, as "Regional Union of Healthcare Professions".
26 Author's translation.

knowledge of population movements, patient habits and the structuring of road networks, including territorial authorities, to best meet patients' needs. The second area of collaboration involves projects currently under development. This concerns mutual aid, the forms and contours of which are to be defined collectively, and the links to be built between actors not necessarily accustomed to collaborating.

This communication work is an essential step in establishing cognitive proximity (sharing a common knowledge base: a TPHC, a shared diagnosis of territory problems) and also social proximity (creating links) and institutional proximity (agreeing on common values: putting the patient at the heart of the project). This phase of information exchange and dialogue enables the identification of concerns on which the action plan can be built. It acknowledges the desire of territory actors to work together. The project group took the time to discuss the project with the local public hospital (which hosted an on-call medical center). The hospital's director was involved, as was the entire medical team, with whom the project team members have worked closely for many years (social and organizational proximity). It was decided to domicile the association (the TPHC project's initiator) within the hospital. This neutral location made it possible to distance the association from any partisan spirit, symbolically displaying the desire for a public–private mix and, ultimately, asserting shared values (institutional proximity).

7.3.3.4. *Collectively identifying courses of action*

After the awareness and information phase, a second essential step is to draw up a shared diagnosis of the territory. The situation in the territory is analyzed on the basis of quantitative data, focusing on two main areas: healthcare provision in the territory, based on RHA data, and healthcare consumption in the territory, based on health insurance data. This detailed diagnosis highlights the particularly problematic situation facing elderly patients:

> As the TPHC territory is located in semi-rural and rural areas, there are many elderly people and still many farmers. A significant proportion of the population has low retirement

> incomes, making it impossible to envisage an *EHPAD*[27], and has to cope with end-of-life dependency at home. 700 end-of-life patients at home/year: leading to a large number of hospitalizations, which are costly and very uncomfortable for our patients[28] (Extract from the diagnosis of the Sud Toulousain TPHC).

This stage identifies the problematic health and care situation(s) on which healthcare professionals wish to act and thus defines the territory and scope of the project. They identify major missions:

– improving access to healthcare, in particular to the attending physician;

– organizing multiprofessional care paths around the patient, to improve healthcare for the elderly through closer collaboration between professional networks and professionals;

– developing prevention by promoting vaccination among the elderly and healthcare professionals;

– making the territory more attractive to healthcare professionals by involving local and regional authorities, welcoming interns and facilitating the training of healthcare professionals within the territory.

Today, the involvement of 253 professionals in the project attests to the pertinence of this type of approach. The TPHC gives rise to the signing of an interprofessional agreement to promote the development of coordinated practice, enabling funding to be obtained from the *Caisse Nationale d'Assurance Maladie*[29] and the Regional Health Agency.

This case study illustrates the need to be aware of the resources that can be mobilized (relational, organizational, expertise, etc.) in order to set up a territorial collective action, "a facilitation, a strong initial network and a good understanding of the healthcare actors within the territory, as well as digital tools designed to facilitate coordination"[30].

---

27 *EHPAD: Établissement d'hébergement pour personnes âgées dépendantes* is the most widespread type of French residential care for senior citizens.

28 Author's translation.

29 France's national health insurance fund.

30 Author's translation.

7.3.4. *The Thiers Ambert Local Health Contract (LHC)*

Another collaborative arrangement is the Local Health Contract (LHC). This second case study focuses on the first LHC to be signed at Auvergne in 2012 for a three-year period (2015), known as the "Thiers Dore Montagne contract". This was followed by a second (2016–2019), and then a third for the period 2020–2023, known as the "Thiers Ambert contract". The experience accumulated over 10 years in designing and managing LHCs enabled them to develop a shared territorial culture in the field of health.

7.3.4.1. *The Local Health Contract: thinking about local collective action*

The LHC is a tool enshrined within the 2009 HPST[31] law. It is jointly managed by the Regional Health Agency and a local authority. Its aim is to reduce territorial and social inequalities in healthcare, and is a means of expressing territory dynamics. It is based on a vision shared by all stakeholders, and is characterized by a jointly defined strategy and objectives, a multiyear program of actions co-constructed on the basis of local needs, monitoring of implementation and joint evaluation of results. The aim is to implement solutions for local healthcare provision as close as possible to the population. The signatories to the contract are territorial authorities and the RHA. Prefects, government departments, healthcare actors and associations may also be involved. The scheme is designed to pool resources to meet local health needs and consolidate local partnerships over the long term. Rural areas are a privileged setting for application.

7.3.4.2. *A collective response to a territorial issue*

The Thiers Ambert LHC (a territory located in central France in the Puy-de-Dôme department) follows a one-year diagnostic phase on the health status of the population and the medical needs of the territory. This diagnosis revealed "a territory with unfavorable indicators in many health fields, with a higher mortality rate in the basin than in the rest of the department"[32] (Thiers Ambert LHC coordinator). On the basis of this diagnosis, five major orientations were defined: health education from an early age, access to healthcare (both financial and in terms of geographical proximity), local

---

31 Proposed translation of *HPST: Hôpital Patients Santé et Territoires*, as "Hospital, Patients, Health and Territories (HPHT)".

32 Author's translation.

hospital care, support for aging and mental health (addictions, suicides, etc.). A number of actions were devised in response to these guidelines, translated into eight action sheets. These include, for example, the prevention of breast and colorectal cancers, the provision of oral and dental care in medico-social establishments, the fight against addiction, etc.

The first LHC, signed in 2012, enabled the development of a local health strategy, shared by the territorial authorities, the RHA, *CPAM*[33] and the local hospitals of the towns of Thiers and Ambert. In 2019, the steering committee, building on the experience gained from the two previous contracts, implemented a method based on several working groups to update the local health diagnosis and identify new axis of intervention. The project benefitted from dedicated resources: coordination of preventive actions (full-time staff), coordination of primary healthcare services (part-time staff) and the involvement of partners and signatories. The LHC is structured around five main themes:

– promote health among different target groups (people in precarious situations, people of foreign origin, young people, schoolchildren, the elderly, people with disabilities, etc.) in a comprehensive, coordinated approach, combining screening, vaccinations and therapeutic education;

– reduce social and territorial inequalities in access to healthcare;

– organize local hospital care to meet the needs of local populations;

– improve livelihoods and healthcare paths and the quality of care for the elderly;

– organize prevention and healthcare responses in terms of mental health and addictions.

The many actions developed contribute to reducing territorial inequalities by providing adapted and innovative responses (e.g. a healthcare relay managed by the hospital center of the town of Thiers, a town of 12,000 inhabitants), free workshop events for the population (conferences, forums, health villages, film debates, memory workshops, balance workshops, therapeutic home education, etc.), and consistency of actions with other

33 Translation of *CPAM: Caisse primaire d'assurances maladie*, a primary health insurance fund in France.

schemes and/or services (e.g. the parenthood collective, the Thiers network for women victims of violence, etc.). In 2016, in the face of worsening medical demographics and growing healthcare needs, the collective launched an initiative aimed at welcoming new healthcare professionals by considering salaried employment as a possible response integrated into the installation process. The campaign was based on communication via social networks, using a humorous film. This collective action makes it possible to welcome two new general practitioners and a speech therapist.

When the first LHC was evaluated, the pilots and partners reiterated the relevance of the LHC in responding to local health issues in a territory marked by a high degree of rurality:

> The LHC has enabled us to create a dialogue and forge partnerships with all the actors concerned by the global dimension of health, the implementation of numerous preventive actions as close as possible to patients, and to legitimize the action of territorial authorities alongside "carers"[34].

They underlined the limits that constitute the main lines of work for future contracts:

> A lack of clarity in all the actions carried out, the absence of certain key co-signatories (*Conseil départemental du Puy-de-Dôme, Éducation nationale, Centre hospitalier universitaire de Clermont-Ferrand*, etc.) and the limitation posed by a scope of intervention that differs from institutional perimeters[35].

They identified the conditions for success:

An open framework and co-constructed actions, the involvement of actors (healthcare professionals, elected representatives, the Regional Health Agency, partners), dedicated leadership and a partnership policy, as well as the obstacles to be overcome in the future: distrust among actors (professionals towards elected representatives, towards the Regional Health Agency, vice versa, etc.), overlapping intervention perimeters depending on the actors and partners and the involvement of patients to be strengthened.

34 Author's translation.
35 Author's translation.

This feedback confirms the reality and value of local community dynamics in providing solutions for improved access to healthcare. While they cannot eradicate medical deserts, they can help to mitigate some of their effects.

7.4. Conclusion

Recent studies in public management highlighted the ability of local actors to take the initiative in responding to user needs by devising relevant and, above all, sustainable solutions. In the field of healthcare, collective territorial dynamics are part of the framework of government-sponsored schemes. They are the manifestation of an institutionalization of collective action, illustrating the governmentality of "stimulating collective exploration"[36].

However, if the state provides an administrative framework, it is up to the actors in the field to make the most of it. These tools provide a mechanism for supporting, or even educating, collective action, which would probably have difficulty expressing itself outside any framework. In the end, the dynamic is supported (and in some cases guided) and may even be triggered by state-sponsored schemes. Even so, it is essential, first, to gain a detailed and qualitative understanding of territorial health issues; and, second, to devise relevant actions to benefit users.

These two examples demonstrate that the emergence of a collective dynamic requires preparation and acculturation to new action logics. The latter are based on an open approach involving a wide range of actors, the identification of available and potentially mobilizable resources and the fine-tuning of initiatives within a shared diagnosis (Rochette and Chaze 2022), and a common territorial project.

Collective initiative, while essential, will not be enough to solve the problem of medical deserts. This issue is first linked to a lack of resources, to a sharp increase in demand for care that hospitals under pressure are struggling to absorb, and to the need to design a healthcare system calibrated to face the challenges of tomorrow.

36 Author's translation.

7.5. References

Aggeri, F. (2017). How can performativity contribute to management and organization research? *M@n@gement*, 20(1), 28–69.

Atwal, A. and Caldwell, K. (2002). Do multidisciplinary integrated healthcare pathways improve interprofessional collaboration? *Scandinavian Journal of Caring Sciences*, 16(4), 360–367.

Bartoli, A. and Sebai, J. (2015). L'expérience des maisons de santé pluriprofessionnelles face aux enjeux de coordination territoriale. *Gestion 2000*, 32(6), 17–37.

Berland, Y. (2005). Commission démographie médicale. Rapport auprès du ministre de la Santé et de la Protection sociale. Report.

Berland, Y. and Gausseron, T. (2002). Démographie des professions de santé. Report, 135.

Boschma, R. (2005). Role of proximity in interaction and performance: Conceptual and empirical challenges. *Regional Studies*, 39(1), 41–45.

Campbell, H., Hotchkiss, R., Bradshaw, N., Porteous, M. (1998). Integrated healthcare pathways. *BMJ*, 316(7125), 133–137.

Campbell, J., Buchan, J., Cometto, G., David, B., Dussault, G., Fogstad, H., Tangcharoensathien, V. (2013). Human resources for health and universal health coverage: Fostering equity and effective coverage. *Bulletin of the World Health Organization*, 91, 853–863.

Cazin, L. (2017). Regrouper pour mieux gouverner ? Le cas des hôpitaux publics français. PhD Thesis, Paris Sciences et Lettres, Paris.

Chaze, M. and Rochette, C. (2022). Promotion des activités physiques et lutte contre la sédentarité. Diagnostic territorial et enjeux d'action publique. L'exemple de Billom Communauté. Research Paper, ONAPS.

Chevillard, G., Lucas-Gabrielli, V., Mousques, J., Dill, L.L. (2018). "Medical deserts" in France: Current state of research and future trends. *L'Espace géographique*, 47(4), 362–380.

Crozier, M. and Thoenig, J.C. (1976). The regulation of complex organized systems. *Administrative Science Quarterly*, 21(4), 547–570.

Duran, P. and Thoenig, J.C. (1996). L'État et la gestion publique territoriale. *Revue Française de Science Politique*, 46(4), 580–623.

Foucault, M. (1986). La gouvernementalité in Michel Foucault. *Actes (Paris)*, 54, 6–15.

Gesler, W. (1986). The uses of spatial analysis in medical geography: A review. *Social Science & Medicine*, 23(10), 963–973.

Ghorob, A.M.P.H. and Bodenheimer, T. (2012). Sharing the care to improve access to primary healthcare. *The New England Journal of Medicine*, 366(21), 1955–1957.

Giusti, I., Sardas, J.C., Kletz, F., Pieri, X. (2019). Accès aux soins et territoires : comment articuler action collective locale et action publique ? *Management Avenir Santé*, 1, 11–29.

Guagliardo, M.F. (2004). Spatial accessibility of primary healthcare: Concepts, methods and challenges. *International Journal of Health Geographics*, 3(1), 1–13.

Gulliford, M.C. (2002). Availability of primary healthcare doctors and population health in England: Is there an association? *Journal of Public Health*, 24(4), 252–254.

Hald, A.N., Bech, M., Burau, V. (2021). Conditions for successful interprofessional collaboration in integrated care – Lessons from a primary healthcare setting in Denmark. *Health Policy*, 125(4), 474–481.

Hall, P.A. (1993). Policy paradigms, social learning, and the state: The case of economic policymaking in Britain. *Comparative Politics*, 25(3), 275–296.

Hassenteufel, P. (2011). Les transformations du mode de gouvernement de l'assurance maladie : une comparaison France/Allemagne. *La Revue de l'IRES*, 70(2011/3), 35–64.

Hassenteufel, P., Schweyer, F.X., Gerlinger, T., Reiter, R. (2020a). Les "déserts médicaux" comme leviers de la réorganisation des soins primaires, une comparaison entre la France et l'Allemagne. *Revue Française des Affaires Sociales*, 1, 33–56.

Hassenteufel, P., Schweyer, F.X., Gerlinger, T., Henkel, R., Lückenbach, C., Reiter, R. (2020b). The role of professional groups in policy change: Physician's organizations and the issue of local medical provision shortages in France and Germany. *European Policy Analysis*, 6(1), 38–57.

Hunter, D.J. and Killoran, A. (2004). *Tackling Health Inequalities: Turning Policy into Practice*. NHS Health Development Agency, London.

Lemke, T. (2015). *Foucault, Governmentality, and Critique*. Routledge, London.

Luo, W. and Qi, Y. (2009). An enhanced two-step floating catchment area (E2SFCA) method for measuring spatial accessibility to primary healthcare physicians. *Health & Place*, 15(4), 1100–1107.

Mizen, A., Fry, R., Grinnell, D., Rodgers, S.E. (2015). Quantifying the error associated with alternative gis-based techniques to measure access to health care services. *AIMS Public Health*, 2(4), 746–761.

Neveu, E. (2017). *Sociologie des Problèmes Publics*. Armand Colin, Paris.

Penchansky, R. and Thomas, J.W. (1981). The concept of access: Definition and relationship to consumer satisfaction. *Medical Care*, 19(2), 127–140.

Rochette, R. and Chaze, M (2022). Intercommunalité, mobilité et santé. L'intérêt du diagnostic partagé entre acteurs. Le cas d'un EPCI (Etablissement Public de Coopération Intercommunale). *Colloque Communautés, Métropoles et Santé. Vers un Renouvellement des Acteurs et Politiques Publiques Locales en Santé ?* Université d'Orléans, November.

Thoenig, J.C. (2005). Territorial administration and political control: Decentralization in France. *Public Administration*, 83(3), 685–708.

Torre, A. and Talbot, D. (2018). Proximités : retour sur 25 années d'analyse. *Revue d'Économie Régionale Urbaine*, 5, 917–936.

Véran, O. (2013). Des bacs à sable aux déserts médicaux : construction sociale d'un problème public. *Les Tribunes de la Santé*, 2, 77–85.

Weinhold, I. and Gurtner, S. (2014). Understanding shortages of sufficient health care in rural areas. *Health Policy*, 118(2), 201–214.

8

Identifying and Valorizing Human Resources Within Territories

8.1. Introduction

Territory is the subject of multiple disciplinary approaches (Simone et al. 2018; Paasi et al. 2020) and, in parallel, the territorial dimension of management situations (Raulet-Croset 2021) has been studied in a growing number of research works over the past 20 years. For Simone et al. (2018), the territory is "a complex system located in a specific geographical space that emerges from the co-evolution of a bundle of heterogeneous processes (anthropological-cultural, relational, cognitive and economic-productive) that characterizes that space in a unique and unrepeatable way"[1]. While some territories focus on exploiting their natural resources, others develop expertise, regional know-how or an innovation ecosystem (Kritz et al. 2018), offering a territorial competitive advantage, thanks to a skilled workforce and the social capital it produces (Stoop et al. 2021).

In order to identify and valorize the skills of organizations and inhabitants, the issue of prioritizing Human Resources (HR) lies at the heart of the territory's concerns (Evon 2018; Loubès et al. 2021). Over the last 15 years or so, these projects have been deployed under various names: "territorial HRM" (T-HRM)[2], "Territorialization of HRM"[3], "HR-focused territory projects"[4], "Territorial Strategic Workforce Planning" (TSWP)[5] or

Chapter written by Ingrid MAZZILLI, Truong GIANG PHAM and Isabelle BORIES-AZEAU.

1 Authors' translation.

2 Proposed translation of: *GRH Territoriale (GRH-T).*

3 Proposed translation of: *territorialisation de la GRH.*

4 Proposed translation of: *projets de territoire orientés RH.*

"Territorial Management of Jobs and Skills"[6] (Loubès et al. 2021). The term "T-HRM" will be retained in this chapter. Behind the multiplicity of contexts, these projects aim to collectively resolve employment and/or skills management and HRM issues at the territorial level, by fostering close links between public and private actors, through collective and structured actions (Geddes 2008; Purkarthofer et al. 2021). Some projects have been successful, while others have encountered great difficulties (Couteret et al. 2019; Mazzilli 2021). Several groups of actors are usually involved in identifying and developing human resources and skills. Territorial authorities, businesses and the voluntary sector are all brought in to coordinate their actions, sometimes from a new angle, with the aim of creating new or evolving intervention tools. Citizens can be mobilized as beneficiaries or future entrepreneurs (Geddes 2008). Implementing a T-HRM project therefore requires a great deal of collaborative work with local actors, in order to identify the issues and needs of all concerned, and to propose actions to meet them. This dynamic can also lead to changes in the norms and rules that prevail between actors. The analysis of this institutional work (Lawrence and Suddaby 2006) investigates the black box that reveals the dynamics of projects aimed at identifying and valorizing human resources and skills within a territory.

The aspect examined in this chapter, which is inherent to territorial HRM, is that of developing new collaborative practices that respond to a need to identify and valorize a territory's human resources. In order to better understand this process, we propose an analytical framework showing the key antecedents that determine the success, or not, of a T-HRM project.

The chapter first proposes an analytical framework based on three key dimensions of T-HRM, supplemented by an analysis based on institutional work (Cloutier et al. 2016). Two case studies on T-HRM projects will then be presented to illustrate concretely how our analytical framework can be mobilized (section 8.3). Finally, the lessons learned from these case studies will be put into perspective, highlighting benefits for both the researcher and the practitioner.

5 Proposed translation of: *Gestion prévisionnelle des emplois et des compétences territoriales (GPEC).*

6 Proposed translation of: *Gestion territoriale des emplois et des compétences (GTEC).*

8.2. HRM and the territory: identifying and valorizing human resources

The complexity of T-HRM projects requires us to approach them from different angles. First of all, academic literature teaches us that these T-HRM projects can be viewed as three dimensions:

– The first provides an understanding of the territorial context that favors the emergence of T-HRM projects.

– The second sheds light on their purpose and the methodology deployed.

– The third highlights the collective and partnership dimension.

Activating these three dimensions requires us to take into account the work of institutional creation, that is, the implementation and adoption of new practices or institutional routines (Lawrence and Suddaby 2006).

8.2.1. *Three key dimensions for analyzing T-HRM projects*

The first dimension focuses on identifying the contextual elements that can foster the emergence of T-HRM projects and impact them. According to Simone et al. (2018), several processes shape the territory: physical (environment, etc.), structural (frameworks, organizations, laws, rules, etc.), cultural (representations, values, etc.) and social (individual and collective actors and their actions). They constitute the territory's own resources (natural, organizational, localized knowledge and know-how, etc.). However, this potential can only be developed if it is identified and mobilized (Colletis and Pecqueur 2005). The existence of relationships of trust based on skills and expertise between territorial actors (Kritz et al. 2018), fostered by geographical, organizational and institutional proximity (Raulet-Croset 2021), makes it possible to activate or reactivate a territorial project (Evon 2018). If the territory is apprehended as a network of concrete and material interactions (Simone et al. 2018; Usher 2019) between actors, and between these actors and their environment, then social capital represents a condition and a result of these interactions (Stoop et al. 2021), but also as a territorial resource. Territorial social capital thus designates a collective resource present in cooperation, trust and reciprocity (Stoop et al. 2021), and operating in collective projects. The activation of territorial resources can then, in certain contexts, contribute to forging territorial competencies (Evon 2018). These underlying mechanisms contribute to the development of T-HRM projects.

The second dimension concerns the purpose and methodology of T-HRM projects. One of the common goals is to preserve, build or activate a territorial competency that enables the territory to display a specialization. To achieve this, T-HRM projects rely on tools to analyze and diagnose the territory's human resources, and then propose measures to support companies, working people and job-seekers. These projects sometimes include a territorial prospective approach, that is, anticipating changes through territorial mutations in order to formulate a territorial project (Pham and Aubert 2013) based on a shared vision of future skills and employment requirements. The diagnosis provides an inventory of the territory's human resources and specific competences (Pham and Aubert 2013). Deploying the action plan involves coordinating the implementation of actions and tools, at various scales (for one or more partners). Finally, two approaches to T-HRM projects coexist, based either on a logic of prescribed or constructed actions. In the first case, the project is based on the implementation of generally centralized, top-down public policies. In the second case, the project results from the initiative of local, socio-economic and public actors (local authorities, territorial public organizations, mixed syndicates, etc.) who organize themselves on a territory (Bories-Azeau and Loubès 2015). However, the involvement of the territorial public actor seems to impact leadership in the governance of T-HRM projects. Indeed, when territorial elected officials are the sponsors of these projects, a politic leadership tends to impose itself, legitimized by predominantly public funding and political stakes. However, this political leadership relies on the expertise of socio-economic actors, particularly in terms of territorial development. A qualitative appraisal of the project's emerging effects can then be used to complement the quantitative evaluation required by project funders (Loubès et al. 2021; Mazzilli 2021).

The three main causes for the failure of T-HRM projects are as follows:

- lack of capacity for coordination among the actors involved;
- lack of common understanding of HRM issues;
- divergent time frames.

Box 8.1. *Three main causes of T-HRM project failure (source: Couteret et al. (2019))*

Dimension linked to the territorial context favoring the emergence of T-HRM projects
– Pre-existing social capital to activate or reactivate resources (Stoop et al. 2021); – specific territorial resources (skilled labor, quality of cooperation between territorial or historical actors) (Kritz et al. 2018), when identified and valorized, lead to the emergence of a territorial competency (Evon 2018).
Dimension relating to the purpose and methodology of T-HRM projects
– Project aimed at preserving, building or activating a territorial competency (Evon 2018); – a territorial prospective methodology (Pham and Aubert 2013); – using a participatory territorial diagnosis to identify skill and competency requirements (Pham and Aubert 2013) that can lead to the development of an action plan.
The collective action and partnership dimension
– Territorial and collaborative governance, favoring collective decision-making (Geddes 2008; Loubès et al. 2021; Mazzilli 2021); – action logics that depend not only on the project sponsor, but also on the type of leadership, whether political or expert (Loubès et al. 2021); – a fragile collaborative dynamic, to be engaged from the outset of the project, supported throughout the process, evaluated and assessed from different angles (Mazzilli 2021); – a qualitative assessment of the project's emerging effects can complement the quantitative evaluation required by project funders (Loubès et al. 2021).

Table 8.1. *Three key dimensions of T-HRM projects*

Regarding the third dimension, collective action and partnership, regardless of the project's orientation, indicate that broad support is needed for the instauration of collaborative working practices amongst the territory's socio-economic actors (Geddes 2008; Evon 2018) to develop: employment, training, recruitment and insertion (Loubès et al. 2021; Mazzilli 2021). This observation calls for a collaborative conception of the territorial governance of the T-HRM project based on a shared global vision (Kritz et al. 2018), to collectively solve one or more complex societal problems (Geddes 2008). Although at the core of T-HRM, the collaborative dynamic remains fragile.

Initiated at the start of the project, it needs to be sustained throughout and any tensions encountered need to be taken into account (Mazzilli 2021) to avoid the risk of ending in failure (Couteret et al. 2019).

Table 8.1 summarizes the main findings found in the literature, structured around the three dimensions that characterize T-HRM.

Analyzing a T-HRM project in terms of its three key dimensions is the first step towards understanding its complexity. An analysis of the collaborative dynamics of these projects sheds additional light on the way they are implemented.

8.2.2. *Collective institution-building as the driving force behind T-HRM projects*

The concept of institutional work sheds light on the ability of public and private actors to jointly regulate jobs and skills on a territorial scale. The aim is to develop new rules, standards and frames of reference that encourage coordinated, collaborative action around common issues. This approach involves analyzing how stakeholders with heterogeneous values and logics engage in institutional work to create, maintain and even change institutions (Lawrence and Suddaby 2006).

Institution-building, that is, the introduction and adoption of new practices or institutional routines (Lawrence and Suddaby 2006), is one of the challenges facing T-HRM projects. The aim is to legitimize new practices vis-à-vis stakeholders, who may support or oppose them, and create a coalition of stakeholders (Lawrence et al. 2009). The aim is to engage in institutional work to develop and/or adjust the field's institutional constraints (legal rules, regulations, professional standards, etc.) and produce its own operating rules. Nevertheless, this process generates tensions.

As Loubès et al. (2021) point out:

> Overcoming tensions in policy frameworks and relationships between territorial actors therefore requires an agreement to evolve and/or adjust institutional constraints in the HRM field

(legal framework, regulations, professional standards, etc.) around issues common to the territory[7].

– Structural work: efforts by a manager or project leader to define roles, rule systems, organizational principles and resource allocation.

– Conceptual work: developing a system of beliefs, norms and interpretation schemes consistent with the institutional change project.

– Relational work: initiatives to build relationships of trust and collaboration between stakeholders.

– Operational work: implementation of concrete actions leading actors to change their behavior.

Box 8.2. *Four forms of institutional work (source: Cloutier et al. (2016))*

The concept of institutional work also highlights the actions taken by actors to engage members in the process of creating new practices and gaining the support of stakeholders in the organizational field (Gawer and Phillips 2013).

In our view, T-HRM projects can be likened to collective institution-building work based on the development of new practices and regulatory modalities that foster collaboration between territorial actors.

The typology of institutional work proposed by Cloutier et al. (2016) complements this analytical framework already adopted for the study of territorial collective dynamics (Arnaud and Serval 2020).

These four forms of institutional work (structural, conceptual, relational and operational) will be mobilized as analytical frameworks for the two T-HRM projects presenting collective dynamics. Our aim here is to gain a better understanding of how a project manager can initiate new collaborative working practices in a T-HRM context.

8.3. T-HRM projects in the Erdre et Gesvres and Sud Lozère territories

This analytical framework (the three dimensions of T-HRM and the institutional work carried out during the project) is shown in Figure 8.1.

7 Authors' translation

Based on two T-HRM projects with different collective dynamics, we demonstrate the need for significant institutional work.

8.3.1. *Two case studies concerning the provision of operational support*

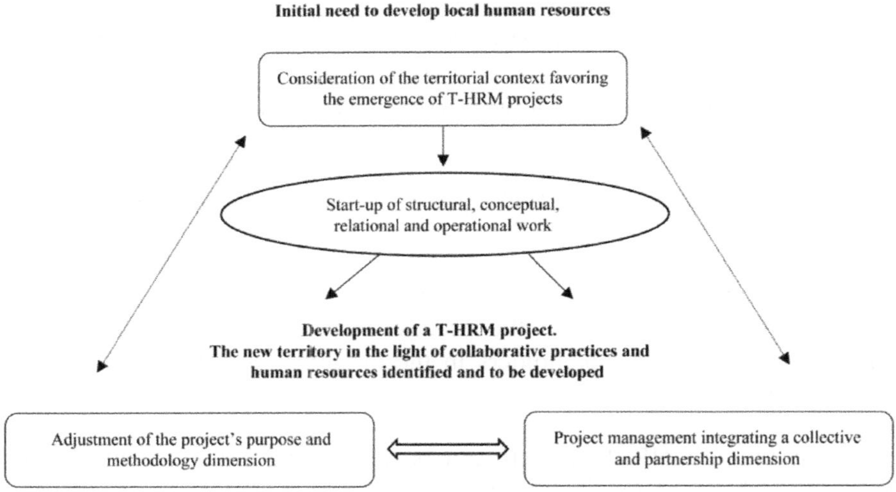

Figure 8.1. *T-HRM analytical framework*

Two case studies were built on the basis of an action-research methodology. The research team was involved in two different territorial projects and was provided with operational support by the "consulting team". The research team analyzed the materials collected from the two territories[8].

In the *Erdre et Gesvres* region, the consulting team was called in by the "Employment Center of the Erdre et Gesvres Community of Communes"[9]. The preparation and implementation of a diagnostic method were drawn up in consultation with the client, in order to identify the territory's skill requirements. This methodology was deployed

8 The empirical materials collected were subjected to a thematic content analysis, with a first level of reading based on the analytical framework of the three characteristic dimensions of T-HRM presented in section 8.2.1. A second level of reading consisted of cross-referencing these initial results with the analytical framework of the four modalities of institutional work proposed by Cloutier et al. (2016).

9 Proposed translation for: *Maison de l'Emploi de la Communauté de communes d'Erdre et Gesvres.*

between 2017 and 2019 across the entire territory. Structured into two distinct phases, the territorial diagnosis, geared towards identifying and enhancing HR, was based on a participative prospective approach before proposing a strategy and actions. During the prospective approach (2017–2018), 34 people were interviewed as part of a survey on the identification of current skills and the attractiveness of the territory. Of these, 14 were local elected officials or heads of public institutions, 12 were business leaders and eight represented local associations or citizens. At the end of the inventory, the aim was to identify the main factors for territorial change that could have an impact on the evolution of skills in the territory and in companies.

In this residential territory, more than one in two workers work outside the territory, most of them in neighboring Nantes. The territory is experiencing very strong demographic growth. The particularly dynamic economic fabric is based on a strong presence of industry, construction, agriculture and personal services. The majority of jobs and business creations concern face-to-face activities (personal services, education, health, social action, commerce and construction).

The dominant desire of local elected officials is to control this rapid growth, so as to preserve the territory's resources (natural spaces, presence of an active network of entrepreneurs, etc.), while developing the quality of life and the desire of residents to live fully in the territory, and not just reside there. This vast subject involves many actors (elected officials, businesses, citizens, etc.), none of whom have the means to act alone. Preparatory discussions with elected officials and technical managers of the community of municipalities, and led by the advisory team, led to linking the subject of skills to that of the attractiveness of the territory. At the end of the prospective workshops, skills have become the heart of reflections upon which to guide strategic actions. These workshops also revealed that the actions envisaged could not be the sole responsibility of one actor, and that the question of attractiveness and skills had to be extended to employment conditions. Recruitment in industrial companies, in the building sector and in particular, that of eco-construction, which is booming in the territory, posed a recurring problem when reviewing the skills of candidates, who thus require training.

However, there is no suitable public transport to reach the training places in Nantes, and Nantes candidates have difficulty traveling to companies in the absence of access to public transport. Mobility, which requires a private car, thus constitutes one of the obstacles to hiring, beyond the question of skills. The company's stakeholders, unable to take charge of this subject, transmitted this to the local public institutions, themselves linked to regional policies. The strategy implemented will then be to agree on a local public transport policy that focuses on priority areas. This issue is coordinated by local public institutions whose action must be supported by local business leaders.

Most of the local actors already knew each other before the process; nevertheless, the new objective was for them to build a new partnership around issues specific to the strategic sectors identified. Ultimately, the actors of the territory were asked to get involved in collaborative work, gradually becoming aware that the resolution of employment-skills problems necessitated the involvement and coordination of actors within the territory to help solve cross-disciplinary issues such as transport and mobility.

Box 8.3. *Case study of a T-HRM project carried out in the Erdre et Gesvres territory*

The territory of Sud Lozère is located in Occitanie on the border of south Gard and west Aveyron[10]. Since 2017, it has been organized around the Sud Lozère *PETR*[11], which brings together two communities of municipalities (Gorges Causses Cévennes and des Cévennes au mont Lozère), bringing together 36 municipalities. One of the main missions of the Employment Pool Committee (EPC)[12] within the current scope of the *PETR* is to carry out a diagnosis of the territory's HR.

The demographic issue is at the heart of policies for this territory, alongside the corresponding interventions by PETR. Since the 1980s, local stakeholders have strongly supported a policy of welcoming new populations, facilitating their settlement in an exceptionally preserved living environment. The challenges of territorial transition are important in terms of sustainable mobility, energy management with a low carbon footprint, local food supply, parsimonious consumption of water and available space. Low density and isolation have long encouraged actors to collaborate. With the arrival of new populations, how can we develop the territory and its HR while preserving existing collaborative dynamics?

The consulting team first carried out a combined analysis of bibliographical documents, statistics and surveys of territorial stakeholders in order to identify the specific skills of the territory. A series of workshops during winter 2019 made it possible to identify the most shared scenarios, the conditions for involving local stakeholders and the territory's resources to make these scenarios a reality. For this territorial project, 42 people representing the main components of the territory were involved and interviewed: associative and citizen actors, entrepreneurial actors, institutional actors and elected

10 The territory is distinguished by the dispersion of habitats and a low population density (eight inhabitants/km²). The Lozère department, the only French department without a large urban area, is mainly made up of rural communes.

11 *PETRs* (*Pôle d'équilibre rural et territorial*) are public establishments that aim to constitute a collaborative tool available to territories located outside metropolitan areas, rural or not. *PETR* relies on strong representation of elected officials in its governance bodies and on significant investment from civil society to offer shared governance. This work habit is linked to the initial composition of the EPC representatives (civil society, businesses, elected officials, employees) of which it is the heir. The permanent employees of the EPC are the same as those of the *PETR*.

12 Proposed translation for: *Comité de bassin d'emploi (CBE).*

officials. At the end of five participatory prospective workshops then organized, these actors were again invited, along with other elected officials and administrative officials, to engage in reflection on the factors of change, the main components of the territory, the hypotheses of evolution and the shared development scenarios using a prospective approach ("Sud Lozère 2040"). In 2020, this consolidated into a territorial project and saw preparations towards a territorial action strategy. This approach was operationalized by the establishment of an international cooperation project and the rewriting of the existing action plan.

For example, the creation of new activities, such as poly-activities, is booming. For three days in October 2018, local stakeholders met their partners and the services of other dedicated territories to support project leaders and discuss the most original and change-making initiatives. This includes supporting agri-food project leaders by supporting the "professionalization of artisanal production" (sterilization, hygiene, etc.), or even facilitating the transmission of traditional know-how requiring a high level of technicality (e.g. the dry-stone construction technique).

These initiatives open up real prospects for exchanging skills in a territory with new inhabitants. The dynamics involved have modified the representations of the major issues in the territory. A large part of the economic strategies, institutional skills of municipalities, communities of municipalities and the creation of associations are focused on this common project of attracting new populations to slow down the rural exodus. Furthermore, the recently commissioned diagnostics shed little light on the conditions for social inclusion, facilitation of interpersonal links and ecological transition. It is now a matter of bringing these new issues to the surface, sharing them with other local stakeholders and establishing an action plan in an approach that is intended to be prospective.

Box 8.4. *Case study of a T-HRM project carried out in the Sud Lozère territory*

The main characteristics of the two case studies are presented in Table 8.2.

	Erdre et Gesvres case study	**Sud Lozère case study**
Project observation period	Prospective interviews: January–June 2016 Workshops: May–December 2017 Putting scenarios and interviews into action: September 2018–January 2019	Interviews: April–June 2019 Workshops: September 2019–January 2020

Territory concerned	Loire-Atlantique: perimeter of the community of communes of Erdre et Gesvres, 55,000 inhabitants	Two communities of communes (Gorges Causses Cévennes and from Cévennes to Mont Lozère), 11,878 inhabitants
Project objective	Identify and develop key skills for the future	Prepare the territorial project and describe the scenarios for the evolution of the territory by 2040
Sponsor	Community of municipalities and employment center	Sud Lozère PETR
Key actors	Business stakeholders, public institutions, community stakeholders and citizens	Business stakeholders, public institutions, community stakeholders and citizens
Project terms	Territorial diagnosis and territorial prospective	Territorial project and prospective study Sud Lozère 2040, pre-designed in 2020 to prepare the territorial action strategy

Table 8.2. *Overview of two case studies*

8.3.2. *Identification of common characteristics and points of differentiation by applying the three dimensions of T-HRM*

The two case studies studied share common characteristics identified using the analytical framework for T-HRM projects. First, we note the existence and mobilization of pre-existing territorial networks (network of entrepreneurs in Erdre et Gesvres, network of territorial actors in Sud Lozère). In both case studies, a T-HRM project was initiated as part of a prospective approach materialized by workshops to identify the key skills, current and future, of the territory. This facilitated a *rapprochement* between public and private actors to adopt a common reading of HRM issues in the territory; through proximity effect, these forms of collaboration generated a collective learning process which focused on the coordination of activities and behaviors (Loubès et al. 2021). A logic of constructed actions has favored local adjustments based on pre-existing territorial activities and practices, often within the framework of cooperation, and in connection with the constructed territories (Raulet-Croset 2021). These T-HRM projects also have the common challenge of developing the attractiveness of the territory.

	Erdre et Gesvres case study: project aimed at improving employment conditions	Sud Lozère case study: project in favor of strengthening a territorial dynamic
Dimension relating to contextual factors	Proximity to a metropolitan area Residential territory Very strong population growth Economical fabric, particularly dynamic	Rural territory Low population density Strong focus on demographic issues Preserved living environment Pre-existing social capital within communities of actors
Dimension relating to purpose and methodology	Purposes: – improvement of employment conditions – increased territorial attractiveness Methodology: – territorial diagnosis – territorial prospective	Purposes: – facilitate the installation of project leaders – maintaining and strengthening social ties – increased territorial attractiveness Methodology: – territorial project – territorial prospective
Collective and partnership dimension	Public and private actors Organization by sector Partnership work Business leaders reluctant at first Raising awareness among elected officials about business activity Workshop to identify the most important actions to take	Dominant public actors and involving private actors Pre-existing collaborative dynamics Participatory prospective workshops

Table 8.3. *Three dimensions of T-HRM projects*

However, these two projects present elements of differentiation. First, if the territory of Erdre et Gesvres is located close to a metropolitan territory, with a dynamic economic fabric, the Sud Lozère territory is rural. However, rurality seems to favor the construction of territorial social capital based on collaborative dynamics pre-existing the T-HRM project, unlike the case study on Erdre et Gesvres. Next, the question of maintaining and strengthening social ties seems central in the Sud Lozère territory project, and less significant in the Erdre et Gesvres territory. Finally, in the Erdre et Gesvres case study, the collaborative dynamic struggled to emerge, due to business leaders who were sometimes reluctant due to lack of time. The characteristics of these two T-HRM projects are listed in Table 8.3.

8.3.3. *A territory newly considered in the light of human resources to be valued and collaborative practices engaged*

It is now a matter of analyzing the two case studies from the perspective of the institutional work initiated at the start of the two T-HRM projects supported by the consulting team. For each case study, the aim is to characterize the institutional change in its entirety and identify the modalities of this work in the sense of Cloutier et al. (2016): structural, relational and conceptual work[13]. Finally, these three institutional work modalities are put into perspective with the dimensions of T-HRM mobilized during this approach.

8.3.4. *In the Erdre et Gesvres territory*

At the start of the project, the stakeholders had divergent representations of their role. However, thanks to the support work, the actors understood the need for a partnership approach centered on the attractiveness of the territory and HR. The institutional work facilitated the integration of questions on housing, transport, living conditions, etc., into the initial problem, the identification of the key skills required by the territory. This work then focused on the engagement of a dynamic of collective work between stakeholders (companies, institutional and political actors, associative actors and citizens) who a priori were not (or if so, then only slightly) linked, neither by hierarchical relationships nor by the sharing of experiences or common values. The work of bringing actors together finally allowed for the emergence of a shared vision and a necessary cross-disciplinary approach to

---

13 The operational work could not be observed in these case studies, as the support of the consulting team during these T-HRM projects only focused on the diagnosis phase and not on that of deployment of an action plan.

HRM issues (recruitment, training, employment conditions). This institutional work was facilitated by a favorable territorial context.

Indeed, in Erdre et Gesvres, the actors were already used to working together on territorial projects. This pre-existing social capital (Stoop et al. 2021) favored the activation of territorial competency (Evon 2018). The institutional change linked to the T-HRM project can be understood as a form of creation of new rules and standards, having led the stakeholders to consider the human resources of the territory as one of the key resources of its attractiveness. More specifically, this change can be analyzed from the perspective of three forms of institutional work (structural, conceptual, relational, operational) (Cloutier et al. 2016).

The structural work focused on efforts to formalize new roles in the T-HRM project, leading local authorities and businesses to understand that everyone could have the capacity to identify and participate in the valorization of human resources and skills considered specific to the territory. The consulting team contributed to this by involving project governance stakeholders in the diagnosis, then by offering broader stakeholders the opportunity to participate in collective territorial prospective workshops. In this project based on a large-scale participatory methodology, structural work and relational work are linked. Indeed, the relational work consisted of leading this participatory approach throughout the project so that each actor could get involved and express their vision of the future of the territory. Changes in posture could thus be observed at the level of relations between institutions and the network of business leaders. Conceptual work was undertaken to promote the emergence of a new shared vision on the necessary cross-disciplinarity of T-HRM issues (recruitment, training, employment conditions). The participatory approach led by the advisory team helped to initiate a collaborative dynamic, favoring reflection on skills, and more broadly, on the complex socio-economic issues of the territory (transport, living conditions, housing, etc.).

8.3.5. *In the Sud Lozère territory*

The institutional work has led the actors of the T-HRM project to consider the territorial human resources as central to their attractiveness. This new conception of the territory implied recognition of the need to develop networks and social links to support economic activity. It was a question of moving from a conception of territory attractiveness based on the valorization of natural resources (landscapes, geography, climate) to a multifactorial approach to attractiveness. This institutional work was initiated thanks to determining cultural factors: in fact, the notion of solidarity is very locally anchored within this territory, which has, throughout history, been the refuge of several communities. Today, although the links within the same community can be very strong, they are less obvious between communities.

Structural work was carried out during the T-HRM project. Therefore, *PETR* and its institutional partners in the communities of municipalities have questioned their strategies for supporting private entrepreneurship, and in particular, the support for entrepreneurs with entrepreneurial projects. The relationships between local public institutions, such as those which govern them with businesses and associations, were thus questioned in the participatory prospective workshops. The intervention made it possible to open up new debates and reveal the positions of the actors. This modality of structural work is strongly linked to relational work.

Over the course of this work, new issues emerged from the workshops: the discussions led to the consideration of new relational modes, namely the informal links created during socializing occasions such as parties or meeting places, beyond formal links to inside associations and companies. The conceptual work was decisive: initially, the consulting team was asked to think about the territorial project. The conclusions and those of the actors of the T-HRM project surprised them. Indeed, initially, everyone thought that the territory was already considered attractive because of the beauty of its landscapes and its natural resources. However, the conceptual work carried out via the territorial diagnosis, then the territorial prospective workshops, modified this interpretation and brought about a shared vision. A large part of the economic strategies, the institutional skills of municipalities and communities of municipalities, and the creation of associations, should focus on a common project to attract new populations.

Within these two territories, institutional work mobilizes several key dimensions of T-HRM in a cross-disciplinary manner. The structural, conceptual and relational work was made possible thanks to a shared territorial diagnosis and the organization of participatory territorial governance to carry out this project. The fragile collaborative dynamic was supported throughout the process, guaranteeing the progressive involvement of the project stakeholders. The results show that institutional work is decisive to the extent that it allows the interpretation patterns of the stakeholders of a territorial project to evolve. The dimensions and facets of T-HRM are thus reaffirmed as key elements in the activation of the different modalities of institutional work (structural, relational and conceptual work). In this, T-HRM promotes the development of a collective response to a problem of identification and valorization of the human resources of a territory.

8.4. Conclusion

This chapter highlights the weight of the relational dimension during the emergence and sustainability of T-HRM projects. More specifically, it underlines that institutional work is necessary to consider a global approach to the territory during the process of identifying and developing human resources. Activities linked to the T-HRM project and its territorial dynamics can be then assimilated to the "work" of a multitude of actors who are committed to reshaping institutions, that is, building new collective practices of "co-construction" and experimentation. The implementation workshops (Erdre et Gesvres case study) and the prospective workshops (two case studies), which bring together businesses, institutional and political actors, associative actors and citizens, are an illustration of this.

The analysis of the two case studies calls for a new understanding of the issues at the heart of HRM: it is no longer a question of dealing only with a particular HRM problem, such as that of the difficulties in recruiting business leaders in the Erdre et Gesvres, but of beginning a broader reflection on employment conditions (mobility, living environment). The emergence of a common understanding on HRM issues within a territory implies a formalization and clarification of roles. The rules of the game must then be constructed through consultations and the empowerment of stakeholders. This testifies to the evolution from an instrumental conception to a partnership conception of territorial HRM (Uzan et al. 2017), more open and more qualitative, and the issue of which may be the attractiveness of the territory. It is no longer a question of only assessing the development of the territory with regard to the number of jobs maintained or created, or the establishment of businesses, but also of considering the improvement of local employment conditions and the emergence, or even strengthening, of territorial social capital.

8.5. References

Arnaud, C. and Serval, S. (2020). Les formes de travail institutionnel et les rôles du territoire dans la phase d'émergence d'un RTO de l'ESS. *Management International*, 24(4), 84–98.

Bories-Azeau, I. and Loubès, A. (2015). *Territoire prescrit, territoire construit et nouvelle régulation sociale : état des pratiques*. Colloque international du CRIMT, Montreal.

Cloutier, C., Denis, J.L., Langley, A., Lamothe, L. (2016). Agency at the managerial interface: Public sector reform as institutional work. *Journal of Public Administration Research and Theory*, 26(2), 259–276.

Colletis, G. and Pecqueur, B. (2005). Révélation de ressources spécifiques et coordination située. *Revue Économie et Institutions*, 6/7, 445–463.

Couteret, P., Bornarel, F., Virgili, S. (2019). L'échec de la mise en œuvre d'une GTEC : une étude longitudinale. *Gestion 2000*, 36, 33–50.

Evon, J. (2018). L'attractivité territoriale : de l'existence des ressources à leur valorisation en compétences. PhD Thesis, Université de Tours, Tours.

Gawer, A. and Phillips, N. (2013). Institutional work as logics shift: The case of Intel's transformation to platform leader. *Organization Studies*, 34(8), 1035–1071.

Geddes, M. (2008). Inter-organizational relationships in local and regional development partnerships. In *The Oxford Handbook of Inter-Organizational Relations*, Cropper, S., Ebers, M., Huxham, C., Smith Ring, P. (eds). Oxford University Press, Oxford, 201–230.

Kriz, A., Bankins, S., Molloy, C. (2018). Readying a region: Temporally exploring the development of an Australian regional quadruple helix. *R&D Management*, 48(1), 25–43.

Lawrence, T.B. and Suddaby, R. (2006). Institutions and Institutional work. In *Handbook of Organization Studies*, Clegg, S.R., Hardy, C., Nord, W.R., Lawrence, T.B. (eds). Sage, London, 215–254.

Lawrence, T.B., Suddaby, R., Leca, B. (eds) (2009). Introduction: Theorizing and studying institutional work. In *Institutional Work: Actors and Agency in Institutional Studies of Organization*. Cambridge University Press, Cambridge.

Loubès, A., Bories-Azeau, I., Defélix, C. (2021). Territoire et GRH : question ancienne, approche récente. In *Les grands courants en gestion des ressources humaines*, Beaujolin, R., Oiry, E. (eds). EMS, Caen, 315–334.

Mazzilli, I. (2021). How to organise territorial competency management? In *Managing Competences: Research, Practice, and Contemporary Issues*, Grasser, B., Loufrani-Fedida, S., Oiry, E. (eds). Taylors & Francis, Milton Park, 131–144.

Paasi, A., Harrison, J., Jones, M. (2020). *Handbook on the Geographies of Regions and Territories*. Edward Elgar Publishing, Cheltenham.

Pham, T.G. and Aubert, F. (2013). Diagnostic des enjeux territoriaux de GRH, retour d'expérience de Fougères et de Figeac. *Colloque JRSS*.

Purkarthofer, E., Humer, A., Mäntysalo, R. (2021). Regional planning: An arena of interests, institutions and relations. *Regional Studies*, 55(5), 773–777.

Putnam, R. (2001). Social capital: Measurement and consequences. *Canadian Journal of Policy Research*, 2(1), 41–51.

Raulet-Croset, N. (2021). La question du territoire en sciences de gestion – Point de vue sur le territoire comme ressource pour les organisations. *Question(s) de management*, 33, 33–36.

Simone, C., Barile, S., Calabrese, M. (2018). Managing territory and its complexity: A decision-making model based on the viable system approach (VsA). *Land Use Policy*, 72, 493–502.

Stoop, E., Brandsen, T., Helderman, J.-K. (2021). The impact of the cooperative structure on organizational social capital. *Social Enterprise Journal*, 17(4), 548–565.

Usher, M. (2019). Territory incognita. *Progress in Human Geography*, 44(6), 1019–1046.

Uzan, O., Bonneveux, É., Bories-Azeau, I., Condomines, B., Delattre, M., Houessou, B., Loubès, A., Raulet-Croset, N. (2017). De la GRH instrumentale à la GRH partenariale : l'impact des stratégies territoriales. *Revue de gestion des ressources humaines*, 103, 20–39.

9

Attracting and Retaining Talents in Organizations and Territories

9.1. Introduction

Attractiveness objectives evolve over time, and residential attractiveness is now a central objective for many territories (attracting and anchoring inhabitants).

Indeed, in addition to talent (qualified as such because it is recruited in the knowledge-based economy sector), many territories are struggling to fill jobs in all the sectors already present on the territory. Companies and territorial authorities are faced with a common challenge: how to retain and recruit employees in areas where organizations are short of manpower. This challenge arises in the specific context of "big quitting" or "quiet quitting", with an increase in resignations from permanent and fixed-term contracts. According to the DARES[1], "The Directorate of Research, Economic Studies and Statistics" of the French Ministry of Labor, resignations have increased by 25% between 2019 and 2021, which confirms the emergence of new aspirations from employees who increasingly wish to combine Quality of Life within the territory and Quality of Life at work $(QLW)^2$.

In this chapter, we will be looking at talent retention and its new challenges through $(QLW)^2$ and territorial employer branding (see Box 9.1).

Chapter written by Christophe ALAUX and Ève SAINT-GERMES.

1 Translation of: *DARES: Direction de l'animation de la recherche, des études et des statistiques*.

Employer Brand: the set of functional, economic and psychological benefits inherent in employment, with which the company, as employer, is identified (Ambler and Barrow 1996).

Territorial Employer Brand: efforts made by a territory's actors and stakeholders to promote, both internally and externally, an image of what makes it different and attractive to a talent, a company or a public actor (Loufrani-Fedida and Saint-Germes 2020, p. 163).

Territorial attractiveness: a mechanism for the development, current and future quality of life throughout territories. It aims to attract and/or anchor the various internal and external stakeholders within territories: residents, market and non-market organizations, tourists, events, etc. (*Chaire attractivité et nouveau marketing territorial 2021*[2]).

$(QLW)^2$: a combination of Quality of Work Life and Quality of Territorial Life. It includes both objective global elements and subjective elements of individual perception, making it possible to measure these two forms of complementary quality for the territorial employer brand.

Box 9.1. *Definitions*

In this new context, we need to look at the employer branding strategies of recruiters who symbolize quality of work life, and also at the attractiveness strategies of territories based on quality of territorial life. Indeed, if the workplace can now be further away from the home, thanks to increased flexibility by telecommuting, employees will tend to prefer residential locations that meet their expectations, and not just the criterion of proximity to their workplace. To meet these territorial challenges, innovative collective dynamics are being created between companies and territorial authorities, as well as new actors such as local attraction agencies. These are structured around territorial employer brands, which will be analyzed through the case study of the "Attitude Manche" attraction agency.

9.2. Territorial attractiveness in a context of employee shortages

9.2.1. *The employment context: an employee shortage*

The number of job vacancies in France stood at 355,400 in the second quarter (Q2) of 2022[3]. It has risen by 69% since the fourth quarter (Q4) of

2 Proposed translation: "Chair in New Place Marketing and Attractiveness".

3 See: https://dares.travail-emploi.gouv.fr/donnees/les-emplois-vacants.

2019. This sharp rise has affected all sectors, but particularly industry, with an increase of 91%; the non-market tertiary sector, with an increase of 78% (administration, health, social action); the market tertiary sector, with an increase of 64% (trade, retail, accommodation-restaurants), and the construction sector, with an increase of 46%.

Many economic sectors are no longer able to fill the jobs they offer. This shortage concerns many of the activities of the residential economy, which INSEE[4] defines as "activities implemented locally for the production of goods and services aimed at satisfying the needs of people present in the area, whether they are residents or tourists"[5].

9.2.2. *Decline in the residential economy and territorial attractiveness*

Difficulties in recruiting in the residential sector are the starting point for the negative spiral, as seen through the lens of residential attractiveness, within territories. Indeed, Talandier (2016) explains that "the challenge of local economic development is threefold. It is about creating wealth through the productive economy; capturing wealth through the residential economy; and circulating this wealth throughout the sphere or 'presential' economy, to use the INSEE terminology"[6] (Talandier 2016, p. 6).

Recruitment difficulties are the starting point for this process, detailed in Figure 9.1. The sectors experiencing shortages often constitute a significant residential income base for those spending their income within the territory, complementing the productive base for companies operating in the territory. As explained in Figure 9.1, this shortage affects the territory's residential and productive incomes (double difficulty in recruiting in exporting and residential companies), leading to a reduction in the territorial supply (risks of productive relocation and cuts in residential services: health, personal care, leisure activities, etc.). Public and social foundations alone are no longer enough to ensure local development. The labor shortage affecting the residential and productive bases then impacts the territory's basic income; that is, that which comes from outside the territory, which then circulates within it, thanks to the residential economy.

4 INSEE: *Institut national de la statistique et des études économiques*, the French "National Institute of Statistics and Economic Studies".

5 Authors' translation.

6 Authors' translation.

This decline in supply objectively reduces the territory's quality of life, which in turn makes it less attractive for residents and businesses. In concrete terms, companies will turn away from territories where there are recruitment difficulties. Similarly, potential residents will no longer target territories that do not offer the expected quality of life.

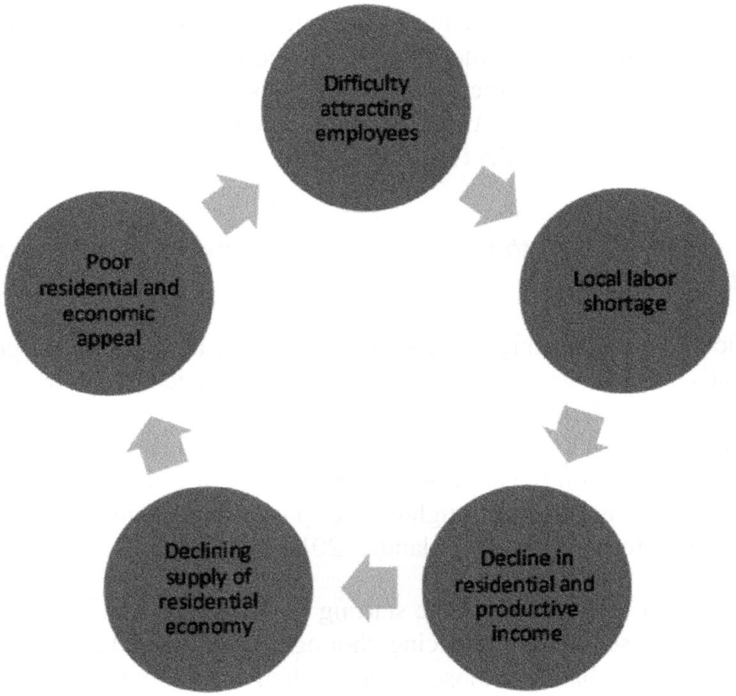

Figure 9.1. *From recruitment difficulties to declining attractiveness (source: authors)*

9.3. Explanatory factors for this shortage

This labor shortage is the result of a dual movement: the retirement of the Baby Boomer generation and the arrival on the job market of the Y and Z generations, with their new expectations and desires for change (Loufrani-Fedida and Saint-Germes 2015).

9.3.1. *A desire for change in quality of life at work*

The recent phenomenon of the "big resignation" illustrates these new aspirations. We are seeing an increase in resignations and a desire to move towards a new job. In the first quarter (Q1) of 2022, there were 523,107 resignations, of which 469,610 were from open-ended contracts (*CDI* in French)[7]. This phenomenon is described as high, but not necessarily unprecedented, as it is similar to data already observed during the 2008 economic crisis. The "Global Workforce Hopes and Fears" study, carried out in 2022 by the consultancy firm Price Waterhouse Coopers[8], confirmed that one in five workers (one in six in France) said they were likely to change employer in the next 12 months (27% of 18- to 25-year-olds and 23% of 26- to 41-year-olds).

This phenomenon of resignations and planned mobility is partly explained by the employees' new aspirations in terms of quality of work life. According to this study, the quality of life at work is a combination of complex expectations, both tangible and psychological. In fact, when considering a change of job, an employee's top priority is to find a salary they consider to be fair (71%). However, just after this salary criterion come motivations linked to meaning: the search for a fulfilling job (69%), one that corresponds to their values (66%) and where they are concerned about the well-being of employees (60%). This study confirms the primordial importance of flexibility for employees wishing to change jobs, perceived as a guarantee of quality of life at work.

France is part of this international dynamic, with high psychological expectations. While the salary criterion remains the primary concern for 58% of them, it is almost on a par with professional fulfillment (55%) and alignment with personal values (51%).

These new aspirations are a challenge not only for companies, but also for territorial authorities working to improve the quality of life within the territories they administer. The phenomenon therefore does not appear to be marginal, which explains why many territorial authorities are initiating

7 DARES [Online]. Available at: https://dares.travail-emploi.gouv.fr/publication/la-france-vit-elle-une-grande-demission.

8 The Global Workforce Hopes and Fears survey was conducted in March 2022 by PwC, a consulting and auditing firm. It covers 52,195 employees worldwide, including over 2,100 in France.

strategies in collaboration with territorial actors to help companies in their search for candidates.

9.3.2. *Employees in search of a better-territorial quality of life*

While working conditions still seem to be the most important factor in attracting employees (salary, meaning, flexibility), almost half of them want to choose where and when they work. This expectation, probably reinforced by the development of telecommuting, confirms that territory quality of life is an increasingly decisive factor in attracting employees to a company. This may mean attracting them to a company that offers telecommuting or to a company that recruits from a territory that is attractive for its quality of life. Employees also pay close attention to the location of their place of residence and the quality of life associated with it, especially as their home may be a long way from their workplace[9]. The balance between quality of life (at work and throughout the territory) and professional opportunities is also the main criterion for being attracted to a job for the over-35s who are already working[10].

9.4. The singular strategies of (QLW)²

Faced with labor shortages and new expectations on the part of working people in terms of employment and working conditions, seeking to combine the development of quality of work life in organizations and quality of life in territories is a relevant and innovative strategy. These singular (QLW)² approaches combine a reinforcement of the attractiveness of organizations and territories with new marketing approaches, based on employer brands and territorial employer brands.

9.4.1. *Employer branding to embody quality of work life*

Employer branding is a concept developed by companies to enhance their attractiveness as employers. It represents "the set of functional, economic and psychological benefits inherent in employment with which the company,

9 In 2013, two-thirds of workers did not live in the municipality in which they worked. INSEE (2016). [Online]. Available at: https://www.insee.fr/fr/statistiques/2019022.

10 Universum 2018.

as employer, is identified"[11] (Ambler and Barrow 1996, p. 187). Companies are developing strategies to improve the performance of their employer brand, both to create external value for future recruits and internal value for those already in post. "Employer brand" therefore refers to the value created by a company to attract and retain employees (Berthon et al. 2005).

This value is described around five main dimensions (Charbonnier-Voirin and Lissillour 2018, see Figure 9.2). The *attractiveness value* refers to the interest of the work on offer. The *social value* refers to the atmosphere and team cohesion. The *economic value* corresponds to remuneration and job security. The *development value* covers the professional opportunities on offer. Finally, a fifth value corresponds to the *transmission value*, which is "the opportunity to apply what the employee knows and pass it on"[12] (Charbonnier-Voirin and Lissillour 2018, p. 101).

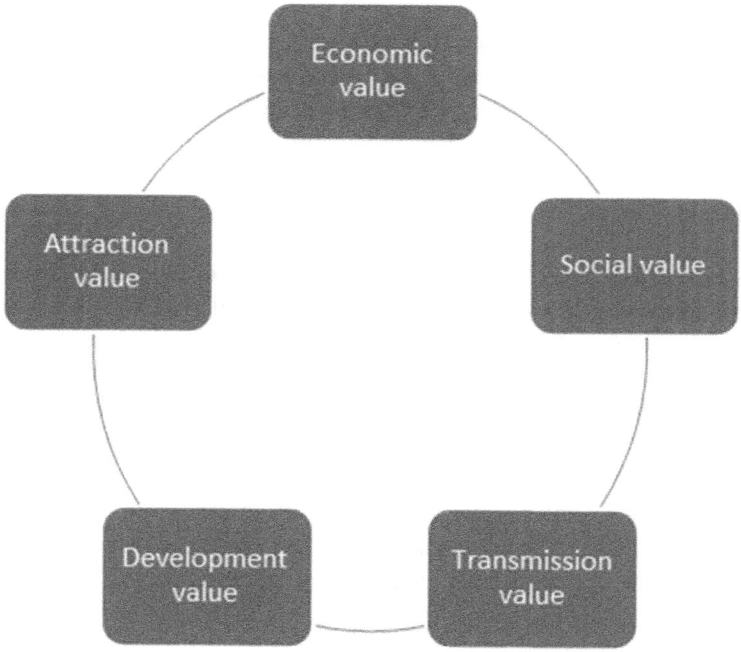

Figure 9.2. *Dimensions of the value created by employer branding (source: Charbonnier-Voirin and Lissillour (2018))*

11 Authors' translation.

12 Authors' translation.

This employer brand focuses on the characteristics offered by the company. Territory, as a concept, therefore does not figure in this recruitment and retention equation, even though it is becoming a major issue in the location of populations (Arnoult and Duhautois 2019). To speak of a territorial employer brand is to consider the company's location and/or the employee's place of residence as a source of complementary value and as a factor of attractiveness. This extension of employer branding to the territory has already been addressed by the literature (Loufrani-Fedida and Saint-Germes 2015).

9.4.2. *Territorial attractiveness and brands: indicators of quality of territorial life*

Territorial attractiveness was initially defined by its ability to attract, without integrating its ability to anchor:

> The ability of a territory to be chosen by an actor as a location zone (temporary or lasting) for all or part of its activities; this attractiveness is a perceived attractiveness that involves only natural persons, individuals, households or teams, for example the management teams of a company or a public administration[13] (Gérardin and Poirot 2010, p. 27).

This definition, which primarily focused on external attractiveness as a means of attracting resources, has been broadened. Indeed, the concept of territory is a construct that integrates several dimensions, both internal and external. We can thus identify the system of geographic space that makes it up (landscapes, location, etc.), the actors attached to it (residents, workers, tourists, market and non-market organizations) and the representations of this space that are associated with it (identity and image/reputation of the territory). For these stakeholders, who are both internal and external (Zenker and Beckmann 2013), "the relational paradigm suggests focusing on internal attractiveness as a complement to external attractiveness"[14] (Alaux et al. 2015, p. 67).

As specified by the *Chaire attractivité et nouveau marketing territorial*[15] (2021), attractiveness therefore also integrates the ability of territories to anchor their internal stakeholders and not only to attract external

13 Authors' translation.

14 Authors' translation.

15 Translation: Chair in New Place Marketing and Attractiveness.

stakeholders. It is clearly defined in its aim to develop and improve the current (and future) quality of life within territories. Territorial attractiveness thus pursues multiple goals depending on the stakeholders it targets, even though many objectives, such as quality of life, are common to both internal and external stakeholders.

Attractiveness also has a dual tangible/intangible dimension (see Table 9.1). The tangible dimension refers to the attraction and retention of resources (human, financial, material). The attractiveness of talent and the creative class has thus figured prominently in the attractiveness strategies implemented by international metropolises over the past 20 years (Zenker 2009). Today, international metropolises are also focusing on the talent already present in their territory to retain it. This dimension provides measurable attraction criteria, such as jobs, available surface areas, amenities and reception capacities (Hatem 2007).

On the contrary, the intangible dimension refers to the mental depictions that a territory can have on people's attitudes. For example, a territory can be attractive if it has a very positive reputation, as is the case with major international cities (Alaux et al. 2020).

The *tangible* dimension of attractiveness	**The *intangible* dimension of attractiveness**
Attraction of resources human, financial, material	Reputation of the territory and attitudes of stakeholders towards the territory
Measurable criteria (e.g. number of new projects, number of inhabitants, number of tourists)	Intangible dimensions and representations (e.g. brand awareness, image dimensions, reputation content, e-reputation measurement)

Table 9.1. *The dimensions of territorial attractiveness (source: Hatem 2007; Alaux et al. 2020)*

9.4.3. *Moving towards an increasingly attractive lifestyle*

Attractiveness objectives evolve over time, and residential attractiveness is now a central objective for many territories (attracting and anchoring inhabitants). Indeed, as highlighted in section 9.2, some territories have difficulty filling jobs in the sectors present in their territory. To develop their attractiveness, these territories are turning to the promotion of a superior quality of life, combining professional opportunities with territorial well-being. This explains the interest in tools for measuring quality of territorial life. This objective measurement of quality of life is based on indicators (human development, socio-economic conditions, living environment, etc.). It complements more subjective approaches to measuring perceived territorial well-being (Jany-Catrice 2016).

9.4.4. *Pioneering territories*

As early as 2007, several regions were already focusing on the well-being of their territories. They adopted vernacular to target inhabitants disappointed by urban and metropolitan life. A decade ago, Auvergne summarized "Today's World" as "Urbanophiles". Ten years later, Brittany offered Parisians "metro/work/sleep" and posters of old sea dogs converted into "hipsters", with the hashtag: #passezàlouest [16]. This desire to be elsewhere was also illustrated by the strong development of support services for individuals, territories and businesses, such as the start-ups LAOU[17] and "Parisjetequitte"[18]!

Various methods can be used to achieve these internal and external attractiveness objectives. We can clearly identify the development of territorial marketing approaches that focus on the capture, creation, communication and deliverance of value (Braun and Klijn 2013). Territorial brand management has also developed alongside marketing, around place branding approaches (Herezniak and Anders-Morawska 2015).

9.4.5. *The development of territorial brands*

Although all types of territory face recruitment challenges, not all of them necessarily have the brand awareness and image that could help them cope. For these territories, the challenge is more often building an image, or even a territorial identity, than making use of already existing brand equity (Alaux et al. 2015). The contributions of relationship marketing in the management of internal stakeholders can then be used to build territorial identities that will subsequently make it possible to disseminate images associated with mental representations.

16 Translation: #movetothewest.

17 See: https://www.laou.fr.

18 See: www.paris-jetequitte.com.

Territories are identified through four dimensions of representations perceived by internal and external stakeholders (Chamard et al. 2013; Alaux et al. 2020, see Figure 9.3). The first factor is dynamism in economic terms. The second factor relates to quality of life: the quality of human relations, the climate, and the aesthetics of the city. The third dimension concerns the territory's cultural heritage. The fourth relates to the territory's personality (its values, its emotional perception).

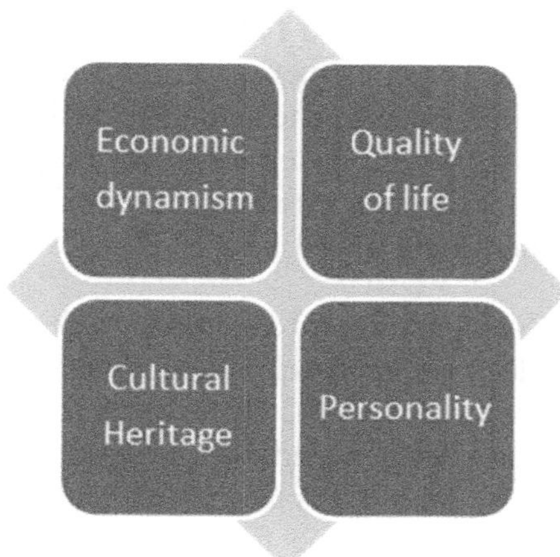

Figure 9.3. *Dimensions of territorial branding (source: Chamard et al. (2013); Alaux et al. (2020))*

In this collective, cross-functional approach, territorial attractiveness brands can be enriched by the contributions and expectations of companies already located within the territory. Indeed, as proposed by Loufrani-Fedida and Saint-Germes, territories will increasingly be called upon to build territorial employer brands along the lines of the employer brands developed by companies (Loufrani-Fedida and Saint-Germes 2015).

9.4.6. *An integrating concept: the territorial employer brand*

The recent development of a territorial employer brand has been inspired both by work on an organization's employer brand and by work on Territorial Human Resource Management (T-HRM), as well as by developments in HR marketing and territorial marketing. In fact, territorial employer branding is progressively seen as a transposition of an organization's internal employer brand management practices to the territorial level, and also as an extension of territorial corporate employer brands and territorial marketing, creating positive synergies between the different brands and perceived images. It can also be seen as the development of new and innovative HRM practices within a territory, thanks to the networking of different public and private stakeholders (Loufrani-Fedida and Saint-Germes 2020).

Therefore, the employer branding[19] (Backhaus and Tikoo 2004) and HR marketing approaches are transposed onto the territorial, regional or place employer branding level. The construction of a territorial employer brand is then defined "as the efforts made by the actors and stakeholders of a territory to promote, both internally and externally, an image of what makes it different and attractive for a talent, a company or a public actor"[20] (Loufrani-Fedida and Saint-Germes 2020, p. 163).

In building this positive territorial reputation, marketing human resources and skills becomes a decisive approach to federating stakeholders around a territorial dynamic (Evon and Hulin 2020). A territorial employer brand is thus necessarily multi-stakeholder, and also multi-targeted, with the aim of improving the image for employees and talent within (and without) the territory (with an international scope for certain territories), for local and external companies; and finally for territorial and national public organizations. This image objective is not confined to the creation of classic territorial promotional campaigns. It is often accompanied by the creation of new services, new structures and HRM innovations with a marketing approach.

Lastly, it is the HRM practices developed on the ground that help develop and position a territorial employer brand. As with an organization's employer brand, recruitment, selection and integration practices (Russell and Brannan 2016) are decisive in forging an attractive, loyalty-building image. More broadly, the territorial employer brand is shaped by all the talent management practices developed by territorial actors (Loufrani-Fedida and Saint-Germes 2020). These practices and their marketing help to forge the image of an attractive and dynamic territory for economic actors, a breeding ground for talent and skills, and also one that offers a genuine quality of life for these talents and skills.

---

19 Building an employer brand is a set of activities, a process implemented by an organization and a set of actors to make its image attractive.

20 Authors' translation.

9.5. Case study: the strategy of *Attitude Manche,* the attractiveness agency for the Manche department[21]

9.5.1. *Context and diagnosis*

La Manche is a French department with a population of 495,983 (see Box 9.2), spread across 433 municipalities (as at January 1, 2020), 77% of which have fewer than 1,000 inhabitants. Cherbourg-en-Cotentin is the largest, with 79,144 inhabitants, and Saint-Lô the second largest, with 19,024.

– 495,983 inhabitants, 433 municipalities. – 72,200 salaried jobs.
– 1 attractiveness agency: Attitude Manche, 36 employees, average age 41.8 years, first attractiveness agency and Great Place To Work® certified Manche organization. – 441 member companies within the agency. – 182 new agency contacts, installed in 2021 in the Manche department. – 15.7 million tourist nights, 6,043 tourist jobs on annual average. – 9 out of 10 residents express a strong attachment and feel like they are *Manchois*.

Box 9.2. *Key figures: attractiveness of the Manche department and (QLW)*²

9.5.2. *Quality of life at work*

It is difficult to obtain global information on the quality of work life at the departmental level. We can, however, point to the leadership of the attractiveness agency, the first Manche organization to obtain a "Great Place to Work®" certification. In this way, "Attitude Manche" aims to show the way for local companies wishing to improve their quality of work life. La Manche is already enjoying a very favorable economic situation, with one of the lowest unemployment rates in mainland France: 5.8% in the fourth quarter (Q4) of 2020 (5.3% by the end of 2022) versus 8% in France in the fourth quarter (Q4) of 2020 (7% by the end of 2022). Despite this positive momentum, many job vacancies remain unfilled: 19,018 recruitment projects for 2021, 30% of which are seasonal. This dynamism is due to the presence

21 This case study is based on public documents from the attractiveness agency *Latitude Manche* and interviews with management, in particular its director, Paul-Vincent Marchand and the manager in charge of talent attraction, Olivier Chartrain.

of sectors of excellence (agri-food, luxury goods, renewable energies and industry). The territory's main problem is the difficulty of filling certain types of jobs: executives, qualified technicians and doctors.

9.5.3. *Quality of life within the territory*

This quality of life was confirmed by a survey conducted in 2020 by "Lattitude Manche":

> Residents recognize a tranquil (95% of residents) and safe (99% of residents) living environment. 8/10 is the average score given to quality of life, with 76% of respondents giving a score = or > 8/10). 100% of residents link their attachment to La Manche to the environment/quality of life. 96% of residents recommend La Manche as a place to live (73% of whom would recommend it)[22].

9.5.4. *The actors*

The *Conseil départemental de la Manche* is one of the territorial authorities behind the creation of Attitude Manche, formerly "Latitude Manche". Attitude Manche is the attractiveness agency for the Manche region. Its governance is structured around five cross-functional institutions:

- departmental elected representatives;
- college of institutional actors;
- tourism actors;
- business actors;
- institutional influencers.

In 2021, the agency had 441 member companies (301 companies in 2018) contributing to part of its funding.

22 Taken from *memento chiffres clés* [Online]. Available at: https://drive.google.com/file/d/1FuWclNH850QeKdCJ5Cg9D7-0EUD8_S6r/view?usp=sharing. Excerpt translated by authors.

9.5.5. *The vision*

Launched in 2017, the Manche approach was structured around the creation of an attractiveness agency:

> Born of a collective desire to truly showcase the Manche region, the agency's mission is to raise the department's profile beyond its borders and to unite private and public actors in this large-scale project[23].

The objectives of the attractiveness initiative are summarized in the Attitude Manche agency presentation:

– to make La Manche a welcoming and privileged territory for new talent (employees and project leaders), by promoting the territory's living environment and career opportunities;

– to stimulate the matching of companies and employee profiles to facilitate recruitment;

– to augment the territory's healthcare system by attracting new healthcare professionals (general practitioners and specialists, dentists) and encouraging them to settle here;

– to create a "Manche spirit" to federate a network of influencers made up of local residents, entrepreneurs and the media.

9.5.6. *Strategy and actions: targets, services and communication*

The attractiveness agency and the Departmental Council identified various targets:

– influencers: companies, local residents, personalities, media;

– new talent: employees, project leaders;

– tourists: French market, UK, Germany, Benelux;

– healthcare professionals: general practitioners, specialists, dentists.

23 See: https://www.maviedanslamanche.fr/latitude-manche/. Excerpt translated by authors.

It has developed services for residents and businesses involved in the attractiveness drive:

– grouping of job offers in La Manche (6,688 offers as of August 19, 2022)[24];

– bringing together job seekers and employers[25];

– a CV library available to companies, enabling them (with the candidate's consent) to forward the CVs of unsuccessful candidates to other companies looking for profiles;

– the "hospitality" service helps new talent being recruited by local companies to settle in La Manche: finding accommodation, schools, nurseries, etc.;

– weekend discovery stays in La Manche for candidates at the end of the recruitment process;

– a spousal support program since 2017. This service enables the spouse of a talent recruited by a company in the department to also find a position in the region, thereby facilitating family mobility.

In 2019, Latitude Manche also launched an extensive communications campaign entitled "*Ma nouvelle vie dans la Manche, c'est ici que tout commence*"[26]. The aim was to promote the territory and its career opportunities to talented individuals from outside the Manche region.

Employment actors in La Manche went out to meet talent in nine targeted employment areas in the northern half of France. A total of 14 recruitment events were held between September 26 and October 17, 2019, in the cities of Le Havre, Lille, Amiens, Paris, Nancy, Metz, Dunkirk, Le Mans and Rouen.

A month before the events, trailers on the quality of life in La Manche were shown in cinemas, and *afterworks* were organized to invite talented people to "discover possible recruitment prospects, the territory's economic dynamism, companies and the quality of life that La Manche has to offer"[27].

24 See: https://www.maviedanslamanche.fr/sinstaller/travailler-dans-la-manche/offres-travail/.

25 See: https://www.monemploidanslamanche.fr.

26 Translation: My new life in La Manche – it all starts here.

27 Authors' translation.

9.5.7. *The results*

In 2018, 60 talents were able to benefit from the support package for their spouses and families. As a follow-up to the 2019 promotional actions and the services developed, the following were the talent attraction results for 2021: 892 qualified contacts, 400 candidates accompanied, 81 discovery stays offered and 182 contacts installed. The contact transformation rate was extremely high, at 20%.

9.6. Conclusion

Against a backdrop of recruitment shortages, companies and territorial authorities need to work in synergy around the concept of a territorial employer brand.

Moving beyond the boundaries of corporate HRM, by using the concepts of employer branding and quality of work life, into approaches of attractiveness and quality of territorial life, it will make it possible to combine the two forms of attractiveness from the angle of $(QLW)^2$. Although the workplace and the home are becoming increasingly dissociated, the concept of territorial employer branding from a $(QLW)^2$ perspective opens up new perspectives by thinking in terms of these two concepts of quality of life. Table 9.2 enables territorial actors and recruiters to identify the different combinations of $(QLW)^2$ by identifying their combined challenges.

	QLW territory –	**QLW territory +**
QLW company –	Risk of residential migration Risk of relocation of activities	Attracting new businesses and residents Risk of not keeping employees in local jobs
QLW company +	Risk of a degraded residential economy Increased use of teleworking	Employee loyalty and territorial attractiveness

Table 9.2. *$(QLW)^2$ combinations for companies and territories*

Reasoning in terms of $(QLW)^2$ is more qualitative than binary reasoning in terms of a shortage of jobs or a territory's lack of attractiveness. In the past, the lack of jobs and low quality of life were used to explain the lack of attractiveness of certain areas. $(QLW)^2$ enables us to develop a two-way approach that simultaneously questions the company and territorial actors in their strategies. This decompartmentalization enables us to better adapt to the changing aspirations of future employees. In this way, areas labeled as unattractive can build up a new "squared" attractiveness, both economic and residential, based on the combined action of companies in favor of quality of life at work, and territorial authorities in favor of quality of territorial life.

9.7. References

Alaux, C., Serval, S., Zeller, C. (2015). Le marketing territorial des Petits et Moyens Territoires : identité, image et relations. *Gestion et Management Public*, 4(2), 61–78.

Alaux, C., Carmouze, L., Serval, S. (2020). What's in a place name: Reputation components and drivers. A comparison of five European metropolises' images. *Management International/International Management/Gestión Internacional*, 24, 139–149.

Ambler, T. and Barrow, S. (1996). The employer brand. *Journal of Brand Management*, 4(3), 185–206.

Arnoult, É., and Duhautois, R. (2019). Une analyse spatiale des mouvements de l'emploi et de la population en France. *Travail et Emploi*, 160(4), 23–46.

Backhaus, K. and Tikoo, S. (2004). Conceptualizing and researching employer branding. *Career Development International*, 9(5), 501–517.

Berthon, P., Ewing, M., Hah, L.L. (2005). Captivating company: Dimensions of attractiveness in employer branding. *International Journal of Advertising*, 24(2), 151–172.

Braun, E. and Klijn, E. (2013). Place marketing as governance strategy: An assessment of obstacles in place marketing and their effects on attracting target groups place. *Public Administration Review*, 73, 507–516.

Chaire Attractivité & Nouveau Marketing Territorial (2021). Manifeste de l'attractivité territoriale et du marketing territorial [Online]. Available at: https://anmt.univ-amu.fr/sites/anmt.univ-amu.fr/files/public/le_manifeste_compressed.pdf.

Chamard, C., Liquet, J.-C., Mengi, M. (2013). L'image de marque des régions françaises : évaluation du "capital territoire" par le grand public. *Revue Française Du Marketing*, 244/245(4/5-5), 27–43.

Charbonnier-Voirin, A. and Lissillour, M. (2018). La marque employeur comme outil de fidélisation organisationnelle. *Recherches en Sciences de Gestion*, 125(2), 97–119. doi: 10.3917/resg.125.0097.

Evon, J. and Hulin, A. (2020). La contribution des marques employeurs à la formation de l'image territoriale. In *Marque employeur et travail expérientiel. La GRH dans l'économie des marques*, Guillot-Soulez, C. and Pezet, E. (eds). Vuibert, Paris.

Gérardin, H. and Poirot, J. (2010). L'attractivité des territoires : un concept multidimensionnel. *Mondes en Développement*, 38(1) 27–41. doi: 10.3917/med.149.27.

Hatem, F. (2007). *Le marketing territorial. Principes, méthodes et pratiques*. EMS Éditions, Caen.

Herezniak, M. and Anders-Morawska, J. (2015). City brand strategy evaluation: In search of effectiveness indicators. *Journal of Place Management and Development*, 8(3), 187–205. doi: 10.1108/JPMD-06-2015-0023.

INSEE (2016). *France, portrait social*. Paris.

Jany-Catrice, F. (2016). La mesure du bien-être territorial. Travailler sur ou avec les territoires ? *Revue de l'OFCE*, 145, 63–90.

Loufrani-Fedida, S. and Saint-Germes, E. (2015). Quand le territoire s'organise pour attirer à l'international et fidéliser en local les talents : le cas du cluster technologique de Sophia Antipolis. *@GRH*, 2, 99–125.

Loufrani-Fedida, S. and Saint-Germes, E. (2020). La construction de la marque employeur territoriale par les pratiques de management global des talents : le cas du cluster technologique de Sophia-Antipolis. In *Marque employeur et travail expérientiel. La GRH dans l'économie des marques*, Guillot-Soulez, C. and Pezet, E. (eds). Vuibert, Paris, 161–184.

Russell, S. and Brannan, M.J. (2016). "Getting the Right People on the Bus": Recruitment, selection and integration for the branded organization. *European Management Journal*, 34(2), 114–124.

Talandier, M. (2016). L'économie résidentielle à l'horizon 2040. *Futuribles*, 35–49.

Zenker, S. (2009). Who's your target? The creative class as a target group for place branding. *Journal of Place Management and Development*, 2(1) 23–32. doi: 10.1108/17538330910942771.

Zenker, S. and Beckmann, S.C. (2013). My place is not your place – Different place brand knowledge by different target groups. *Journal of Place Management and Development*, 6(1). doi: 10.1108/17538331311306078.

List of Authors

Christophe ALAUX
CERGAM
Aix-Marseille Université
Aix-en-Provence
France

Anne ALBERT-CROMARIAS
CleRMa
ESC Clermont Business School
France

Thérèse ALBERTINI
Université de Corse-Pascal-Paoli
Corte
France

Alexandre ASSELINEAU
CEREN
BSB
Dijon
France

Christophe ASSENS
LAREQUOI
UVSQ
Versailles
France

Isabelle BORIES-AZEAU
MRM
Université de Montpellier
France

François COLÉNO
SADAPT
INRAE
AgroParisTech
Université Paris-Saclay
Palaiseau
France

Guillaume DETCHENIQUE
ESSCA School of Management
Angers
France

Camille FIORE
CERGAM
Aix-Marseille Université
Aix-en-Provence
France

Colette FOURCADE
MRM
Université de Montpellier
France

Truong GIANG PHAM
Le Cube
Le Mans
France

Solange HERNANDEZ
CERGAM
Aix-Marseille Université
Aix-en-Provence
France

Christophe LEYRONAS
TBS Education
Toulouse
France

Thomas LOILIER
NIMEC
IAE de Caen
Université de Caen Normandie
France

Stéphanie LOUP
LGTO
Université-Toulouse-III-Paul-Sabatier
France

Magali MALHERBE
NIMEC
IAE Caen
Université de Caen Normandie
France

Ingrid MAZZILLI
LEST, CNRS
Aix-Marseille Université
Aix-en-Provence
France

Nathalie RAULET-CROSET
Sorbonne Recherche en Management
IAE Paris Sorbonne Business School
Université Paris 1 Panthéon Sorbonne
France

Corinne ROCHETTE
CleRMa
IAE Clermont Auvergne
Université Clermont-Auvergne
France

Ève SAINT-GERMES
GREDEG
Université Côte d'Azur
Nice
France

Patrice TERRAMORSI
Université de Corse-Pascal-Paoli
Corte
and
Labex Entreprendre
Université de Montpellier
France

Yamina VIERGE
Sorbonne Recherche en Management
IAE Paris Sorbonne Business School
Université Paris 1 Panthéon Sorbonne
France

Index

A, B

C, D

N, O

P, Q

R, S

T, U, V, W

Other titles from

iSTE

in

Innovation, Entrepreneurship and Management

2024

BRASSEUR Martine, BARTOLI Annie, CHABAUD Didier, GROUIEZ Pascal, ROUET Gilles
Inclusive Territories 2: Role of Institutions and Local Actors
(Territorial Entrepreneurship and Innovation Set – Volume 2)

COURIE-LEMEUR Aline
Innovation, Collective Intelligence and Resiliency in Healthcare Organizations
(Health and Innovation Set – Volume 4)

DIMOTIKALIS Yannis, SKIADIS Christos H.
Data Analysis and Related Applications 3: Theory and Practice – New Approaches
(Big Data, Artificial Intelligence and Data Analysis Set – Volume 11)

PARMENTIER Guy
Organizational Creative Capabilities: Management Factors, Processes and Devices
(Organizational Creativity Set – Volume 1)

RUIZ Émilie
The Creative Capabilities of Open Organizations
(Organizational Creativity Set – Volume 2)

VERNIER Marie-France
Eco-Design and Ecological Transition: Questioning the Economic Model
(Smart Innovation Set – Volume 42)

2023

BOLLINGER Sophie
Management Control and Creativity: Challenges of Managing Innovation Processes
(Smart Innovation Set – Volume 41)

BOUVIER-PATRON Paul
Frugal Innovation and Innovative Creation
(Smart Innovation Set – Volume 40)

BRASSEUR Martine, BARTOLI Annie, CHABAUD Didier, GROUIEZ Pascal, ROUET Gilles
Inclusive Territories 1: Role of Enterprises and Organizations
(Territorial Entrepreneurship and Innovation Set – Volume 1)

CASADELLA Vanessa, UZUNIDIS Dimitri
Agri-Innovations and Development Challenges: Engineering, Value Chains and Socio-economic Models
(Innovation in Engineering and Technology Set – Volume 8)

DARTIGUEPEYROU Carine, SALOFF-COSTE Michel
Futures: The Great Turn
(Innovation and Technology Set – Volume 18)

PEYROUX Élisabeth, RAIMOND Christine, VIEL Vincent, LAVIE Émilie
Development and Territorial Restructuring in an Era of Global Change: Theories, Approaches and Future Research Perspectives

SAULAIS Pierre
Knowledge and Ideation: Inventive Knowledge Analysis for Ideation Stimulation
(Innovation and Technology Set – Volume 17)

2022

AOUINAÏT Camille
Open Innovation Strategies
(Smart Innovation Set – Volume 39)

BOUCHÉ Geneviève
Productive Economy, Contributory Economy: Governance Tools for the Third Millennium
(Innovation and Technology Set – Volume 15)

BRUYÈRE Christelle
Caring Management in Health Organizations: A Lever for Crisis Management
(Health and Innovation Set – Volume 3)

ENJOLRAS Manon
Innovation and Export: The Joint Challenge of the Small Company
(Smart Innovation Set – Volume 37)

FLEURY Sylvain, RICHIR Simon
Immersive Technologies to Accelerate Innovation: How Virtual and Augmented Reality Enables the Co-Creation of Concepts
(Smart Innovation Set – Volume 38)

HELLER David
Valuation of the Liability Structure by Real Options
(Modern Finance, Management Innovation and Economic Growth Set – Volume 5)

MATHIEU Valérie
A Customer-oriented Manager for B2B Services: Principles and Implementation

MORALES Lucía, DZEVER Sam, TAYLOR Robert
Asia-Europe Industrial Connectivity in Times of Crisis
(Innovation and Technology Set – Volume 16)

NOËL Florent, SCHMIDT Géraldine
Employability and Industrial Mutations: Between Individual Trajectories and Organizational Strategic Planning
(Technological Changes and Human Resources Set – Volume 4)

DE SAINT JULIEN Odile
The Innovation Ecosystem as a Source of Value Creation: A Value Creation Lever for Open Innovation
(Diverse and Global Perspectives on Value Creation Set – Volume 4)

SALOFF-COSTE Michel
Innovation Ecosystems: The Future of Civilizations and the Civilization of the Future
(Innovation and Technology Set – Volume 14)

SOULÉ Bastien, HALLÉ Julie, VIGNAL Bénédicte, BOUTROY Éric, NIER Olivier
Innovation in Sport: Innovation Trajectories and Process Optimization
(Smart Innovation Set – Volume 35)

VALLIER Estelle
Innovation in Clusters: Science–Industry Relationships in the Face of Forced Advancement
(Smart Innovation Set – Volume 36)

VAYRE Emilie
Digitalization of Work: New Spaces and New Working Times
(Technological Changes and Human Resources Set – Volume 5)

ZAFEIRIS Konstantinos N, SKIADIS Christos H, DIMOTIKALIS Yannis, KARAGRIGORIOU Alex, KARAGRIGORIOU-VONTA Christina
Data Analysis and Related Applications 1: Computational, Algorithmic and Applied Economic Data Analysis
(Big Data, Artificial Intelligence and Data Analysis Set – Volume 9)
Data Analysis and Related Applications 2: Multivariate, Health and Demographic Data Analysis
(Big Data, Artificial Intelligence and Data Analysis Set – Volume 10)

2021

ACH Yves-Alain, RMADI-SAÏD Sandra
Financial Information and Brand Value: Reflections, Challenges and Limitations

ARCADE Jacques
Strategic Engineering
(Innovation and Technology Set – Volume 11)

BÉRANGER Jérôme, RIZOULIÈRES Roland
The Digital Revolution in Health
(Health and Innovation Set – Volume 2)

BOBILLIER CHAUMON Marc-Eric
Digital Transformations in the Challenge of Activity and Work: Understanding and Supporting Technological Changes
(Technological Changes and Human Resources Set – Volume 3)

BUCLET Nicolas
Territorial Ecology and Socio-ecological Transition
(Smart Innovation Set – Volume 34)

DIMOTIKALIS Yannis, KARAGRIGORIOU Alex, PARPOULA Christina, SKIADIS Christos H
Applied Modeling Techniques and Data Analysis 1: Computational Data Analysis Methods and Tools
(Big Data, Artificial Intelligence and Data Analysis Set - Volume 7)
Applied Modeling Techniques and Data Analysis 2: Financial, Demographic, Stochastic and Statistical Models and Methods
(Big Data, Artificial Intelligence and Data Analysis Set – Volume 8)

DISPAS Christophe, KAYANAKIS Georges, SERVEL Nicolas, STRIUKOVA Ludmila
Innovation and Financial Markets
(Innovation between Risk and Reward Set – Volume 7)

GAUDIN Thierry, MAUREL Marie-Christine, POMEROL Jean-Charles
Chance, Calculation and Life

GASMI Nacer
Corporate Innovation Strategies: Corporate Social Responsibility and Shared Value Creation
(Smart Innovation Set – Volume 33)

GIORGINI Pierre
The Contributory Revolution
(Innovation and Technology Set – Volume 13)

GOGLIN Christian
Emotions and Values in Equity Crowdfunding Investment Choices 1: Transdisciplinary Theoretical Approach
Emotions and Values in Equity Crowdfunding Investment Choices 2: Modeling and Empirical Study

GRENIER Corinne, OIRY Ewan
Altering Frontiers: Organizational Innovations in Healthcare
(Health and Innovation Set – Volume 1)

GUERRIER Claudine
Security and Its Challenges in the 21st Century
(Innovation and Technology Set – Volume 12)

HELLER David
Performance of Valuation Methods in Financial Transactions
(Modern Finance, Management Innovation and Economic Growth Set – Volume 4)

LEHMANN Paul-Jacques
Liberalism and Capitalism Today

LIMA Marcos
Entrepreneurship and Innovation Education: Frameworks and Tools
(Smart Innovation Set – Volume 32)

MACHADO Carolina, DAVIM J. Paulo
Sustainable Management for Managers and Engineers

MEUNIER François-Xavier
Dual Innovation Systems: Concepts, Tools and Methods
(Smart Innovation Set – Volume 31)

UZUNIDIS Dimitri, KASMI Fedoua, ADATTO Laurent
Innovation Economics, Engineering and Management Handbook 1: Main Themes
Innovation Economics, Engineering and Management Handbook 2: Special Themes

2020

ANDREOSSO-O'CALLAGHAN Bernadette, DZEVER Sam, JAUSSAUD Jacques, TAYLOR Robert
Sustainable Development and Energy Transition in Europe and Asia
(Innovation and Technology Set – Volume 9)

BEN SLIMANE Sonia, M'HENNI Hatem
Entrepreneurship and Development: Realities and Future Prospects
(Smart Innovation Set – Volume 30)

CHOUTEAU Marianne, FOREST Joëlle, NGUYEN Céline
Innovation for Society: The P.S.I. Approach
(Smart Innovation Set – Volume 28)

CORON Clotilde
Quantifying Human Resources: Uses and Analysis
(Technological Changes and Human Resources Set – Volume 2)

CORON Clotilde, GILBERT Patrick
Technological Change
(Technological Changes and Human Resources Set – Volume 1)

CERDIN Jean-Luc, PERETTI Jean-Marie
The Success of Apprenticeships: Views of Stakeholders on Training and Learning (Human Resources Management Set – Volume 3)

DELCHET-COCHET Karen
Circular Economy: From Waste Reduction to Value Creation
(Economic Growth Set – Volume 2)

DIDAY Edwin, GUAN Rong, SAPORTA Gilbert, WANG Huiwen
Advances in Data Science
(Big Data, Artificial Intelligence and Data Analysis Set – Volume 4)

DOS SANTOS PAULINO Victor
Innovation Trends in the Space Industry
(Smart Innovation Set – Volume 25)

GUILHON Bernard
Venture Capital and the Financing of Innovation
(Innovation Between Risk and Reward Set – Volume 6)

JURCZENKO Emmanuel
Machine Learning for Asset Management: New Developments and Financial Applications

LATOUCHE Pascal
Open Innovation: Human Set-up
(Innovation and Technology Set – Volume 10)

MAKRIDES Andreas, KARAGRIGORIOU Alex, SKIADAS Christos H.
Data Analysis and Applications 3: Computational, Classification, Financial, Statistical and Stochastic Methods
(Big Data, Artificial Intelligence and Data Analysis Set – Volume 5)
Data Analysis and Applications 4: Financial Data Analysis and Methods
(Big Data, Artificial Intelligence and Data Analysis Set – Volume 6)

MASSOTTE Pierre, CORSI Patrick
Complex Decision-Making in Economy and Finance

MICHAUD Thomas
Science Fiction and Innovation Design
(Innovation in Engineering and Technology Set – Volume 6)

MONINO Jean-Louis
Data Control: Major Challenge for the Digital Society
(Smart Innovation Set – Volume 29)

MORLAT Clément
Sustainable Productive System: Eco-development versus Sustainable Development (Smart Innovation Set – Volume 26)

SAULAIS Pierre, ERMINE Jean-Louis
Knowledge Management in Innovative Companies 2: Understanding and Deploying a KM Plan within a Learning Organization
(Smart Innovation Set – Volume 27)

UZUNIDIS Dimitri
Systemic Innovation: Entrepreneurial Strategies and Market Dynamics

2019

AMENDOLA Mario, GAFFARD Jean-Luc
Disorder and Public Concern Around Globalization

BARBAROUX Pierre
Disruptive Technology and Defence Innovation Ecosystems
(Innovation in Engineering and Technology Set – Volume 5)

DOU Henri, JUILLET Alain, CLERC Philippe
Strategic Intelligence for the Future 1: A New Strategic and Operational Approach
Strategic Intelligence for the Future 2: A New Information Function Approach

FRIKHA Azza
Measurement in Marketing: Operationalization of Latent Constructs

FRIMOUSSE Soufyane
Innovation and Agility in the Digital Age
(Human Resources Management Set – Volume 2)

GAY Claudine, SZOSTAK Bérangère L.
Innovation and Creativity in SMEs: Challenges, Evolutions and Prospects
(Smart Innovation Set – Volume 21)

GORIA Stéphane, HUMBERT Pierre, ROUSSEL Benoît
Information, Knowledge and Agile Creativity
(Smart Innovation Set – Volume 22)

HELLER David
Investment Decision-making Using Optional Models
(Economic Growth Set – Volume 2)

HELLER David, DE CHADIRAC Sylvain, HALAOUI Lana, JOUVET Camille
The Emergence of Start-ups
(Economic Growth Set – Volume 1)

HÉRAUD Jean-Alain, KERR Fiona, BURGER-HELMCHEN Thierry
Creative Management of Complex Systems
(Smart Innovation Set – Volume 19)

LATOUCHE Pascal
Open Innovation: Corporate Incubator
(Innovation and Technology Set – Volume 7)

LEHMANN Paul-Jacques
The Future of the Euro Currency

LEIGNEL Jean-Louis, MÉNAGER Emmanuel, YABLONSKY Serge
Sustainable Enterprise Performance: A Comprehensive Evaluation Method

LIÈVRE Pascal, AUBRY Monique, GAREL Gilles
Management of Extreme Situations: From Polar Expeditions to Exploration-Oriented Organizations

MILLOT Michel
Embarrassment of Product Choices 2: Towards a Society of Well-being

N'GOALA Gilles, PEZ-PÉRARD Virginie, PRIM-ALLAZ Isabelle
Augmented Customer Strategy: CRM in the Digital Age

NIKOLOVA Blagovesta
The RRI Challenge: Responsibilization in a State of Tension with Market Regulation
(Innovation and Responsibility Set – Volume 3)

PELLEGRIN-BOUCHER Estelle, ROY Pierre
Innovation in the Cultural and Creative Industries
(Innovation and Technology Set – Volume 8)

PRIOLON Joël
Financial Markets for Commodities

QUINIOU Matthieu
Blockchain: The Advent of Disintermediation

RAVIX Joël-Thomas, DESCHAMPS Marc
Innovation and Industrial Policies
(Innovation between Risk and Reward Set – Volume 5)

ROGER Alain, VINOT Didier
Skills Management: New Applications, New Questions
(Human Resources Management Set – Volume 1)

SAULAIS Pierre, ERMINE Jean-Louis
Knowledge Management in Innovative Companies 1: Understanding and Deploying a KM Plan within a Learning Organization
(Smart Innovation Set – Volume 23)

SERVAJEAN-HILST Romaric
Co-innovation Dynamics: The Management of Client-Supplier Interactions for Open Innovation
(Smart Innovation Set – Volume 20)

SKIADAS Christos H., BOZEMAN James R.
Data Analysis and Applications 1: Clustering and Regression, Modeling-estimating, Forecasting and Data Mining
(Big Data, Artificial Intelligence and Data Analysis Set – Volume 2)
Data Analysis and Applications 2: Utilization of Results in Europe and Other Topics
(Big Data, Artificial Intelligence and Data Analysis Set – Volume 3)

VIGEZZI Michel
World Industrialization: Shared Inventions, Competitive Innovations and Social Dynamics
(Smart Innovation Set – Volume 24)

2018

BURKHARDT Kirsten
Private Equity Firms: Their Role in the Formation of Strategic Alliances

CALLENS Stéphane
Creative Globalization
(Smart Innovation Set – Volume 16)

CASADELLA Vanessa
Innovation Systems in Emerging Economies: MINT – Mexico, Indonesia, Nigeria, Turkey
(Smart Innovation Set – Volume 18)

CHOUTEAU Marianne, FOREST Joëlle, NGUYEN Céline
Science, Technology and Innovation Culture
(Innovation in Engineering and Technology Set – Volume 3)

CORLOSQUET-HABART Marine, JANSSEN Jacques
Big Data for Insurance Companies
(Big Data, Artificial Intelligence and Data Analysis Set – Volume 1)

CROS Françoise
Innovation and Society
(Smart Innovation Set – Volume 15)

DEBREF Romain
Environmental Innovation and Ecodesign: Certainties and Controversies
(Smart Innovation Set – Volume 17)

DOMINGUEZ Noémie
SME Internationalization Strategies: Innovation to Conquer New Markets

ERMINE Jean-Louis
Knowledge Management: The Creative Loop
(Innovation and Technology Set – Volume 5)

GAUDIN Thierry, LACROIX Dominique, MAUREL Marie-Christine,
POMEROL, Jean-Charles
Life Sciences, Information Sciences

GILBERT Patrick, BOBADILLA Natalia, GASTALDI Lise,
LE BOULAIRE Martine, LELEBINA Olga
Innovation, Research and Development Management

VAN HOOREBEKE Delphine
The Management of Living Beings or Emo-management

IBRAHIMI Mohammed
Mergers & Acquisitions: Theory, Strategy, Finance

LEMAÎTRE Denis
Training Engineers for Innovation

LÉVY Aldo, BEN BOUHENI Faten, AMMI Chantal
Financial Management: USGAAP and IFRS Standards
(Innovation and Technology Set – Volume 6)

LOISY Catherine, COULET Jean-Claude
Competence and Program-based Approach in Training: Tools for Developing Responsible Activities
Innovation and Responsibility Set – Volume 1)

MILLOT Michel
Embarrassment of Product Choices 1: How to Consume Differently

PANSERA Mario, OWEN Richard
Innovation and Development: The Politics at the Bottom of the Pyramid
(Innovation and Responsibility Set – Volume 2)

RICHEZ Yves
Corporate Talent Detection and Development

SACHETTI Philippe, ZUPPINGER Thibaud
New Technologies and Branding
(Innovation and Technology Set – Volume 4)

SAMIER Henri
Intuition, Creativity, Innovation

TEMPLE Ludovic, COMPAORÉ SAWADOGO Eveline M.F.W.
Innovation Processes in Agro-Ecological Transitions in Developing Countries
(Innovation in Engineering and Technology Set – Volume 2)

UZUNIDIS Dimitri
Collective Innovation Processes: Principles and Practices
(Innovation in Engineering and Technology Set – Volume 4)

2017

AÏT-EL-HADJ Smaïl
The Ongoing Technological System
(Smart Innovation Set – Volume 11)

D'ANDRIA Aude, GABARRET Inés
Building 21st Century Entrepreneurship
(Innovation and Technology Set – Volume 2)

BAUDRY Marc, DUMONT Béatrice
Patents: Prompting or Restricting Innovation?
(Smart Innovation Set – Volume 12)

BÉRARD Céline, TEYSSIER Christine
Risk Management: Lever for SME Development and Stakeholder Value Creation

CHALENÇON Ludivine
Location Strategies and Value Creation of International Mergers and Acquisitions

CHAUVEL Danièle, BORZILLO Stefano
The Innovative Company: An Ill-defined Object
(Innovation between Risk and Reward Set – Volume 1)

CORSI Patrick
Going Past Limits To Growth

DAIDJ Nabyla
Cooperation, Coopetition and Innovation
(Innovation and Technology Set – Volume 3)

FERNEZ-WALCH Sandrine
The Multiple Facets of Innovation Project Management
(Innovation between Risk and Reward Set – Volume 4)

FOREST Joëlle
Creative Rationality and Innovation
(Smart Innovation Set – Volume 14)

GUILHON Bernard
Innovation and Production Ecosystems
(Innovation between Risk and Reward Set – Volume 2)

HAMMOUDI Abdelhakim, DAIDJ Nabyla
Game Theory Approach to Managerial Strategies and Value Creation
(Diverse and Global Perspectives on Value Creation Set – Volume 3)

LALLEMENT Rémi
Intellectual Property and Innovation Protection: New Practices and New Policy Issues
(Innovation between Risk and Reward Set – Volume 3)

LAPERCHE Blandine
Enterprise Knowledge Capital
(Smart Innovation Set – Volume 13)

LEBERT Didier, EL YOUNSI Hafida
International Specialization Dynamics
(Smart Innovation Set – Volume 9)

MAESSCHALCK Marc
Reflexive Governance for Research and Innovative Knowledge
(Responsible Research and Innovation Set – Volume 6)

MASSOTTE Pierre
Ethics in Social Networking and Business 1: Theory, Practice and Current Recommendations
Ethics in Social Networking and Business 2: The Future and Changing Paradigms

MASSOTTE Pierre, CORSI Patrick
Smart Decisions in Complex Systems

MEDINA Mercedes, HERRERO Mónica, URGELLÉS Alicia
Current and Emerging Issues in the Audiovisual Industry
(Diverse and Global Perspectives on Value Creation Set – Volume 1)

MICHAUD Thomas
Innovation, Between Science and Science Fiction
(Smart Innovation Set – Volume 10)

PELLÉ Sophie
Business, Innovation and Responsibility
(Responsible Research and Innovation Set – Volume 7)

SAVIGNAC Emmanuelle
The Gamification of Work: The Use of Games in the Workplace

SUGAHARA Satoshi, DAIDJ Nabyla, USHIO Sumitaka
Value Creation in Management Accounting and Strategic Management: An Integrated Approach
(Diverse and Global Perspectives on Value Creation Set –Volume 2)

UZUNIDIS Dimitri, SAULAIS Pierre
Innovation Engines: Entrepreneurs and Enterprises in a Turbulent World (Innovation in Engineering and Technology Set – Volume 1)

2016

BARBAROUX Pierre, ATTOUR Amel, SCHENK Eric
Knowledge Management and Innovation
(Smart Innovation Set – Volume 6)

BEN BOUHENI Faten, AMMI Chantal, LEVY Aldo
Banking Governance, Performance And Risk-Taking: Conventional Banks Vs Islamic Banks

BOUTILLIER Sophie, CARRÉ Denis, LEVRATTO Nadine
Entrepreneurial Ecosystems
(Smart Innovation Set – Volume 2)

BOUTILLIER Sophie, UZUNIDIS Dimitri
The Entrepreneur
(Smart Innovation Set – Volume 8)

BOUVARD Patricia, SUZANNE Hervé
Collective Intelligence Development in Business

GALLAUD Delphine, LAPERCHE Blandine
Circular Economy, Industrial Ecology and Short Supply Chains
(Smart Innovation Set – Volume 4)

GUERRIER Claudine
Security and Privacy in the Digital Era
(Innovation and Technology Set – Volume 1)

MEGHOUAR Hicham
Corporate Takeover Targets

MONINO Jean-Louis, SEDKAOUI Soraya
Big Data, Open Data and Data Development
(Smart Innovation Set – Volume 3)

MOREL Laure, LE ROUX Serge
Fab Labs: Innovative User
(Smart Innovation Set – Volume 5)

PICARD Fabienne, TANGUY Corinne
Innovations and Techno-ecological Transition
(Smart Innovation Set – Volume 7)

2015

CASADELLA Vanessa, LIU Zeting, DIMITRI Uzunidis
Innovation Capabilities and Economic Development in Open Economies
(Smart Innovation Set – Volume 1)

CORLOSQUET-HABART Marine, GEHIN William, JANSSEN Jaques, MANCA Raimondo
Asset and Liabilities Management for Banks and Insurance Companies

CORSI Patrick, MORIN Dominique
Sequencing Apple's DNA

CORSI Patrick, NEAU Erwan
Innovation Capability Maturity Model

FAIVRE-TAVIGNOT Bénédicte
Social Business and Base of the Pyramid

GODÉ Cécile
Team Coordination in Extreme Environments

MAILLARD Pierre
Competitive Quality and Innovation

MASSOTTE Pierre, CORSI Patrick
Operationalizing Sustainability

MASSOTTE Pierre, CORSI Patrick
Sustainability Calling

2014

DUBÉ Jean, LEGROS Diègo
Spatial Econometrics Using Microdata

LESCA Humbert, LESCA Nicolas
Strategic Decisions and Weak Signals

2013

HABART-CORLOSQUET Marine, JANSSEN Jacques, MANCA Raimondo
VaR Methodology for Non-Gaussian Finance

2012

POMEROL Jean-Charles
Decision-Making and Action

SZYLAR Christian
UCITS Handbook

2011

LESCA Nicolas
Environmental Scanning and Sustainable Development

LESCA Nicolas, LESCA Humbert
Weak Signals for Strategic Intelligence: Anticipation Tool for Managers

MERCIER-LAURENT Eunika
Innovation Ecosystems

2010

SZYLAR Christian
Risk Management under UCITS III/IV

2009

COHEN Corine
Business Intelligence

ZANINETTI Jean-Marc
Sustainable Development in the USA

2008

CORSI Patrick, DULIEU Mike
The Marketing of Technology Intensive Products and Services

DZEVER Sam, JAUSSAUD Jacques, ANDREOSSO Bernadette
Evolving Corporate Structures and Cultures in Asia: Impact of Globalization

2007

AMMI Chantal
Global Consumer Behavior

2006

BOUGHZALA Imed, ERMINE Jean-Louis
Trends in Enterprise Knowledge Management

CORSI Patrick, CHRISTOFOL Hervé, RICHIR Simon, SAMIER Henri
Innovation Engineering: the power of intangible networks

Printed and bound by CPI Group (UK) Ltd, Croydon, CR0 4YY

13/09/2026

14961047-0001